NICK HILL lives in Devizes, not far from the Ridgeway which he's walked from end to end numerous times. He is also often to be found on the other tracks and footpaths around Wiltshire.

When times allow and the opportunity arises, Nick travels widely, not just in Britain and Europe but also in Asia, a continent he's crossed overland four times. He settled temporarily in Thailand, his four years in Bangkok punctuated by periods in Siberia, China, India and Pakistan.

As part of the Trailblazer team he is author, illustrator and cartographer, drawing many of the maps for the guides. He has also researched and updated the *Trans-Siberian Handbook* and *South Downs Way*. He also produces walkers' maps covering routes in the south-west of England – see 🖥 nickhillmaps.co.uk.

Author

The Ridgeway
First edition: 2006; this fifth edition: **2021**

Publisher: Trailblazer Publications
The Old Manse, Tower Rd, Hindhead, Surrey GU26 6SU, UK
trailblazer-guides.com

British Library Cataloguing in Publication Data
A catalogue record for this book is available from the British Library

ISBN 978-1-912716-20-3

© **Trailblazer** 2006, 2009, 2012, 2017, 2021: Text and maps

Editor and layout: Anna Jacomb-Hood **Proof-reading**: Jane Thomas
Cartography: Nick Hill **Illustrations**: © Nick Hill (pp69-72)
Photographs (flora): © Bryn Thomas
All other photographs: © Nick Hill unless otherwise indicated
Index: Anna Jacomb-Hood

The maps in this guide were prepared from out-of-Crown-
copyright Ordnance Survey maps amended and updated by Trailblazer.

Acknowledgements
FROM NICK: I'd like to thank my parents for dropping me off and picking me up at various
points along the trail. Lots of other people helped me along the way too, whether it was
answering a simple question I had, or taking the time to explain something more in depth.
I'm grateful to all the people who work hard to keep the Ridgeway in such good condition
for the benefit and enjoyment of so many others and to those Ridgeway walkers who I
talked to along the way, or who emailed their helpful comments and updates to Trailblazer
including Janine, Jonathan Billings, Nigel Black, Martin Cox, Bob Crockford, Nick
Goodyer, Thomas Hope, Nigel Kemp, Trevor & Joan Lipscombe, Sarah Morgan, Matthew
Pires, Keith Rogers, Bob Royalty and Frances Shelley. Thanks also to the Trailblazer team.

A request
The author and publisher have tried to ensure that this guide is as accurate as possible.
Nevertheless things change even on these well-worn routes. If you notice any changes or
omissions please write to Trailblazer (address as above) or email us at 📧 info@trailblazer-
guides.com. A free copy of the next edition will be sent to persons making a significant con-
tribution.

Warning: long-distance walking can be dangerous
Please read the notes on when to go (pp14-16) and health and safety (pp58-60). Every effort
has been made by the author and publisher to ensure that the information contained herein
is as accurate and up to date as possible. However, they are unable to accept responsibility
for any inconvenience, loss or injury sustained by anyone as a result of the advice and information given in this guide.

PHOTOS – Front cover and this page: Taking in the view from
Uffington White Horse on a summer afternoon (see p116).
Previous page: Weathered Ridgeway signpost near Blowingstone Hill.
Overleaf: On Liddington Hill, looking north-east along the Ridgeway (p109).

Updated information will be available on: 🖥 www.trailblazer-guides.com

Printed in China; print production by D'Print (☎ +65-6581 3832), Singapore

THE
Ridgeway

**Large-scale maps (1:20,000) for the entire route
& detailed guides to 24 towns and villages**

PLANNING – PLACES TO STAY – PLACES TO EAT

NICK HILL

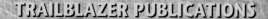

TRAILBLAZER PUBLICATIONS

INTRODUCTION

About the Ridgeway

History 10 – How difficult is the Ridgeway? 12 – How long do you need? 13 – When to go 14

PART 1: PLANNING YOUR WALK

Practical information for the walker

Route finding 17 – GPS 17 – Accommodation 18 – Food and drink 21 – Money 24 – Information for foreign visitors 24 – Other services 26 – Walking companies and luggage transfer 26 – Disabled access 27 – Mountain-biking 28 – Horse riders 28 – Motor vehicles 28 – Walking with a dog 29

Budgeting 29

Itineraries

Which direction? 30 – Suggested itineraries 31 – The best day & two-day walks 31 – Town & village facilities table 33 (eastbound), 35 (westbound) – Side trips 36

What to take

Keep your luggage light 38 – How to carry it 38 – Footwear 38 Clothes 39 – Toiletries 40 – First-aid kit 40 – General items 40 Camping gear 41 – Money 41 – Maps 41 – Recommended reading 43 – Sources of further information 43

Getting to and from the Ridgeway

Getting to Britain 44 – National transport 45 – Public transport map 48 – Local bus services 50 – Local transport 51

PART 2: MINIMUM IMPACT WALKING & OUTDOOR SAFETY

Minimum impact walking

Economic impact 53 – Environmental impact 53 – Access 56 Countryside code 56

Outdoor safety

Avoidance of hazards 58 – Weather forecasts 59 – Health 59

PART 3: THE ENVIRONMENT & NATURE

Conservation of the Ridgeway

Natural England 61 – Ridgeway Partnership 62 – Campaigning & conservation organisations 63

Flora and fauna

Flowers 64 – Butterflies 65 – Trees 66 – Mammals 67 – Birds 69

Contents

PART 4: MARLBOROUGH TO AVEBURY

Marlborough 73 – Marlborough to Avebury walk 77
Avebury and around
Avebury 85 – West Overton 87 – Avebury stone circle 88 – West
Kennett & East Kennett 90 – A walk around Avebury 90
Getting to and from Overton Hill 93

PART 5: ROUTE GUIDE AND MAPS

Using this guide 95   ➜ = walking east   ⬅ = walking west

➜ **Overton Hill to Foxhill** 97 (Ogbourne St George 105,
     Liddington 108)
⬅ **Foxhill to Overton Hill** 111

➜ **Foxhill to Court Hill (& Wantage)** 111 (Bishopstone 113
     Ashbury 114 – Woolstone 115 – Uffington 119 – Sparsholt
     Firs 122 – Sparsholt 122 – Letcombe Regis 123)
⬅ **Court Hill (& Wantage) to Foxhill** 125 (Wantage 126)

➜ **(Wantage &) Court Hill to Goring** 129 (East Ilsley 132
     Compton 133 – Aldworth 137 – Streatley 139)
⬅ **Goring to Court Hill (& Wantage)** 140 (Goring 141)

➜ **Goring to Watlington** 143 (South Stoke 144 – North Stoke 146
     Wallingford 147 – Crowmarsh Gifford 151 – Nuffield 157)
⬅ **Watlington to Goring** 158 (Watlington 160)

➜ **Watlington to Princes Risborough** 161 (Lewknor 162 – Aston
     Rowant 163 – Chinnor 165)
⬅ **Princes Risborough to Watlington** 160 (Princes Risborough 170)

➜ **Princes Risborough to Wigginton (& Tring)** 173
     (Wendover 176)
⬅ **Wigginton (& Tring) to Princes Risborough** 183
     (Wigginton 184 – Tring 184)

➜ **(Tring &) Wigginton to Ivinghoe Beacon** 188 (Aldbury 190)
⬅ **Ivinghoe Beacon to Wigginton (& Tring)** 194
     (Aldbury 190 – Ivinghoe 195 – Pitstone 195)

APPENDICES

A: Walking with a dog 196   B: The Greater Ridgeway 198
C: Map key 199   D: GPS waypoints 200

INDEX 203

OVERVIEW MAPS & PROFILES 209

Contents

ABOUT THIS BOOK

This guidebook contains all the information you need. The hard work has been done for you so you can plan your trip without having to consult numerous websites and other books and maps.

Track through Fyfield Down National Nature Reserve (see p80).

When you're all packed and ready to go, there's comprehensive public transport information to get you to and from the trail and detailed maps (1:20,000) and town plans to help you find your way along it. The guide includes:

● Where to stay: from campsites to luxurious hotels
● Details of walking companies if you'd prefer an organised holiday and luggage-transfer services if you just want your luggage carried
● Itineraries for all levels of walkers
● Answers to all your questions: when to go, how challenging it is, what to pack and the approximate cost of the whole walking holiday.
● Walking times and GPS waypoints
● Details of cafés, pubs, teashops, takeaways and restaurants as well as shops and supermarkets for supplies
● Rail, bus and taxi information for all places along the path
● Street plans of the main towns and villages
● Historical, cultural and geographical background information

---

❏ MINIMUM IMPACT FOR MAXIMUM INSIGHT

Nature's peace will flow into you as the sunshine flows into trees. The winds will blow their freshness into you and storms their energy, while cares will drop off like autumn leaves. **John Muir** (one of the world's earliest and most influential environmentalists, born in 1838)

It is no surprise that, since the time of John Muir, walkers and adventurers have been concerned about the natural environment; this book seeks to continue that tradition. By developing a deeper ecological awareness through a better understanding of nature and by supporting rural economies, local businesses, sensitive forms of transport and low-impact methods of farming and land-use we can all do our bit for a brighter future.

As we work harder and live our lives at an ever faster pace a walking holiday is a chance to escape from the daily grind and the natural pace gives us time to think and relax. This can have a positive impact not only on our own well-being but also on that of the area we pass through. There can be few activities as 'environmentally friendly' as walking.

INTRODUCTION

The Ridgeway stretches for **87 miles (139km)** across the very heart of England, on a meandering journey through no fewer than five counties – Wiltshire, Oxfordshire, Berkshire Hertfordshire and Buckinghamshire (see back of the book for overview map). Though now one of the 15 National Trails of England and Wales, the path actually started life around 5000 years ago – a thoroughfare for prehistoric man to make his way across the country on higher (and thus drier) ground. It's no surprise, therefore, you'll often see it described in promotional literature as the oldest road in the country – and there may well be some truth to that.

The Ridgeway stretches for 87 miles (139km) across the very heart of England

Perhaps the main joy of the Ridgeway is that so much evidence of its extensive history is still visible. The highlight is magical **Avebury** at the western end of the trail – a UNESCO World Heritage Site thanks to the concentric **stone circles** that ring the village, including the largest stone circle in the whole of Western Europe – but there are many more prehistoric sites both in this area and further east. On the edge of the village is **West Kennet Avenue**, originally

Pausing for a breather near Pitstone Hill (see p192).

The Thames between Goring and Streatley where another national trail, the Thames Path, crosses the Ridgeway.

lined with about 100 pairs (give or take a few) of giant sarsen stones in parallel lines; only some of which now remain. And not far from the official start of the path at **Overton Hill**, your gaze is diverted towards a set of three tumuli to the west of the path – ancient barrows (burial mounds) that are almost as old as the road itself.

Also close to the western end of the trail are the huge Iron Age forts of **Barbury Castle** and **Liddington Castle** and the wonderfully preserved **Neolithic long barrow at Wayland's Smithy** – at around 5500 years old it's as old as the trail itself! Add to this list the most striking ancient landmark of them all, the magnificent **Uffington White Horse**: lines of trenches filled with crushed chalk that, together, form a highly stylised outline of a 100m-long white horse. So striking and enigmatic is it that it is said to have influenced not only all the other white horses that adorn many a hillside round these parts, but it has also even been described as a forerunner of much of modern-day's minimalist art.

But the Ridgeway's charms are not merely confined to remnants of its distant past, as fascinating as these may be. There are the landscapes through which it passes and the panoramas you can enjoy from it too. The western half of the trail, across the voluptuous Wessex Downs, is open to the elements but it is exhilarating. On sunny days the air is wonderful, filling you with energy and physical well-being. It is also one of the most enjoyable sections of the Ridgeway; in blissful solitude you can look down at the towns and villages far below, with only the occasional friendly dog-walker or fellow Ridgeway trekker to break the isolation every once in a while.

The river **Thames** at the pretty Siamese twin villages of **Streatley** and **Goring** marks the halfway point of the Ridgeway and is a great place to break your walk and relax a while.

The eastern half of the trail is dominated by the **Chiltern Hills** with luxuriant woodland bearding the trail's many ascents and descents. But scattered amongst the trees are several small, picturesque villages, such as **Wigginton** and **Aldbury**, as well as a number of market towns – **Princes Risborough**, **Wendover** and **Tring** – all of which lie either on the trail or within easy walking distance of it. Plus there's also the rare opportunity to walk through the Chequers Estate, the traditional country home of the prime minister!

Towards the eastern end of the trail there is the butterfly mecca of Aldbury Nowers, home to over 30 species of butterfly. But it's **Ivinghoe Beacon** that marks the eastern extremity of the Ridgeway and offers some quite spectacular, panoramic views of the countryside below.

Whether you decide to walk the trail eastwards from Overton Hill to Ivinghoe Beacon, or vice versa, you are guaranteed some excellent walking punctuated by a wide variety of interesting distractions, plus the warm feeling that comes with having completed one of the country's great walks.

Prehistoric sites, gorgeous rolling countryside and exquisite little villages huddled around cosy, half-timbered pubs. And, if that's not enough, it should also be pointed out that walking the Ridgeway is *not* difficult. It can be done in five days but this won't leave much time for relaxation, or for enjoying the

Below: Wayland's Smithy (see p115) is a Neolithic long barrow. Legend tells that the shoes for the Uffington White Horse were forged here.

countryside you are walking through. So allow time to explore, to dally, to soak in the sun and smell the flowers. The Ridgeway, after all, is a path to savour, not hurry through; so allow six or, even better, seven days for your hike along this most ancient of trails – you'll be mightily glad that you did.

History

The Ridgeway is very ancient. It's often described as '**the oldest road in Britain**' and it's clear that parts of the route were in use 5000 years ago or more. The Ridgeway, as we know it today, is in fact the middle section of the **Greater Ridgeway** (see pp198-9), an ancient system of tracks that stretches from Lyme Regis on the Dorset coast up to Hunstanton on the Norfolk coast. These tracks evolved over centuries as people chose the driest and most suitable paths across the countryside, for themselves and their animals – which usually meant following the higher ground.

> **It's often described as the 'oldest road in Britain' ... parts were in use 5000 years ago or more**

During your walk you will still be able to see and touch stone structures dating back to the **prehistoric days** of the Ridgeway; the burial mound known as Wayland's Smithy (see box on p115) dates back to around 3590BC. Bronze Age (2500BC to 800BC) stone structures still stand, with the Avebury stone circle (see box pp88-9) and West Kennet Avenue (see box on p90) being by far the most famous and accessible of these. Additionally, you can see numerous Bronze Age burial mounds dotted along the Ridgeway.

From the **Iron Age** (beginning about 800BC) there are several important hill forts to investigate including Barbury Castle (see pp102-4) and Uffington Castle (see p117) plus earthworks such as Grim's ditch (see box on p154) also

dating from this time. During the **Dark Ages** the Ridgeway was used as a major transport route for invading Danish Viking armies. By the late **9th century** they had conquered most of Saxon England and had turned their attention to the kingdom of Wessex. In 871 they marched west along the Ridgeway from their base by the Thames at Reading only to be defeated by King Alfred at the Battle of Ashdown, which some think took place in the area around White

Avebury Stone Circle (see p88), near the western end of the walk.

Horse Hill (see box on p118).

Up until the **18th century** the Ridgeway still consisted of a collection of routes broadly heading in approximately the same direction across the country but then the Enclosures Acts were passed by parliament and these initiated the division of previously communal open land into privately owned fields. These fields were then hedged in to protect them from passing livestock and as a result the Ridgeway was forced to follow a single, defined route.

At North Stoke (see p146) the Ridgeway runs through the churchyard of St Mary's. The church dates back to the 14th century.

As **coaching routes** to London developed they avoided the actual course of the Ridgeway so it was left largely neglected – although several towns on the path, such as Marlborough and Wendover, were important rest stops. For several hundred years, therefore, the main users of the path were **drovers** transporting their sheep from the West Country, and even Wales, to the large sheep fairs at East Ilsley (see p132). The width of the Ridgeway in this area, sometimes up to 20 metres, gives an idea of just how much livestock was transported on this route. At their peak the fairs held auctions for up to 80,000 sheep a day though by the early 20th century these fairs were in decline: the last one was held in 1934. From then on the path was used mainly by farmers for access to their land.

This was especially the case during **World War II** when many of the hillsides around the Ridgeway saw a change in use from sheep-grazed areas to cultivated fields. This was the result of a government-initiated effort to provide sufficient food for the population as imports were threatened owing to the fighting. This not only changed the visual landscape of many areas of the Ridgeway but also damaged the indigenous wildlife as powerful chemical fertilisers were used to improve the poor soil.

The first calls for the Ridgeway to be recognised as a long-distance walking trail were made in 1947 by the National Parks Committee and in the 1950s the Ramblers' Association (now Ramblers; see box on p43) joined the appeal. However, it wasn't until 1973 that it was officially opened as a **National Trail**, since when the most common use for the path has been for recreation. Only minor alterations have

The Ridgeway was once used mainly by drovers taking their sheep to the sheep fairs at East Ilsley. You'll see far fewer sheep now.

been made to its course since then which enable everyone to make their way along the 87-mile (139km) trail in the footsteps of the first Ridgeway pioneers from thousands of years ago.

How difficult is the Ridgeway?

If you are reasonably fit you won't encounter any problems walking the Ridgeway. There are no sections that are technically difficult and despite having a couple of steep climbs during each day's walking, it's nothing like as demanding as many other National Trails. The most important thing to do is plan your

It's nothing like as demanding as many other National Trails

walking based on your own abilities. If you try to walk too far in one day, not only will you lose the chance to

really enjoy the countryside you are walking through but you will end up exhausted and won't feel much like walking the next day.

If anything, the half of the Ridgeway west of the Thames could be considered more difficult than the half east of it owing to its remote and exposed con-

ditions that become very apparent during bad weather. East of the Thames, the Ridgeway is often in woodland, or passing through fields, and goes through, or near to, numerous towns and villages.

How long do you need?

This depends on your fitness and experience. Do not try to do too much in one day if you are new to long-distance walking. Most people find that eight days is enough to complete the walk and still have time to look around the villages and enjoy the views along the way. Alternatively, the entire path can be done in

Most people find that eight days is enough to complete the walk and have time to look around the villages ... but it can be done in five days if you are fit enough

five days if you are fit enough, but you won't see much of the surrounding countryside.

If you're camping don't underestimate how much a heavy pack laden with camping gear will slow you down. It is also worth bearing in mind that those who take it easy on the Ridgeway see a lot more than those who sweat out long days and tend to only ever see the path in front of them. If you are walking on your own you can dictate the pace, but when walking with someone else you need to take their abilities into account and take time to enjoy their company – this may slow you down. If you don't take time to do this, you might as well be walking separately and simply meet up at the end of the day.

On all sections, but particularly the western part of the trail, you'll also need to consider how far off the path your accommodation is and build that distance into your daily total. Although some B&Bs will collect you from the Ridgeway and drop you back the next morning, not all offer this service so you do need to check when reserving a room. On p32 and p34 there are some suggested

Left: Ivinghoe Beacon – journey's end, or the start of your walk.

INTRODUCTION

**See p32 and p34 for some
suggested itineraries covering
different walking speeds**
itineraries covering different
walking speeds that will give you
an idea of what you can expect to
achieve each day.

If you only have a few days it
makes sense to concentrate on the 'best' parts of the Ridgeway; there is a list of
recommended day/two-day walks on pp31-7.

When to go

SEASONS

The western half of the Ridgeway follows the high ground and is very exposed
so if it rains you'll certainly know about it. Likewise, if it is sunny, you'll get
very hot. To compound this there is very little in the way of shelter on the western section. The eastern section, on the whole, follows lower ground and is
often in sheltered woodland. You are also far closer to human habitation on this
section should the weather turn really bad. The **main walking season** is from
Easter (March/April) to the end of September.

The biggest attraction of walking the Ridgeway in the **spring** is to see the
wild flowers in bloom, especially the carpets of bluebells in the woods. You'll
also get good walking weather at this time but there will be a risk of showers

Below: Descending Kingston Hill (see p120), heading towards Sparsholt Firs.

and thick fog can obscure pretty much everything in the early to mid morning. Unsurprisingly, the Easter holiday is a busy time.

Obviously **summer** is the busiest season for walkers on the Ridgeway owing to the fact that it is the main holiday period and the weather should be good. You probably still won't see many people on the western section, but the eastern section is very popular with dog-walkers and day-trippers. If you are walking on your own it can be nice to stop and chat to other walkers every once in a while. Although summer is your best bet, the weather in England is not always good at this time. Look at the forecast before you go and be prepared.

Autumn can be one of the best times of year to walk the Ridgeway. Most walkers have finished their holidays but you can still have good, clear weather and the sections of woodland walking are especially colourful. The western section is less inviting at this time owing to its exposed conditions.

The cold and often unpredictable weather in the **winter** makes walking the Ridgeway low on most people's lists of priorities. It certainly wouldn't be much fun on some of the open western sections but there is still plenty of opportunity for some good day walks on other parts if the weather is clear.

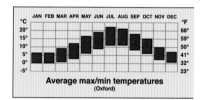

Average max/min temperatures
(Oxford)

TEMPERATURE & RAINFALL

As the English climate is temperate, walking can be enjoyed at most times of the year. However, there will be plenty of days in the winter where it will be too cold for comfortable walking but equally in the summer it can sometimes be too hot. The air **temperature** will generally be fine, it's the rain you need to watch out for. On average it rains on about one day in three in England, though more often in the winter.

Rainfall in July can be as little as half that of January in the Ridgeway area, but that's not much consolation if you are caught in a summer downpour.

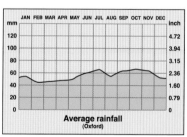

Average rainfall
(Oxford)

DAYLIGHT HOURS

If walking in autumn, winter and early spring, you must take account of how far you can walk in

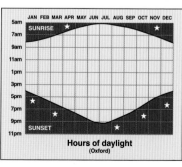

Hours of daylight
(Oxford)

the available light. It may not be possible to cover as many miles as you would in summer. The sunrise and sunset times in the table (see p15) are based on information for Oxford on the first of each month. This gives a rough picture for the Ridgeway. Also bear in mind that you will get a further 30-45 minutes of usable light before sunrise and after sunset depending on the weather.

❏ FESTIVALS AND ANNUAL EVENTS

Due to COVID-19 most of the events planned for 2020 – country fairs, festivals, concerts and organised walks – were cancelled, though at the time of research many that are held annually were planning to return in 2021.

Year-round
● **Organised events along the Ridgeway** The National Trails Office (🖳 national-trail.co.uk/ridgeway/events) promotes walks and activities along the Ridgeway **year-round**. Most weekends, especially in the summer months, there will be something going on, be it a walk along a particularly interesting section accompanied by a knowledgeable guide, a focus on specific wildlife, or a class in navigating skills.

Throughout the summer months
● **Morris dancing** During the **summer months** you can see Morris groups perform-ing at festivals and pubs along the first half of the Ridgeway. Most performances are arranged well in advance which allows you to plan your trip to coincide with them if you so desire. See box on p119 for more information about Morris dancing.

May
● **The Ridgeway 40** (🖳 ridgeway40.co.uk) This is a 40-mile walk along the Ridgeway from Overton Hill to the YHA hostel at Streatley. You are expected to com-plete the walk in one day and there are checkpoints along the route. There is also a separate event for runners. The Ridgeway 40 is held annually on a weekend in May; you may want to avoid doing your walk over this weekend.

June
● The **summer solstice** (20-21st June) draws a lot of people to Avebury Stone Circle.

July
● **Goring & Streatley Regatta** (🖳 goringgapbc.org.uk) This regatta, held in mid July, is organised by Goring Gap Boat Club. The focus is on providing a family day out with a funfair and live entertainment, in addition to the boat races on the Thames.

August
● **Uffington White Horse Show** (🖳 whitehorseshow.co.uk) This traditional country show, held on ground between Uffington and Kingston Lisle villages, is a well-organ-ised event attracting over 10,000 visitors. Past attractions have included a fly-past by a Vulcan Bomber, stunt horses, ferret racing, morris dancing, a heavy horse show and a falconry display. It's held on the Bank Holiday weekend at the end of August.

(**Opposite**) Top: Silbury Hill. **Bottom left**: Easy walking on Overton Hill (see p98).
Bottom right: Moulsford double-arched railway viaduct across the Thames (see p144).

(**Overleaf**) Left: Grim's Ditch east of Bachelor's Hill (see p154). **Right, top and middle (L)**: Exploring West Kennet Long Barrow (p91). **Middle (R)**: On the alternative walkers' path near Watlington (p157). **Right, bottom**: Chinnor station (p165), the start of the four-mile Chinnor to Princes Risborough Railway.

PLANNING YOUR WALK

1

Practical information for the walker

ROUTE FINDING

You shouldn't have any problems staying on the Ridgeway. At nearly all the junctions there are special 'Ridgeway' signposts showing the direction of the trail and these are usually also marked with the National Trail **acorn symbol**. For many stretches you barely even need these signposts as the path is clear and well-trodden. Other branching paths are also shown.

In some places the standard system of chevrons and identifying colours is used. An acorn and a **yellow** chevron or yellow writing indicates that this route is a footpath, ie exclusively for pedestrians. **Blue** indicates that the trail is a bridleway and can therefore also be used by horses and cyclists. **Purple/plum** quaintly adds a pony and trap. The word '**Byway**' in either **red** or **white** warns that the route can also be used by motorists.

Since other footpaths may be indicated on the waymark posts you won't go wrong if you just **follow the acorn**. All path junctions are included on the maps in this book along with relevant notes.

GPS

GPS technology is an inexpensive, well-established if non-essential, navigational aid. Within a minute of being turned on and with a clear view of the sky, **GPS receivers** will establish your position and elevation anywhere on earth to an accuracy of within a few metres. Most **smartphones** also have a GPS receiver built in and mapping software available to run on it (see box on p42). Don't treat a GPS as a replacement for maps, a compass and common sense. Every electronic device is susceptible to battery failure or some electronic malfunction that might leave you in the dark. GPS should be used merely as a backup to more traditional route-finding techniques and is best used in conjunction with a paper map.

(**Opposite**): The superb view from the Uffington White Horse. The flat-topped Dragon Hill below was where St George is said to have slain the dragon, its blood poisoning the grass and leaving a bare area of chalk on the hill.

Using GPS with this book – waypoints

Though a GPS system is not essential on the Ridgeway, for those who have one, GPS waypoints for the route are provided. **Waypoints** are single points like cairns. This book identifies key waypoints on the route maps. The book's waypoints correlate to the list on pp200-2 which gives the grid reference and a description. You can download the complete list as a GPS-readable .gpx file of grid references (but with no descriptions) from ⌨ trailblazer-guides.com. It's anticipated that you won't tramp along day after day, ticking off the book's waypoints, transfixed by the screen on your GPS or smartphone; the route description and maps should be more than adequate most of the time.

It's worth repeating that 98% of people who've ever walked the Ridgeway did so without GPS so there's no need to rush out and buy one – or a new GPS-enabled smartphone for that matter. Your spending priorities ought to be on good waterproofs and above all, footwear.

ACCOMMODATION

Although there is plenty of accommodation along the Ridgeway, nearly all of it falls into the B&B category. There are some campsites, but only one hostel and one bunkhouse on/near the path, both of which were closed at the time of writing.

On the western section, up to Streatley, there is virtually no accommodation on the Ridgeway itself and the nearest place to stay might be a mile or two off the path: for this reason, you really should book ahead otherwise you might find yourself very tired and without a bed for the night.

Camping

Wild camping (see also p55) is not strictly allowed on the Ridgeway: it's private land and although it's a public right of way this does not entitle you to stop and camp. However, if you pitch your tent on the path and move on the next morning leaving no trace of yourself, you shouldn't have any problems. In many places the path is wide enough to pitch a tent and leave room for anyone else passing by. Unless you have personally asked permission from the landowner, do not pitch your tent in fields, or woods, next to the Ridgeway.

There are some official campsites with basic facilities such as toilets and showers with prices around £5-10 per person (pp) which makes this the cheapest accommodation option. The campsites aren't usually open in winter (Oct-Mar), which is a strong hint that camping at this time of year really isn't much fun.

There simply aren't enough official campsites along the Ridgeway for you to stay at one every night of your walk so sometimes you'll have to engage in a spot of wild camping, splash out on a B&B, or book an Airbnb unless the (YHA) hostel and bunkhouse on the route are open again.

Hostels and bunkhouses

There is only one (YHA) hostel actually on the Ridgeway – at Streatley – and one independent bunkhouse, at Court Hill. At the time of writing both were closed due to COVID-19 but to check the latest contact the YHA (**Youth**

Hostels Association of England and Wales (☎ 01629 592700, freephone ☎ 0800 019 1700, 🖳 yha.org.uk) and for the bunkhouse see pp124-5.

Bed and breakfasts (B&B)

Anyone who has not stayed in a B&B has missed out on something very British. They consist of a bed in someone's house and usually a big cooked breakfast (see p21) in the morning though at the time of writing some places were no longer offering a cooked breakfast (see box on p21). For visitors from outside Britain it can provide an interesting insight into the way of life here as you often feel like a guest of the family.

What to expect The B&Bs in this guide are included primarily due to their proximity to the Ridgeway. They basically all offer the same thing but can vary greatly in terms of quality, style and price.

Many B&Bs offer en suite rooms but often this can mean a shower and toilet have been squeezed into a corner of the room. For a few pounds less you can usually get a standard room and it's rarely far to the bathroom, which may have the choice of a bath or a shower, though admittedly you might have to share it with other guests. At the end of a long day's walking some people prefer to stretch out in a bath rather than squash into a shower.

A **single** room has one bed, though not all B&Bs have a single room so if you are walking alone you might have to book a twin or double room and pay a supplement (see p30). **Twin** rooms and **double** rooms are often confused but a twin room comprises two single beds while a double room has one double bed (or two twins pushed together). **Triple/quad** rooms are for three/four people: they often have one double bed and one or two single beds but sometimes these are bunk beds. Proprietors often describe rooms that sleep more than two as family rooms; in some cases the additional beds are suitable for children only.

If you think you would like an **evening meal** ask when you are booking as most B&Bs require advance warning. Alternatively, the owner may give you a lift to and from the nearest eating place if there isn't a pub or restaurant within

PLANNING YOUR WALK

❏ BOOKING ACCOMMODATION

You should always book your accommodation in advance. In summer, at weekends and on public holidays there can be stiff competition for beds and in winter there's the distinct possibility that the place could be closed.

Most B&Bs, pubs/inns, guesthouses and hotels have their own website and offer online/ email booking but for some B&Bs you will need to phone; it is also possible to book some places through agencies but almost always it will end up costing a bit more.

Most places ask for a deposit (about 50%) which is generally non-refundable if you cancel at short notice. Some places may charge 100% if the booking is for one night only. Always let the owner know as soon as possible if you have to cancel your booking so they can offer the bed to someone else.

B&Bs have various ways of taking payment. Most common is to request the deposit and balance to be paid by bank transfer, though some might prefer cash on arrival or a cheque. Some places now also take credit and debit cards.

walking distance. Some proprietors will make a **packed lunch** as long as you request it by the night before.

B&B owners may also provide a **pick-up service** from the Ridgeway and take you back the next morning, which can be a great help; offering to pay something towards the petrol would be appreciated (but see box below). Some also provide a **luggage-transfer** service for which a charge would be made; see p55.

Guesthouses, pubs, inns and hotels

Guesthouses are usually more sophisticated than B&Bs and offer evening meals and a lounge for guests. Some **pubs** and **inns** offer accommodation; these have the added advantage of food and drink within staggering distance of your bed. However, the noise from tipsy punters might prove a nuisance if you want an early night. **Hotels** are usually aimed more at the motoring tourist than the muddy walker and the tariff is likely to put off the budget traveller. You'll probably arrive there in the late afternoon and leave fairly early the next morning so it's hard to justify the price. However, if you want a few more luxuries in your room, or room service, it may be worth considering a hotel.

Airbnb

The rise and rise of Airbnb (🖥 airbnb.co.uk) has seen private homes and apartments opened up to overnight travellers on an informal basis. Originally based in cities, the concept has spread to tourist hotspots in more rural areas, but do check thoroughly what you are getting and the precise location.

❏ HOW COVID-19 COULD AFFECT RIDGEWAY WALKERS

COVID-19 has had a major impact on life in Britain (and the rest of the world). At the time of writing, many businesses were open again and during research it was encouraging to see plenty of walkers on the Ridgeway, but we don't know what the situation will be when you are reading this. For most of your trip you're going to be out in the countryside with almost no one else around. However, in towns and villages that won't apply; it's always been a good idea to ring ahead to double-check that somewhere is open, or a place will be serving food when you plan to arrive, but this makes even more sense in the current times. Things to bear in mind are:

Accommodation Most accommodation along the Ridgeway was back open in the summer of 2020, albeit with some changes. The exceptions being the YHA hostel at Streatley and the bunkhouse at Court Hill.

Buffet-style breakfasts are not available anymore and even though some places are still serving 'the full English' at a dining room table, many others were opting for continental-style only, and others still providing a 'breakfast-in-a-bag' delivered to your room. Where social distancing is problematic, some places might have reduced the number of rooms that they are letting out at any one time. At the time of research some places with rooms which share facilities were only offering those rooms to families because of the problems of cleaning between each person.

Some B&B owners offer to pick you up and drop you off on the Ridgeway when you're staying with them. Depending on the situation at the time you book, this offer might, or might not, be available – this is worth checking when booking somewhere.

Places tend to come and go far more frequently than 'normal' B&Bs but there are several possibilities for a Ridgeway walk. However, while the first couple of options listed may be in the area you're after, others may be far too far afield for walkers. At its best, this is a great way to meet local people in a relatively unstructured environment, but do be aware that these places are not registered B&Bs, so standards may vary, yet prices may not necessarily be any lower than the norm. In most of the towns and villages along the route you can find accommodation in an Airbnb.

FOOD AND DRINK

Breakfast and lunch
[See also box below] Almost everywhere you stay, other than if camping, you'll be offered a full English cooked **breakfast**. A cooked breakfast includes some or all of the following: fried bacon, eggs, sausages, tomatoes, mushrooms, baked beans and fried bread – in addition to cereal and toast, washed down with a fruit juice and tea or coffee. This will certainly be enough to set you up for a day's walking – if you are thinking about calories, you'll probably want to spend the day trying to walk it off – but it may be more than you are used to or even want. If so, ask for a continental breakfast. Alternatively, if you want an early start or would prefer to skip breakfast it might be worth asking if you could have a packed lunch instead.

Eating and drinking Most pubs, restaurants and cafés along the Ridgeway were open at the time of writing. Many were already trialling reduced hours, so a pub that was previously open all day might not open until 4pm or so, but in September 2020 new rules were introduced and all places have to close at 10pm.

Obviously the need to social distance reduces the number of people allowed in any pub, restaurant or café and movement around these places is restricted; some were allowing customers in outdoor spaces only. Most restaurants and pubs require you to reserve a table in advance if you want to eat and now table service is a requirement. Some also offered a more limited menu than usual. There will also be hand-sanitising stations near the entrances and special arrangements regarding toilet facilities. It is not necessary to wear a face mask in a pub, café or restaurant.

All this does detract somewhat from the social aspect of eating and drinking out, but businesses are very keen to welcome customers through their doors again.

Public transport At the time of writing the frequency of train and bus services had mostly returned to normal and taxi companies were also operating. However, face coverings were required on (or in) all forms of public transport.

Walking There are very few places on the Ridgeway where social distancing is a problem. Perhaps there are a few pinch-points on enclosed, narrow paths, but everyone I met was courteous and we all made room for each other to pass with no problems. You will need to open and close many gates along the route – I saw someone wearing a glove to do this. If you are concerned, you might like to do the same, or take a small bottle of hand-sanitiser with you.

PLANNING YOUR WALK

❑ REAL ALES ALONG THE RIDGEWAY

Among the many pleasures of strolling on the Ridgeway is coming across country pubs and inns that you would never otherwise have visited. As you'll discover, they all have their own character and you'll end up with some very fond memories of your time spent at some of them. You'll usually have the chance to try some real ales that you might not have tried before. There are too many to list here and many pubs change their beers on a regular basis, but below is a selection of real ales that you are almost guaranteed to see in the course of your walk. (ABV means 'alcohol by volume' and is expressed as a percentage of how much alcohol a drink contains).

For more information about real ales look at the website for **CAMRA** (Campaign for Real Ale) at ❑ camra.org.uk.

● **Arkell's** (❑ arkells.com) This Swindon-based brewery produces a range of beers, but the ones you are most likely to see in their pubs are **3B** (4%), **Hoperation IPA** (4.2%) and **Wiltshire Gold** (3.7%).

● **Brakspear** (❑ brakspear-beers.co.uk) You'll certainly come across Brakspear ales, especially during the middle sections of the walk. The most common is **Brakspear Bitter** which is easy enough for anyone to drink, being only 3.4%. It has an amber colour and a mild taste. It's a good beer for more prolonged rest stops and has won many national awards. Their **Oxford Gold** (4% on draught) is brewed year-round and has a light, golden colour and fruity flavour.

● **Hop Back Brewery** (❑ hopback.co.uk) This brewery is in Downton, near Salisbury. Among the range of ales they produce is one that could be of particular interest to Ridgeway walkers, namely **Crop Circle**. Its ABV of 4.2% is accompanied by crisp and thirst-quenching qualities. It might be hard to find a pint of this on the Ridgeway but it's available in pubs around the south-west of England.

● **Ridgeway Brewing** (❑ ridgewaybrewery.co.uk) Surely the most apt beers for Ridgeway walkers are those produced by Ridgeway Brewing, based in South Stoke in Oxfordshire. Their ales have only been brewed under contract by other breweries since 2003 but already have a good reputation. **Ridgeway Bitter** (ABV 4%) is their standard brew, but if you have time to linger you might like to try their stronger premium bitter, **Oxfordshire Blue** (5%). Stronger still is their **Ridgeway IPA** (5.5%) and there is also **Ivanhoe** (5.2%). These are all available in bottles and sometimes on draught, though from personal experience they can be quite elusive; if you do see any, grab the opportunity!

● **Tring Brewery Co** (❑ tringbrewery.co.uk) Since 1992 this brewery has been busy producing a wide range of beers. Obviously you should try their **Ridgeway** (4.0%), which would be a fitting way to celebrate the end of your walk.

● **Wadworth** (❑ wadworth.co.uk) Mainly around the beginning of the Ridgeway, but even as far as Tring, you will find Wadworth ales. The best known is **6X** (4.1%); this has been brewed in Wadworth's Devizes brewery since 1921 and has a fruity, malty taste and a copper colour.

● **West Berkshire Brewery** (❑ wbbrew.com) Based in Yattendon, only half a dozen miles south of Aldworth, you're most likely to come across their excellent **Good Old Boy** (4.0%) or **Mr Chubb's** (3.4%) in pubs around the area.

● **White Horse Brewery** (❑ whitehorsebrewery.co.uk) Also very fitting for Ridgeway walkers, this company has been brewing since 2004. You are most likely to encounter their **Bitter** (3.7%), which is perfect if you're stopping off for a few. Their excellent **Wayland Smithy** (4.4%) is tastier though has the potential to stop you in your tracks. You might also like to try a pint of their **Village Idiot** (4.1%), which is light and fruity.

Many places to stay can also provide you with a packed **lunch** for an additional cost. Alternatively, packed lunches (and indeed breakfast) can be bought and made yourself. In most towns and villages you should be able to find at least one shop selling sandwiches and usually a café. If you are lucky you may be in town when there is a (farmers') market – if you come across one do have a look as local produce is likely to be on sale.

Remember that certain stretches of the walk are devoid of anywhere to eat so look at the town and village facilities table (p33 and p35) and check the information in Part 5 to make sure you don't go hungry.

Evening meals

There are some lovely **pubs** and **inns** on the Ridgeway but none directly on the path before Streatley. Although there are fewer freehouses than there used to be you can still sample some excellent beers (see box opposite) during or after a day's walking. Most pubs also serve food (at lunchtime and in the evenings, though not always daily) and this ranges from standard 'pub grub' to restaurant quality fare. There will usually be at least one vegetarian choice and sometimes also vegan/gluten-free options.

There are some quality **restaurants** in the larger towns. Additionally, most towns and some of the larger villages are riddled with cheap **takeaway** joints offering kebabs, pizzas, Chinese, Indian and fish 'n' chips; they can come in handy if you finish your walk late in the day, since they usually stay open until at least 11pm.

Buying camping supplies

If you are camping, fuel for your stove, outdoor equipment and food supplies are important considerations. Plan your journey carefully as, particularly on the western half of the Ridgeway, there aren't many opportunities to stock up without embarking on a fair trek to the nearest shop and back.

Drinking water

Depending on the weather you will need to drink as much as two to four litres of water a day. If you're feeling lethargic it may well be that you haven't drunk enough, even if you're not particularly thirsty.

Drinking directly from streams and rivers is tempting, but is not a good idea. Streams that cross the path tend to have flowed across farmland where you can be pretty sure any number of farm animals have relieved themselves. Combined with the probable presence of farm pesticides and other delights it is best to avoid drinking from these streams.

There are drinking **water taps** at some points along the Ridgeway and these are marked on the maps. Where these are thin on the ground you can usually ask a friendly shopkeeper or pub staff to fill your bottle or pouch for you – from a tap, of course. When you are filling your bottle have a good drink from it then fill it again so you leave the tap with a full bottle and don't feel like drinking half of it 100 metres down the path. When you reach a water tap, remember to check that it is working before you drink your remaining water.

MONEY

There are no banks and few post offices on the western half of the Ridgeway. So for this stretch, although most pubs will take cards, you should take enough **cash** for purchases in small shops. Unless you leave the Ridgeway and go to Wantage you won't find a bank/ATM till Goring and after that you'll have to wait until Princes Risborough unless you leave the path. In towns without a

---

❏ INFORMATION FOR FOREIGN VISITORS

● **Currency** The British pound (£) comes in notes of £50, £20, £10 and £5, and coins of £2 and £1. The pound is divided into 100 pence (usually referred to as 'p', pronounced 'pee') which come in 'silver' coins of 50p, 20p, 10p and 5p, and 'copper' coins of 2p and 1p.

A guide to currency **exchange rates** can be found on 🖵 xe.com/currencycon verter; however, the actual rate used by post offices, banks and travel agents varies.

● **Business hours** Most **village shops** are open Monday to Friday 9am-5pm and Saturday 9am-12.30pm but many are open longer and some open on Sundays as well. Occasionally you'll come across a local shop that closes at lunchtime on one day during the week, usually a Wednesday or Thursday; this is a throwback to the days when all towns and villages had an 'early closing day'. **Convenience stores** and **supermarkets** are open Monday to Saturday 8am-8pm (sometimes up to 15 hours a day) and on Sunday from about 9am to 5 or 6pm, though at the time of writing main branches of supermarkets can only open for six hours on a Sunday; most choose 10am-4pm or 11am-5pm.

Main **post offices** generally open Monday to Friday 9am-5pm and Saturday 9am-12.30pm; **banks** typically open at 9.30/10am Monday to Friday and close at 3.30/4pm, though in some places both post offices and banks may open only two or three days a week and/or in the morning, or limited hours, only. **ATMs** (**cash machines**) located outside a bank, shop, post office or petrol station are open all the time, but any that are inside will be accessible only when that place is open.

Pub hours are less predictable (especially now because of COVID-19); although many open daily 11am-11pm, opening hours in rural areas and during quieter periods (early weekdays, or in the winter months) are often more limited: typically Monday to Saturday 11am-3pm & 5 or 6-11pm, and Sunday 11am/noon-3pm & 7-10.30/11pm. The last entry time to most **museums and galleries** is usually half an hour/an hour, before the official closing time.

● **Public (bank) holidays** Most businesses are shut on 1st January, Good Friday (March/April), Easter Monday (March/April), the first and last Monday in May, the last Monday in August, 25th December and 26th December.

● **School holidays** School holiday periods in England are generally: a one-week break late October, two weeks around Christmas/New Year, a week in mid February, two weeks around Easter, a week in late May/early June (to coincide with the bank holiday on the last Monday in May), and six weeks from late July to early September.

● **Documents/entry charges** If you are a member of a National Trust (NT) organisation in your country bring your membership card as you should be entitled to free entry to National Trust properties and sites in the UK. English Heritage (EH) also have a membership card allowing free access to their sites. Some NT and EH properties have two entry charges: one standard charge and one that is proportionately higher because it includes Gift Aid; this can only be used by UK tax payers.

bank there is sometimes an ATM in a petrol station or at a newsagent but be aware that many of these charge £1.25-1.95 regardless of the amount you withdraw. Many ATMs are part of the Link (🖥 link.co.uk) network and the website has an ATM locator search function.

Small independent shops might still require you to pay in cash, as will most B&Bs and campsites. Shops that do take credit/debit cards, such as convenience stores and supermarkets, and some pubs, may advance cash against a card

(see also pp20-1)

● **Travel/medical insurance** At the time of writing the **European Health Insurance Card** (EHIC) entitles EU nationals (on production of their card) to necessary medical treatment under the UK's National Health Service (NHS) while on a temporary visit here. However, it is unlikely this will be the case after Brexit but it may depend on your home country. Anyhow an EHIC card is not a substitute for proper medical cover on your travel insurance for unforeseen bills and for getting you home should that be necessary. Also consider cover for loss or theft of personal belongings, especially if you're camping, as there may be times when you have to leave your luggage unattended.

● **Weights and measures** Milk in Britain is generally sold in pints (1 pint = 568ml), as is beer in pubs, though most other **liquids** including petrol (gasoline) and diesel are sold in litres. Most **food** is sold in metric weights (g and kg) but the imperial weights of pounds (lb: 1lb = 453g) and ounces (oz: 1oz = 28g) are often displayed too.

Road **distances** are given in miles (1 mile = 1.6km) rather than kilometres, and yards (1yd = 0.9m) rather than metres. The population remains divided between those who still use inches (1 inch = 2.5cm) and feet (1ft = 0.3m) and those who are happy with centimetres and millimetres; you'll often be told that 'it's only a hundred yards or so' to somewhere, rather than a hundred metres or so.

The **weather** – a frequent topic of conversation – is also an issue: while most forecasts predict temperatures in °C, many people continue to think in terms of °F (see temperature chart on p15 for conversions).

● **Time** During the winter the whole of Britain is on Greenwich Meantime (GMT). The clocks move one hour forward on the last Sunday in March, remaining on British Summer Time (BST) until the last Sunday in October.

● **Smoking** Smoking in enclosed public places is banned. The ban relates not only to pubs and restaurants, but also to B&Bs, hostels and hotels. These latter have the right to designate one or more bedrooms where the occupants can smoke, but the ban is in force in all enclosed areas open to the public – even in a private home such as a B&B. Should you be foolhardy enough to light up in a no-smoking area, which includes pretty well any indoor public place, you could be fined £50, but it's the owners of the premises who suffer most if they fail to stop you, with a potential fine of £2500.

● **Telephones** From outside Britain the international country **access code** for Britain is ☎ 44 followed by the area code minus the first 0, and then the number you require.

To protect against vandalism some public phones accept debit/credit cards only; the minimum cost for a call is 60p. **Mobile (cell) phone** reception is quite reliable along the Ridgeway. If you're using a mobile phone that is registered overseas, consider buying a local SIM card to keep costs down; also remember to bring a universal adaptor so you can charge your phone.

● **Emergency services** For police, ambulance, fire and mountain rescue dial ☎ 999, or the EU standard number ☎ 112.

PLANNING YOUR WALK

(**cashback**) if you buy something (usually at least £5) at the same time and as long as they have cash as now so many more people pay by card. See also p41 and the town and village facilities table, p33 and p35.

Using the Post Office for banking

Several banks in Britain have agreements with the Post Office allowing customers to make cash withdrawals using a debit card (with a PIN number) at branches throughout the country.

As many towns along the Ridgeway have a post office this can be a very useful service. However, check with the Post Office Helpline (🖳 postoffice.co .uk/branch-finder) that the post offices en route are still open.

OTHER SERVICES

On the western half of the Ridgeway, services are a bit scant, but on the eastern half most villages and all the towns have a small **shop** and a **post office**. Apart from getting cash, post offices can be used for sending home unnecessary equipment that may be weighing you down.

In Part 5 special mention is given to other services that may be of use to the walker such as **pharmacies** and **tourist information centres** – the latter can be used for finding accommodation among other things.

WALKING COMPANIES & LUGGAGE TRANSFER

Several UK-based companies offer self-guided holidays on the Ridgeway but, at the time of writing, none offered a fully guided walk.

Luggage transfer

● **Ridgeway Luggage Transfers** (🖳 ridgewayluggagetransfers.co.uk) They can transfer your luggage the whole length of the Ridgeway, or just a part of it. In addition to this, they also provide passenger transport to/from railway stations/airports and along the trail.

● **Move Along Radio Cars** (☎ 07500 118323, 🖳 aly.murray089@hotmail.co .uk) are happy to transfer luggage on the western half of the Ridgeway up to Streatley and also will pick people and luggage up at Swindon rail or coach station. Text or email contact preferred as Aly is often driving.

● **Village Cars** (☎ 01844 342551, 🖳 www.villagecars.cab; Princes Risborough) Offer a bespoke service for luggage transfer and can take passengers.

Some of the B&Bs listed in this guide (see Part 5) will also take your luggage on to your next overnight stop if you are staying with them. Local taxi companies can also provide this service but may be more expensive.

Self-guided holidays

Self-guided holidays usually include detailed advice and notes on itineraries and routes, maps, accommodation including breakfast, daily baggage transfer and transport arrangements at the start and end of your walk.

● **Absolute Escapes** (☎ 0131 610 1210, 🖥 absoluteescapes.com; Edinburgh) Offer three itineraries: the full route in 7 days and two shorter sections, either the Wessex Downs or the Chiltern Hills, in 4 days.

● **British & Irish Walks** (☎ 01242 254353, 🖥 britishandirishwalks.com; Cheltenham) Offer walks along the southern section of the way, beginning in Marlborough and ending at Ogbourne St George.

● **Celtic Trails Walking Holidays** (☎ 01291 689774, 🖥 celtictrailswalkingholidays.co.uk; Chepstow) Have two itineraries covering the whole walk in 9-10 days and will also tailor-make walks.

● **Contours Walking Holidays** (☎ 01629 821900, 🖥 contours.co.uk; Derbyshire) Operate three itineraries covering the whole route in 6-8 days and two offering part of the route: Avebury to Goring, and Goring to Ivinghoe Beacon. Dog-friendly itineraries are also available.

● **Explore Britain** (☎ 01740 650900, 🖥 explorebritain.com; Durham) Operate one itinerary on the western half from Avebury to Goring.

● **Footpath Holidays** (☎ 01985 840049, 🖥 footpath-holidays.com; Wilts) In addition to offering an 8-day self-guided Ridgeway tour they also, unusually, offer treks along the Wessex Ridgeway (see p198), plus 'Ancient Landscapes of Wessex' which are highlights and include sections of the Ridgeway.

● **Freedom Walking Holidays** (☎ 07733 885390, 🖥 freedomwalkingholidays.co.uk; Goring-on-Thames) Can accommodate a variety of requirements within your holiday package.

● **Hikes & Bikes** (☎ 0330 043 6843, 🖥 hikesandbikes.com; Worcestershire) Offer the whole trail, and in parts as well as highlights.

● **Macs Adventure** (☎ 0141 530 4390, 🖥 macsadventure.com; Glasgow) Operate two itineraries: 8 days/7 nights and 10 days/9 nights, available from April to end September.

● **Responsible Travel** (☎ 01273 823700, 🖥 responsibletravel.com; Brighton) Offer two itineraries of 5 and 8 days' walking along the entire trail.

● **Great British Walks** (☎ 01600 713008, 🖥 great-british-walks.com; Monmouth) Operate itineraries for the whole trail and also for sections; can tailor make as required.

DISABLED ACCESS

There are no officially recognised stretches of the Ridgeway open for wheelchair users, though that doesn't mean it isn't possible to use some stretches of the path. On the western half there are only a few of gates, none of which would prove problematic for a wheelchair user. On the downside though, the route on this section sometimes consists of rutted tracks that can also be very muddy after rain. An area on this half that is accessible is around Barbury Castle (see pp102-4). There is a car park here and although the castle itself would prove very difficult for a wheelchair user, the area around it is beautiful and provides excellent views over the surrounding countryside. The eastern half of the Ridgeway is less isolated and the route passes through several towns that could make good starting points. The path heading east from Wendover (see Map 34, pp178-9) is accessible, but not particularly exciting. Where the Ridgeway cross-es a road there is often a car park and driving to one of these enables you to get into the open countryside quickly and with little effort.

The project to replace stiles with wide gates has now been completed. National Trails staff work to maintain the gates in partnership with landowners. They also work with landowners and others to keep the track in good condition, but weather conditions and use by vehicles still damage some stretches of track.

MOUNTAIN-BIKING

The Ridgeway and trails leading off it are very popular with mountain-bikers. However, not all of it is open to them. The western section from Avebury to Streatley is totally open and has only a short section of road and relatively few gates compared to the eastern section. The paths along this portion are generally wide and shouldn't present a problem for mountain-bikers. From Streatley heading east many sections of the Ridgeway are closed to cyclists – you can see this in detail on the interactive map on the National Trails website (🖳 national trail.co.uk/en_GB/trails/the-ridgeway/custom-itinerary). This, of course, doesn't deter some cyclists who use the designated footpaths despite doing so illegally.

Conditions on the Ridgeway during the summer months are pretty good for cyclists though some sections of heavily rutted path might cause problems. Also be aware of flint on some sections of the path as it can cause punctures.

Details of cycle (repair) shops in towns on or near the route are given in the route guide.

HORSE RIDERS

The same sections of the Ridgeway that are open to cyclists are also open to horse riders. In practice, most horse riders use only short sections of the path which link into many other bridleways. Deeply rutted tracks can be problematic for horses and you should also be aware of the flinty sections of path that can injure horses' hooves.

MOTOR VEHICLES

Despite many people's opposition, motor vehicles are allowed to use selected stretches of the Ridgeway. Since 2006 only five short sections have been open to cars and motorcycles. The total length of these sections is about 17 miles and all but one mile of that is west of the Thames. Of the five sections that are open, four can only be used between May and September.

You will rarely come across a car or 4x4 on the Ridgeway and even motor-cyclists seem to be few and far between nowadays.

It's obvious that motor vehicles do serious damage to the Ridgeway tracks that they use and the effects of this damage are most keenly felt by walkers. It's not much fun walking on a deeply rutted, muddy track for several miles.

WALKING WITH A DOG

[See also pp196-7] You are allowed to take your dog on all sections of the Ridgeway. Indeed, the majority of people you meet will be accompanied by at least one dog. Henry Stedman, who updated the 4th edition of this guide, took his dog Daisy (a veteran of many a long-distance trail) along the whole of the path without any problems. Indeed, **Daisy thinks that the Ridgeway is the best trail for dogs she has yet been on**. The relative lack of fields with livestock in them (only two fields with cows encountered by Henry and Daisy, and only one with sheep – though this of course could vary from year to year) and the small number of busy roads mean that fairly obedient dogs (ie ones that aren't liable to jump fences and will come to heel on command) can be left off the leash for much of the trip. True, the (slight) possibility that motor vehicles will be on the trail is a potential hazard that you won't find on other national trails; but time your walk to a season when these are not allowed and you should have a safe walk for your dog – and a stress-free walk for you. Do be careful near the horse gallops, however, particularly those stretches where there is only a white rail between you and the gallop as dogs can get onto the gallop easily; the sheer speed of the horses and the thunder of their hooves can easily unnerve or excite your pet – and mayhem may ensue.

As the owner, you are fully responsible for your dog's behaviour. Dogs should always be kept on leads while around livestock (see p196). Having said this, if you are harassed by cattle because of your dog, the Ramblers/NFU recommend letting the dog off the lead.

Budgeting

The amount of money you need to take with you depends on your accommodation plans and how you're going to eat. If you camp and cook your own meals your expenses can be very low, but most people prefer to have at least some of their meals cooked for them and even the hardiest camper may be tempted into the occasional B&B when the rain is falling. Also, don't forget all those little things that inevitably push up your daily bill: postcards, stamps, cream teas, ice-creams, beer, buses here, buses there and more beer; it all adds up!

CAMPING

You can survive on as little as £15 per person if you use the cheapest sites and cook all your own food from staple ingredients. Nevertheless, most people find that the best-laid plans to survive on the bare minimum soon fall flat after a couple of hard days' trekking. Always budget for unforeseen expenses and, of course, the end-of-day pint of beer which costs around £3.50. Assuming such liquid treats and the occasional takeaway or pub meal, a budget of £20-25 per day is far more realistic.

B&B-STYLE ACCOMMODATION

Rates can be as little as £25pp per night assuming two people are sharing a room but are more often £30-35pp, particularly for guesthouses and hotels, and can even be £50pp or more for the most luxurious places. If wanting sole occupancy of a room there is likely to be a supplement; this is usually about £10-15 less than the room rate, in some cases you may have to pay the full rate.

Add on the price of lunch (though if you have had a cooked breakfast you may not want much), an evening meal, beer and other expenses and you can expect to need at least £60-80pp per day. However, rates can be substantially less if you are planning to stay in one place for three or more nights and are also usually lower during the winter months. If you are on a budget you could always ask to go without breakfast which will probably result in a reduction.

Itineraries

Part 5 of this book (the Route Guide) has been re-written for this edition so that it can be used by hikers walking the Ridgeway in either an eastward or westward direction, following a colour coding: **E➜** and **W ←**. For more details see below.

This route has been divided into stages but these are not rigid daily stages. It's structured to make it easy for you to plan your own itinerary. If you have a week to spare you can walk the Ridgeway in one go. However, many people decide to walk it in sections over a longer period.

To help you plan your walk the **colour maps** at the back of the book have profile charts; there is also a **planning map** (see opposite inside back cover). The **table of town & village facilities**, see p33 and p35, gives a rundown on the essential information you need regarding accommodation possibilities and services. Alternatively, you could follow one of the suggested **itineraries**, see opposite, that are based on walking speed.

There is also a list of recommended linear **day and two-day (weekend) walks** (see opposite) that cover the highlights of the Ridgeway as well as some suggested side trips (see box on pp36-7).

The **public transport map** and the table of **bus services** are on pp48-51.

Once you have an idea of your approach turn to **Part 5** for detailed information on accommodation, places to eat and drink, as well as other services in each town and village on the route. Also in Part 5 you will find summaries of the route to accompany the detailed trail maps.

WHICH DIRECTION?

The generally accepted way to walk the Ridgeway is from west to east though it really doesn't matter. As the two halves are very different you might base your decision on what type of scenery and terrain you'd like to tackle first. Neither section is particularly demanding but the western section is far more isolated and really isn't much fun in bad weather. The eastern section, being in woodlands for much of the time, is far more sheltered and relaxing. The prevailing wind is generally west to east so this makes walking in that direction more comfortable.

Availability of public transport heading in either direction along the Ridgeway is similar so this shouldn't have much bearing on which direction you choose to walk in. Unless you're walking the whole path in one trip, you might even decide to walk some sections in one direction and others in the other. This could make sense, depending on transport, accommodation options, or just because you fancy it.

Having walked the Ridgeway in both directions my conclusion is that there is no best way – they are both equally enjoyable. In fact, if you have the time I would thoroughly recommend walking the Ridgeway twice – once in either direction. On the second trip you'll be surprised just how different the walking feels while also being able to revisit, and stop longer, in your favourite places from the first trip. In light of all that, this edition has been re-written as a two-direction guidebook. The route descriptions and trail maps are tailored to suit walking in either direction.

SUGGESTED ITINERARIES

The itineraries in the boxes on p34 and p36 cover walking in either direction and are based on different accommodation types: one is for those who prefer to camp where possible; the other is for those who choose to stay in B&B-style accommodation. Each is divided into three options based on walking speeds. They are only suggestions so feel free to adapt them to your needs. **Don't forget** to add your travelling time before and after the walk.

THE BEST DAY AND TWO-DAY WALKS

The desire of most walkers is to tackle the whole Ridgeway in one go but sometimes this isn't possible. Spare time, good weather, transport and money all need to be found at the same time. For this reason many choose to walk the Ridgeway in separate sections, maybe over a series of summer weekends. Others might not be so concerned about walking every inch of the official path and might only want to walk the best bits. Simply getting out and walking any part will be rewarding, but listed below are some especially enjoyable parts all of which can be walked in either direction. If you're feeling ambitious and the weather is on your side, you could try completing a two-day walk in one day. For details of public transport services to/from the places listed below see pp38-51.

Day walks

● **Avebury to Ogbourne St George** 9½ miles/15km (Alternative start route D, see p94, & pp97-105) This path starts at Avebury Stone Circle and walks the quiet high ridge to the Iron Age fort of Barbury Castle where there are magnificent views northwards; it then goes onto Smeathe's Ridge and finally down into the pleasant village of Ogbourne St George where there is a good pub.

(cont'd on p37)

SUGGESTED ITINERARIES
Avebury to Ivinghoe Beacon – walking east

CAMPING

NIGHT	PLACE	DISTANCE MILES/KM		PLACE	DISTANCE MILES/KM		PLACE	DISTANCE MILES/KM	
	Relaxed pace			**Medium pace**			**Fast pace**		
0	Avebury/Overton Hill*			Avebury/Overton Hill*			Avebury/Overton Hill*		
1	Ogbourne St G*	9.6†	15.5	Ogbourne St G*	9.6†	15.5	Ogbourne St G*	9.6†	15.5
2	Sparsholt Firs	14.5	23	Sparsholt Firs	14.5	23	Court Hill#	19	30.5
3	Court Hill#	4.5	7	Court Hill#	4.5	7	Streatley*	14	22.5
4	Streatley*	14	22.5	Streatley*	14	22.5	Watlington	15	24
5	Crowmarsh G	7.3	12	Crowmarsh G	7.3	12	Princes Risboro'*	11.2	18
6	Watlington	9.6	15	Watlington	9.6	15	Ivinghoe Bcn§	17.5	28
7	Princes Risboro'*	11.2	18	Princes Risboro'*	11.2	18			
8	Wigginton*	12.4	20	Ivinghoe Bcn§	17.5	28			
9	Ivinghoe Bcn§	5.1	8						

* No campsite (or hostel) at the time of writing but
alternative accommodation is available nearby

† 11.3 miles/18.25km if walking from Avebury

Camping not available at the time of writing but should be from 2021
(bunkhouse may also be open)

§ Closest campsite is at Ivinghoe, 1.2-miles/2km from the beacon

STAYING IN B&B-STYLE ACCOMMODATION

NIGHT	PLACE	DISTANCE MILES/KM		PLACE	DISTANCE MILES/KM		PLACE	DISTANCE MILES/KM	
	Relaxed pace			**Medium pace**			**Fast pace**		
0	Avebury/Overton Hill¶			Avebury/Overton Hill¶			Avebury/Overton Hill¶		
1	Ogbourne St G	9.6†	15.5	Bishopstone	17.7†	28.5	Bishopstone	17.7†	28.5
2	Bishopstone	8.7	14	Letcombe Rgs	9.9	15.5	East Ilsley	18.7	30
3	Letcombe Rgs	9.9	15.5	Goring	14.8	23.5	Watlington	20.7	33
4	East Ilsley	8.8	14	Watlington	14.7	23.5	Wendover	17.2	26.5
5	Wallingford	11.2	18.5	Princes Risboro'	11	18	Ivinghoe Bcn§	11.3	18
6	Watlington	9.5	15.5	Wigginton	12.4	20			
7	Princes Risboro'	11	18	Ivinghoe Bcn§	5.1	8			
8	Wigginton	12.4	20						
9	Ivinghoe Bcn**	5.1	8						

Note: Airbnb options are not included in the above

¶ There are no B&Bs at Overton Hill but numerous options in
Avebury (1.7 miles/2.75km away) and East Kennett (0.5miles/0.8km away)

† 11.3 miles/18.25km if walking from Avebury

** There are no B&B options at Ivinghoe Beacon/Ivinghoe but The Greyhound at
Aldbury is 3.5 miles/5.6km and Tring is 5.5 miles/8.9km from Ivinghoe Beacon

PLANNING YOUR WALK

VILLAGE AND TOWN FACILITIES
Avebury to Ivinghoe Beacon – walking east

PLACE*	DISTANCE* MILES/KM	BANK* (ATM)	POST OFFICE*	TIC/ TIP*	EATING PLACE*	FOOD SHOP	CAMP- SITE	B&B*/ HOTEL
Marlborough	to...		✓	✓	TIP	✓✓✓	✓		✓✓✓
Avebury	6 9.5		(✓)		TIP	✓✓	✓		✓✓✓
(East Kennett)	(0.5/0.8)								✓
Overton Hill	1.7 2.75 [Start Ridgeway]								
(Ogbourne St G)	9 14.5 (+0.6/1)					✓			✓✓
(Liddington)	6.5 10.5 (+0.6/1)					✓			✓✓
Foxhill	1 1.5					✓			
(Bishopstone)	1.2 2 (+0.6/1)					✓			✓✓
(Ashbury)	1.5 2.5 (+0.6/1)		(✓)			✓✓	✓		✓
(Woolstone)	2 3 (+1.2/2)					✓			✓
(Uffington)	(1.7/2.5)		✓			✓	✓		✓
(Sparsholt Firs area)	2.5 4 (+0.6/1)							✓	✓✓
(Sparsholt)	(1.5/2.5)					✓			✓
(Letcombe Rgis)	3.9 6 (+1.5/2.5)					✓			✓✓
(Court Hill)	0.6 1 (+0.3/0.5)					✓		✓	
(Wantage)	(2/3)	✓	✓	TIP	✓✓✓	✓		✓
(East Ilsley)	8.2 13 (+1/1.5)					✓			✓
(Compton)	(1.5/2.5)		(✓)			✓	✓		✓
(Aldworth)	2.7 4.5 (+1.2/2)					✓			
Streatley	3 5					✓✓			✓✓✓
Goring	0.3 0.5	ATM	✓	TIP	✓✓✓	✓		✓✓✓
South Stoke	1.5 2.5					✓	✓		✓
North Stoke	2.5 4								
(Wallingford)	1.2 2 (+1.2/2)	✓	✓	TIC	✓✓✓	✓		✓✓✓
(Crowmarsh Gifford)	(0.7/1.2)					✓	✓	✓	✓
Nuffield	4 6.5								
(Watlington)	5.5 9 (+0.6/1)	ATM	✓		✓✓✓	✓	✓	✓
(Lewknor)	2.5 4 (+0.5/0.8)					✓			✓
(Aston Rowant)	1 1.5 (+0.5/0.8)					✓			✓
(Chinnor)	2.2 3.5 (+0.3/0.5)	ATM	✓		✓✓✓	✓		✓
P Risborough	5.3 8.5 (+0.2/0.3)	✓	✓	TIC	✓✓✓	✓		✓
Wendover	6.2 10	ATM	✓	TIP	✓✓✓	✓		✓✓
Wigginton	6.2 10					✓	✓		✓
(Tring)	(1/1.5)	ATM	✓	TIC	✓✓✓	✓		✓✓✓
(Aldbury)	2 3 (+0.6/1)	ATM	✓		✓✓	✓		✓
Ivinghoe Beacon	3.1 5 [End Ridgeway]								
(Ivinghoe)	3.4 5.5 (+1.2/2)		✓		✓✓✓	✓	✓	

* NOTES

PLACE Places in brackets eg (Watlington) are a short walk off the route and the distance then given is to the turn-off for the place.

DISTANCE Distances in (**brackets**) indicate how far the place is from the turn-off which is the nearest point on the Ridgeway.

BANK (ATM) ATM = no bank but there is an ATM

POST OFFICE (✓) = limited opening days/hours
TIC/TIP = Tourist information centre/point
EATING PLACE/B&B/HOTEL ✓ = one place
✓✓ = two **✓✓✓** = three or more

Note: At the time of writing neither the (YHA) hostel or bunkhouse on the route was open.

PLANNING YOUR WALK

SUGGESTED ITINERARIES
Ivinghoe Beacon to Avebury – walking west

FROM IVINGHOE BEACON

CAMPING

Night	Relaxed pace PLACE	DISTANCE MILES/KM		Medium pace PLACE	DISTANCE MILES/KM		Fast pace PLACE	DISTANCE MILES/KM	
0	Ivinghoe Beacon§			Ivinghoe Beacon§			Ivinghoe Beacon§		
1	Wigginton*	5.1	8	Princes Risboro'*	17.5	28	Princes Risboro'*	17.5	28
2	Princes Risboro'*	12.4	20	Watlington	11.2	18	Watlington	11.2	18
3	Watlington	11.2	18	Crowmarsh G	9.6	15	Streatley*	15	24
4	Crowmarsh G	9.6	15	Streatley*	7.3	12	Court Hill#	14	22.5
5	Streatley*	7.3	12	Court Hill#	14	22.5	Ogbourne St G*	19	30.5
6	Court Hill#	14	22.5	Sparsholt Firs	4.5	7	Overton Hill*	9.6†	15.5
7	Sparsholt Firs	4.5	7	Ogbourne St G*	14.5	23			
8	Ogbourne St G*	14.5	23	Overton Hill*	9.6†	15.5			
9	Overton Hill*	9.6†	15.5						

§ Closest campsite is at Ivinghoe, 1.2-mile / 2km from the beacon

* No campsite (or hostel) at the time of writing but
alternative accommodation is available nearby.

\# Camping not available at the time of writing but should be from 2021
(bunkhouse may also be open)

†11.3 miles/18.25km if walking on to Avebury

STAYING IN B&B-STYLE ACCOMMODATION

Night	Relaxed pace PLACE	DISTANCE MILES/KM		Medium pace PLACE	DISTANCE MILES/KM		Fast pace PLACE	DISTANCE MILES/KM	
0	Ivinghoe Beacon¶			Ivinghoe Beacon¶			Ivinghoe Beacon¶		
1	Wigginton	5.1	8	Wigginton	5.1	8	Wendover	11.3	18
2	Princes Risboro'	12.4	20	Princes Risboro'	12.4	20	Watlington	17.2	26.5
3	Watlington	11	18	Watlington	11	18	East Ilsley	20.7	33
4	Wallingford	9.5	15.5	Goring	14.7	23.5	Bishopstone	18.7	30
5	East Ilsley	11.2	18.5	Letcombe Rgs	14.8	23.5	Overton Hill**	17.7†	28.5
6	Letcombe Rgs	8.8	14	Bishopstone	9.9	15.5			
7	Bishopstone	9.9	15.5	Overton Hill**	17.7†	28.5			
8	Ogbourne St G	8.7	14						
9	Overton Hill**	9.6†	15.5						

Note: Airbnb options are not included in the above

¶ There are no B&B options at Ivinghoe Beacon/Ivinghoe but The Greyhound at
Aldbury is 3.5 miles/5.6km and Tring is 5.5 miles/8.9km from Ivinghoe Beacon

** There are no B&Bs at Overton Hill but numerous options in
Avebury (1.7 miles/2.75km away) and East Kennett (0.5miles/0.8km away)

†11.3 miles/18.25km if walking on to Avebury

PLANNING YOUR WALK

VILLAGE AND TOWN FACILITIES
Ivinghoe Beacon to Avebury – walking west

◄W FROM IVINGHOE BEACON

PLACE*	DISTANCE* MILES/KM	BANK* (ATM)	POST OFFICE*	TIC/ TIP*	EATING PLACE*	FOOD SHOP	CAMP-SITE	B&B* HOTEL
(Ivinghoe)	to...				✔✔	✔	✔	
Ivinghoe Beacon	3.4 5.5 (+1.2/2) [Start Ridgeway]							
(Aldbury)	3.1 5 (+0.6/1)	ATM	✔		✔✔	✔		✔
(Tring)	(+1/1.5)	ATM	✔	TIC	✔✔✔	✔		✔✔✔
Wigginton	2 3				✔	✔		✔
Wendover	6.2 10	ATM	✔	TIP	✔✔✔	✔		✔✔✔
P Risborough	6.2 10 (+0.2/0.3)	✔	✔	TIC	✔✔✔	✔		✔✔✔
(Chinnor)	5.3 8.5 (+0.3/0.5)	ATM	✔		✔✔✔	✔		✔
(Aston Rowant)	2.2 3.5 (+0.5/0.8)				✔			✔
(Lewknor)	1 1.5 (+0.5/0.8)				✔			✔
(Watlington)	2.5 4 (+0.6/1)	ATM	✔		✔✔✔	✔	✔	✔
Nuffield	5.5 9				✔			✔
(Crowmarsh Gifford)	4 6.5 (+0.7/1.2)		✔		✔	✔	✔	✔
(Wallingford)	(1.2/2)	✔	✔	TIC	✔✔✔	✔		✔✔✔
North Stoke	1.2 2							
South Stoke	2.5 4				✔			✔
Goring	1.5 2.5	ATM	✔	TIP	✔✔✔	✔		✔✔✔
Streatley	0.3 0.5				✔✔			✔✔✔
(Aldworth)	3 5 (+1.2/2)				✔			
(Compton)	2.7 4.5 (+1.5/2.5)		(✔)		✔	✔		✔
(East Ilsley)	(1/1.5)				✔			✔
(Wantage)	8.2 13 (+2/3)	✔	✔	TIP	✔✔✔	✔		✔
(Court Hill)	(0.3/0.5)				✔		✔	
(Letcombe Rgis)	0.6 1 (+1.5/2.5)				✔			✔✔
(Sparsholt)	3.9 6 (+1.5/2.5)				✔			✔
(Sparsholt Firs area)	(0.6/1)						✔	✔✔
(Uffington)	2.5 4 (+1.7/2.5)		✔		✔	✔		✔
(Woolstone)	(1.2/2)				✔			✔
(Ashbury)	2 3 (+0.6/1)		(✔)		✔✔	✔		✔
(Bishopstone)	1½ 2.5 (+0.6/1)				✔			✔✔
Foxhill	1.2 2				✔			
(Liddington)	1 1.5 (+0.6/1)				✔			✔✔
(Og St G)	6.5 10.5 (+0.6/1)				✔			✔✔
Overton Hill	9 14.5 [End Ridgeway]							
(East Kennett)	(0.5/0.8)							✔
Avebury	1.7 2.75		(✔)	TIP	✔✔	✔		✔✔✔
Marlborough	6 9.5	✔	✔	TIP	✔✔✔	✔		✔✔✔

* NOTES

PLACE Places in brackets eg (Watlington) are a short walk off the route and the distance then given is to the turn-off for the place.

DISTANCE Distances in (brackets) indicate how far the place is from the turn-off which is the nearest point on the Ridgeway.

BANK (ATM) ATM = no bank but there is an ATM

POST OFFICE (✔) = limited opening days/hours
TIC/TIP = Tourist information centre/point
EATING PLACE/B&B/HOTEL ✔ = one place
𝒘 = two 𝒘𝒘 = three or more

Note: At the time of writing neither the (YHA) hostel or bunkhouse on the route was open.

PLANNING YOUR WALK

❑ SIDE TRIPS

There are plenty of good circular and linear walks from the Ridgeway. Information about these can be obtained from local tourist information centres/points (see box p43), the National Trails website (see box p63), or from the relevant councils (see box p62).

● **Aldbourne Circular Route** This is a 12-mile (19.5km) route which for several miles uses the Ridgeway. It takes in Aldbourne village, several Bronze Age burial mounds, the deserted village of Snap (see p106), Liddington Castle (see p108) and Sugar Hill. The trail is waymarked and it's also marked on OS Explorer maps No 157 and 170.

● **Ashbury Circular Walk** This 10-mile (16km) walk from the village of Ashbury (see p114) takes the walker through some beautiful countryside once the initial steep climb has been completed. The path crosses the Ridgeway and heads to Alfred's Castle, an Iron Age hillfort, before reaching Ashdown House, a 17th-century Dutch-style property owned by the National Trust. From here it returns to the Ridgeway via a different route and takes in Wayland's Smithy (see box p115), before heading back down the hill to Ashbury. The trail is waymarked and although the paths are marked on OS Explorer map No 170, they aren't labelled.

● **Lambourn Valley Way** This 20-mile (32km) route starts at Uffington White Horse and leads down into the valley to reach the village of Lambourn. It then broadly follows the River Lambourn along the valley to its end in Newbury. This is a very peaceful walk passing through several small villages with only the crossing of the M4 to spoil the atmosphere. The route is waymarked and is also marked on OS Explorer maps No 170 and 158. A *Lambourn Valley Way* walkers' map by Nick Hill is available from 🖥 nickhillmaps.co.uk.

● **East Ilsley/West Ilsley Circular Route** This 6-mile (9.5km) walk is best started and finished in one of the pubs in East Ilsley. The path takes a wayward route to West Ilsley before heading up to the Ridgeway and following it for just over a mile then turning back to East Ilsley. Much of this path is on broad tracks that often run close to racehorse gallops. The route is waymarked and the paths are marked on OS Explorer map No 170.

● **Aston Rowant Discovery Trail** This is a 5.3-mile (8.5km) walk but 6.2 miles (10km) with a hotel/pub extension. The route is waymarked and is also marked on OS Explorer map No 171. See Map 27 (p163), and for full details see 🖥 nationaltrail.co .uk/ridgeway/route/aston-rowant-discovery-trail.

● **The Chiltern Link** This 8-mile (13km) linear walk starts on Wendover High St and meanders through woods and open countryside to the town of Chesham where you can pick up the Chess Valley Walk. Several miles into the walk you reach The Lee, a tiny village with a popular pub – The Cock and Rabbit Inn (🖥 cockand rabbit.uk) – that is well worth visiting. The route is waymarked and is also marked on OS Explorer map No 181.

● **Beacon View Walk** This 5-mile (8km) circular walk is usually started and finished at The Greyhound in Wigginton (see p184) and follows the course of the Ridgeway for about two miles from Hastoe Cross to the bridge over the Grand Union Canal. The route then follows the canal to Cow Roast (a village!) before heading back to Wigginton. The paths comprising the route are marked with standard signs and all paths appear on OS Explorer map No 181.

● **Two Ridges Link** This 8-mile (13km) linear walk runs from Ivinghoe Beacon, the eastern end of the Ridgeway, to Leighton Buzzard at the start of the Greensand Ridge Walk. The walk takes you first through the villages of Ivinghoe Aston and Slapton before joining the Grand Union Canal. The trail is fully waymarked and it's also marked on OS Explorer maps No 181 and 192.

Day walks (cont'd from p31)

● **Foxhill to White Horse Hill** 5 miles/8km (see pp111-18) Start outside The Burj restaurant at the Foxhill crossroads and quickly climb up onto the open high ground for stunning views, visit the ancient burial site at Wayland's Smithy and finish at White Horse Hill, the site of an Iron Age hill fort, Dragon Hill, and the original white horse.

● **White Horse Hill to East Ilsley** 15 miles/24km (see pp116-33) If you fancy a bit of time on your own, this is the most isolated section of the Ridgeway. It keeps to the high ground with only a few road crossings and a handful of farms on the entire stretch. You need good weather – there is virtually no shelter.

● **Streatley to Wallingford** 7 miles/11.5km (see pp139-51) Begin in the Thames-side village of Streatley and walk into Goring before following the bank of the Thames northwards through the delightful villages of South and North Stoke. The path then heads into the old town of Wallingford.

● **Wendover to Ivinghoe Beacon** 10 miles/16km (see pp176-94) From the attractive town of Wendover the path takes you through the best woodland walking on the Ridgeway, coming close to the village of Wigginton should you choose to stop off for lunch. The final section takes on Ivinghoe Beacon, a long, steep climb through woodland and finally some excellent open walking with increasingly fantastic views.

Two-day (weekend) walks

● **Avebury to White Horse Hill** 22 miles/35.5km (Route D, see p94 & pp97-116) This takes in many of the most interesting ancient sites along the Ridgeway. The walking is mainly along broad, grassy tracks with few steep climbs. There is no accommodation near the middle of this walk so, depending on where you stay, you'll either have a short first day and long second, or vice versa.

● **East Ilsley to Watlington** 22 miles/35.5km (see pp132-61) This walk takes in a bit of each of the Ridgeway's main attractions – first, isolated walking, then, the path along the Thames and finally, some fine woodland walking. You can stay in Wallingford to divide the journey neatly into two days.

PLANNING YOUR WALK

● **The Ashridge Drovers' Walk** This 6-mile (9.5km) circular walk starts and finishes at Tring Railway Station (see Map 38, p191). From there it makes for Aldbury (see p190) then up to the Bridgewater Monument where there is a visitor centre and tea shop. The route then follows the high ground to join the Ridgeway which it follows down to the railway station. The walk often follows wide, sunken lanes used in the past for droving (moving livestock). The paths comprising the route are marked with standard signs and all paths appear on OS Explorer map No 181.

● **Ridgeway Link Walk** This 7½-mile (12km) linear walk follows the Icknield Way from Chilterns Gateway Centre, on Dunstable Downs, to Ivinghoe Beacon (see Map 39, p193). Of course, walking the path in reverse might be more practical for Ridgeway walkers, especially if you are heading to Dunstable for transport connections. The walk passes through Whipsnade and Dagnall, both of which have a pub. Chilterns Gateway Centre is open all year and has a café, shop and toilets and there is also a car park. Although the route is well waymarked some of the paths can get rather muddy after rain. The entire route is marked as the Icknield Way on OS Explorer map No 181.

What to take

Deciding how much to take with you can be difficult. Experienced walkers know that you really should take only the bare essentials but at the same time you need to ensure you have all the equipment necessary to make the trip safe and comfortable.

KEEP YOUR LUGGAGE LIGHT

Carrying a heavy rucksack really can ruin your enjoyment of a good walk and can also slow you down, turning an easy 7-mile day into an interminable slog. Be ruthless when you pack and leave behind all those little home comforts that you tell yourself don't weigh that much really. This advice is even more pertinent to campers who have added weight to carry.

HOW TO CARRY IT

The size of your **rucksack** will depend on where you are planning to stay and how you are planning to eat. If you are camping and cooking for yourself you will probably need a minimum 70-litre rucksack which can hold the tent, sleeping bag, cooking equipment and food. Make sure your rucksack has a stiffened back and can be adjusted to fit your own back comfortably. This will make carrying the weight much easier. If you plan to stay in B&B-style accommodation a 30- to 40-litre pack should be more than enough to carry everything you need.

When packing your rucksack (and if you are not using a luggage-transfer service) make sure you have all the things you are likely to need during the day near the top or in the side pockets. This includes map, water bottle or pouch, packed lunch, waterproofs and this guidebook, of course. Make sure the hip belt and chest strap (if there is one) are fastened tightly as this helps distribute the weight with most of it being carried on your hips. Rucksacks are decorated with seemingly pointless straps, but if you adjust them correctly it can make a big difference to your personal comfort while walking.

If using a luggage-transfer service you will need a **day pack** or small **bum bag** for the essentials listed above and also for when you go sightseeing or for a day walk.

It's also a good idea to keep everything in **canoe bags**, **waterproof rucksack liners** or strong plastic bags. If you don't, it's bound to rain.

FOOTWEAR

Your **boots** are the single most important item of gear that can affect the enjoyment of your trek. In the summer you can use a light pair of trail shoes if you're only carrying a small pack. Make sure they have a Gore-Tex lining otherwise you could end up with wet, cold feet if there is any rain. Although the Ridgeway isn't particularly strenuous, some of the terrain can be quite rough so a good pair of walking boots is a safer bet. They must fit well and be properly broken in. It is no good discovering that your boots are slowly murdering your feet two days into a week-long trek. See p59 for more blister-avoidance advice.

The traditional wearing of a thin liner **sock** under a thicker wool sock is no longer necessary if you choose a high-quality sock specially designed for walking. A high proportion of natural fibres makes them much more comfortable. Three pairs are ample. Some walkers like to have a **second pair of shoes** to wear when they are not on the trail. Trainers, sport sandals or flip-flops are all suitable as long as they are light.

CLOTHES

Experienced walkers know the importance of wearing the right clothes. Especially up on the western part of the Ridgeway the wind, rain and sun can all be fierce and there's often no shelter if you are caught out. Modern technology in outdoor attire can seem baffling but it comes down to: a base layer to transport sweat away from your skin; a mid layer or two to keep you warm; and an outer layer or 'shell' to protect you from the wind and rain.

Base layer
Cotton absorbs sweat, trapping it next to the skin which will chill you rapidly when you stop exercising. A thin lightweight **thermal top** made from synthetic material is better as it draws moisture away, keeping you dry. It will be cool if worn on its own in hot weather and warm when worn under other clothes in cooler conditions. A spare would be sensible. You may also like to bring a **shirt** for wearing in the evening.

Mid layers
In the summer a woollen jumper or mid-weight polyester **fleece** will suffice. For the rest of the year you will need an extra layer to keep you warm. Both wool and fleece, unlike cotton, have the ability to stay reasonably warm when wet.

Outer layer
A **waterproof jacket** is essential year-round and will be much more comfortable (but also more expensive) if it's also 'breathable' to prevent the build up of condensation on the inside. This can also be worn to keep out the wind.

Leg wear
Whatever you wear on your legs it should be light, quick drying and not restricting. Many British walkers find polyester tracksuit bottoms comfortable. Poly-cotton or microfibre trousers are also excellent. Denim jeans should never be worn; if they get wet they become heavy, cold and bind to your legs. A pair of **shorts** is nice to have on sunny days. Thermal **longjohns** or thick tights are cosy if you're camping but are probably unnecessary even in winter.

Waterproof trousers are necessary most of the year. In summer a pair of windproof and quick-drying trousers is useful in showery weather. **Gaiters** are not really necessary but may come in useful in wet weather when the vegetation around your legs is dripping wet.

Underwear
Three changes of what you normally wear is fine. Women may find a **sports bra** more comfortable because pack straps can cause bra straps to dig into your shoulders.

Other clothes
A **warm** hat and **gloves** should always be kept in your rucksack, year-round. You never know when you might need them. In summer you should also carry a **sun hat** with you, preferably one that also covers the back of your neck. Also consider a small **towel**, especially if you are camping.

TOILETRIES

Only take the minimum: a small bar of **soap** in a plastic container (unless staying in B&B-style accommodation) which can also be used instead of shaving cream and for washing clothes; a tiny tube of **toothpaste** and a **toothbrush**; one roll of **loo paper** in a plastic bag. If you are planning to defecate outdoors you will also need a lightweight **trowel** for burying the evidence (see pp54-5 for further tips). A **razor**, **deodorant**, **tampons/sanitary towels** and a high-factor **sun screen** should cover all your needs.

FIRST-AID KIT

There is a pharmacy in many towns and villages along the route so you only need a small kit to cover common problems and emergencies: pack it in a waterproof container. A basic kit will contain **aspirin** or **paracetamol** for treating mild to moderate pain and fever; **plasters/Band Aids** for minor cuts; **Moleskin**, **Compeed**, or **Second skin** for blisters; a **bandage** for holding dressings, splints or limbs in place and for supporting a sprained ankle or a weak knee; a small selection of different-sized **sterile dressings** for wounds; **porous adhesive tape**, **antiseptic wipes**, **antiseptic cream**, **safety pins**, **tweezers** and **scissors**.

GENERAL ITEMS

Essential
The following should be in everyone's rucksack: a one-litre **water bottle** or **pouch**; a **torch** (flashlight) with spare bulb and batteries in case you end up walking after dark; **emergency food** (see p58) which your body can quickly convert into energy; a **penknife**; a **watch** with an alarm; and a suitable **bag** for packing out any rubbish you accumulate. These days, of course, also a **face mask** and a small bottle of **hand sanitiser**. A **whistle** is also worth taking. It can fit in a pocket and although you are very unlikely to need it you may be grateful for it in the unlikely event of an emergency (see pp58-9). Although the path is easy to follow, a 'Silva' type **compass** and knowing how to use it is a good idea in case you need to leave the trail when there is heavy fog.

Useful

Many would list a **camera** as essential but it can be liberating to travel without one once in a while; a **notebook** can be a more accurate way of recording your impressions. A **book** helps to pass the time on train and bus journeys. For comfort, particularly in the summer, you may wish to take a pair of **sunglasses**. Also useful are **binoculars** for observing wildlife, a **walking stick** or pole to take the shock off your knees, a **vacuum flask** for carrying hot drinks and a **mobile phone** (reception is quite reliable along the Ridgeway); if you take a mobile phone make sure you also take the charging device.

CAMPING GEAR

Campers will need a **tent** (or bivvy bag if you enjoy travelling light) which is able to withstand wet and windy weather. You should find that a 2- to 3-season **sleeping bag** is sufficient, but obviously in winter a warmer bag is a good idea. You will also need a **sleeping mat**, a **stove** and **fuel**, a **pan** with a lid that can double as a frying pan/plate (this is fine for two people), a **pan handle**, a **mug**, a **spoon** and a wire/plastic **scrubber** for washing up.

MONEY

There are no banks/ATMs on the Ridgeway between Overton Hill and Goring so unless you leave the way you will have to carry most of your money as **cash** or pay by card. Between Goring and Ivinghoe Beacon most towns have at least one **ATM**. A **debit card** is the easiest way to withdraw money (see pp24-6) and debit/credit cards can be used to pay in larger shops, pubs, restaurants and hotels.

MAPS

The hand-drawn maps in this book cover the trail at a scale of just under 1:20,000: $3^1/_8$ inches = one mile (5cm = 1km); they provide plenty of detail and information to keep you on the right track.

If you are only walking on the Ridgeway, you shouldn't need any other maps but for side trips you will need an **Ordnance Survey** map (🖳 ordnancesurvey .co.uk). The entire Ridgeway route is covered on four OS Explorer/ Active maps at a scale of 1:25,000. These maps are: **157** (Marlborough & Savernake Forest), **170** (Abingdon, Wantage & Vale of White Horse), **171** (Chiltern Hills West, Henley-on-Thames & Wallingford), and **181** (Chiltern Hills North, Aylesbury, Berkhamsted & Chesham). The Explorer maps cost £8.99 each and the Active series (which are laminated) are £14.99 each; these maps are widely available in bookshops or can be ordered from the Ordnance Survey website. Members of Ramblers (see box on p43) can borrow up to 10 maps for free from their library, paying only for return postage; contact them for details; UK public libraries often have a selection of OS maps for their members to borrow. Alternatively, members of the LDWA (see box on p43) are entitled to a discount on maps.

Collins (🖳 collins.co.uk/pages/a-z-maps-atlases) now publishes the A-Z Adventure Atlas map series. This is a booklet with OS strip maps covering the entire route at a scale of 1:25,000 (4cm = 1km) and with an index. The Ridgeway one costs £8.95. It's easy to use as there is no need to fold and unfold it, unlike a map.

Harvey Maps (⌨ harveymaps.co.uk) have a map – *Ridgeway* (£14.50) – for the entire trail but it's at a scale of 1:40,000 (2.5cm = 1km). Printed on polyethylene, it's durable, waterproof, weighs only 60g and can also be downloaded digitally for your iPhone, iPad or Android device.

See also box below.

❑ DIGITAL MAPPING

There are numerous apps and software packages that provide Ordnance Survey (OS) maps for a PC, smartphone, tablet or GPS. Maps are supplied by direct download over the internet. The maps are then loaded into an application, also available by download, from where you can view them, print them and create routes on them.

Digital maps are normally purchased for an area such as a National Park, but the Ridgeway walk is available as a distinct product from some vendors. Once you own the electronic version of the map you can print any section as many times as you like.

The real value of the digital maps though, is the ability to draw a route directly onto the map from your computer or smartphone. The map, or the appropriate sections of it, can then be printed with the route marked on it, so you no longer need the full versions of the OS maps. Additionally, the route can be viewed directly on your smartphone or uploaded to a GPS device, providing you with the whole route in your hand at all times while walking. Most smartphones have a GPS chip in them, so you'll be able to see your position overlaid onto the digital map on your phone.

Many websites now have free routes you can download for the more popular digital mapping products. It is important to ensure any digital mapping software on your smartphone uses pre-downloaded maps, stored on your device, and doesn't need to download them on-the-fly, as this could be difficult when you're on the trail.

Taking OS-quality maps with you on the walk has never been so easy. Almost every device with built-in GPS functionality now has some mapping software available for it. One of the most popular manufacturers of dedicated handheld GPS devices is Garmin (⌨ garmin.com), who have an extensive range of map-on-screen devices; prices vary from around £100 to £700.

Smartphones and GPS devices should complement, not replace, the traditional method of navigation (a map and compass) as any electronic device is susceptible to problems and, if nothing else, battery failure. Remember, too, that battery life will be significantly reduced, compared to normal usage, when you are using the built-in GPS and running the screen for long periods.

● **Anquet** (⌨ anquet.com) has the Ridgeway for £14.20 using OS 1:25,000 mapping. They also have a range of Harvey maps.
● **Ordnance Survey** (⌨ shop.ordnancesurvey.co.uk/apps/os-maps) will let you download and use their UK maps (1:25,000 scale) on a mobile or tablet without a data connection for a subscription of £23.99 for a year or £2.99 a month.
● **Harvey** (⌨ harveymaps.co.uk/acatalog/digital-mapping.html) sell a Ridgeway map for £20.49 for use on any device with the Avenza Maps app.
● **Memory Map** (⌨ memory-map.co.uk) sell OS 1:25,000 Explorer mapping covering the whole of the UK for £125.

Stuart Greig (⌨ lonewalker.net)

RECOMMENDED READING

The Ridgeway, John Cleare, Frances Lincoln 2011; hardback; includes a history of the trail but most of the book is filled with beautiful colour photographs.

Both National Trails (NT; Anthony Burton, 2016) and Cicerone (Steve Davison, 2016) publish guides to *The Ridgeway*.

Of course if you are a seasoned long-distance walker, or even if you are new to the game and like what you see, check out the ever-growing list of titles in the Trailblazer series (see pp207-8).

Flora and fauna field guides

RSPB Birds of Britain and Europe (Rob Hume, published by Dorling Kindersley in association with the RSPB; 5th ed 2018; £16.99) is one of many excellent bird guides though is a little bulky for carrying on the trail.

❏ SOURCES OF FURTHER INFORMATION

Trail information

The Ridgeway National Trails Office (NT; 🖳 nationaltrail.co.uk/en_GB/trails/the-ridgeway) The NT website has information concerning all aspects – history, geology, wildlife, events, future projects – of the Ridgeway and leaflets that can be downloaded. Up-to-date information is on the 'Plan your visit' page; there is also an interactive map and videos on the website. For any other queries you can email through the website. Another useful resource is **The Friends of Ridgeway** website (see p63).

Tourist information

● **Tourist Information Centres/Points (TICs/TIPs)** These are found in towns throughout Britain and provide locally specific information; TICs have staff and may be able to book accommodation whereas TIPs usually only have leaflets. There are TICs in **Wallingford** (p147), **Princes Risborough** (p171), and **Tring** (p185) and TIPs in **Marlborough** (p73), **Wantage** (p126), **Goring** (p141) and **Wendover** (p176). At the time of writing the Tring and Goring offices were closed.

● **County/district councils** The websites for the county/district councils (see box on p62) for the area covering the route can also be a useful source of tourist information.

Organisations for walkers

● **Backpackers Club** (🖳 backpackersclub.co.uk) A club for people who are involved or interested in lightweight camping through walking, cycling, skiing or canoeing. They produce a quarterly magazine and provide members with a comprehensive advisory and information service on all aspects of backpacking. They also organise weekend trips and publish a farm-pitch directory. Membership costs £20 per year and £30 for a family.

● **The Long Distance Walkers Association** (LDWA; 🖳 ldwa.org.uk) An association of people with the common interest of long-distance walking. Membership includes a copy of their journal *Strider* three times per year giving details of challenge events and local group walks as well as articles on the subject. Membership is £15 per year or £22.50 for a family.

● **Ramblers** (formerly Ramblers' Association; 🖳 ramblers.org.uk) Looks after the interests of walkers throughout Britain. They publish a large amount of useful information including their quarterly *Walk* magazine and also have an app. Membership costs £36.60/25.60 individual/concessionary, joint/concessionary £49/34.

PLANNING YOUR WALK

The extensive but pocket-sized *Wild Flowers* (Martin Walters; 2012), published by Collins as part of their 'Gem' series, is well worth £5.99; Collins Gem also publishes *Butterflies* (Michael Chinnery; 2012) for £5.99. The Field Studies Council (⌨ field-studies-council.org) publishes a series of inexpensive *Identification Guides* (fold out charts; £2.50-5) which are also practical.

There are also numerous **fieldguide apps** for both iPhone and Android, for identifying flowers, butterflies and birds by their song as well as by their appearance. One to consider for birds is: ⌨ merlin.allaboutbirds.org.

Getting to and from the Ridgeway

Both ends of the Ridgeway can be reached by public transport (though less conveniently so at the eastern end) and its location in the centre of southern England means that it's one of the most accessible long-distance trails in the country.

PLANNING YOUR WALK

❑ GETTING TO BRITAIN

● **By air** Most airlines serve London Heathrow (⌨ heathrow.com) or London Gatwick (⌨ gatwickairport.com). In addition a number of budget companies fly from Europe's major cities to the other London terminals at Stansted (⌨ stanstedairport .com) and Luton (⌨ london-luton.co.uk); the latter is the most convenient airport for the end of the walk (or the start if you choose to walk east to west). There are also flights to Bristol (⌨ bristolairport.co.uk), which is far closer to the official start of the Ridgeway than London Heathrow.

For details of the airlines using these airports and the destinations served visit the relevant airport's website.

● **From Europe by train** The Eurostar (⌨ eurostar.com) terminal in London is St Pancras International at St Pancras station; there are connections from King's Cross St Pancras station on the London Underground to Paddington, the main station for trains to/from Swindon, and to Euston for services to/from Tring (see box on p46).

For more information about rail services from Europe contact your rail service provider or Railteam (⌨ railteam.eu).

● **From Europe by coach** Eurolines (⌨ eurolines.com) have a huge network of long-distance coach services, connecting over 600 destinations in 36 European countries, as well as Morocco, to London. Check carefully, as once expenses, such as food for the journey, are taken into consideration it often does not work out much cheaper than flying, particularly when compared to the prices of some of the budget airlines.

● **From Europe by car** **Ferries** operate between various ports from mainland Europe and ports on Britain's southern and eastern coasts as well as from Ireland to Britain's western coast. Look at ⌨ ferrysavers.com or ⌨ directferries.com for a full list of operating companies, routes and services.

Eurotunnel (⌨ eurotunnel.com) operates a shuttle (**Le shuttle**) train service for vehicles via the Channel Tunnel between Calais and Folkestone taking just 35 minutes.

The obvious advantages of travelling to the Ridgeway by public transport are that you don't have to go back and collect your car at the end of the walk (in fact, you can't/shouldn't leave your car at either end of the Ridgeway for an extended period) and you don't need to worry about the safety aspect of leaving your car unattended.

If you are walking the Ridgeway from one end to the other in one go, you shouldn't need public transport at any point along the trail. If, however, you are just walking one section, or want to skip a certain stretch and move on to the next, you will. For short distances between towns you will be using the bus.

From nearly any town or village on the Ridgeway it is fairly easy to get to a town that has connections to the national public transport network. So, if you decide to walk only a certain section, you shouldn't have any problem getting back home, though it may take some time and a series of buses.

On the whole, services to the majority of towns and villages are frequent on weekdays and mostly on Saturdays, but on Sundays and public holidays there is often just a limited service, or none at all. Even during the week, getting from one place to another isn't always straightforward; you often need to get a bus to a town from where you can then catch a bus to your destination. This can mean that you might have to finish walking early to ensure you get your bus connections. However, at the time of writing, some services were more limited due to COVID-19 (see box on p21) so ensure you check the timetable in advance of travel.

NATIONAL TRANSPORT

By rail   [see box on p46]

The most convenient railway station for the official start of the Ridgeway is **Swindon** (12½ miles/20km away). Swindon is on the main line from London Paddington to Bristol; it takes about an hour from London to Swindon and about half an hour from Bristol to Swindon (services are operated by GWR). From Swindon you'll need to take one of the local bus services (see box on pp50-1) to Marlborough and change there for Swindon's Bus Company No 42 service which stops at West Kennett, just a few hundred metres from Overton Hill. Alternatively, take the Stagecoach No 49 service from Swindon to Avebury and walk from there.

In the middle of the Ridgeway, GWR has services to **Goring & Streatley** on the London Paddington to Oxford line.

Chiltern Railways operate services to **Princes Risborough** and **Wendover** (both on the Ridgeway). There are also some services to Little Kimble and Saunderton, both of which are fairly close to the Ridgeway.

The nearest railway station to Ivinghoe Beacon at the eastern end of the Ridgeway is **Tring** (3¾ miles/6km away); conveniently it is on the Ridgeway. Tring is a stop on services operated by London Northwestern Railway (Euston to Tring takes about 40 mins) and Southern.

All timetable and fare information can be found at **National Rail Enquiries** (☎ 03457 484950, 🖳 nationalrail.co.uk, or through their app). You can either purchase tickets at any railway station in the UK, or online through the relevant train operating company (see box below) or their app, or alternatively through 🖳 thetrainline.com or 🖳 qjump.co.uk.

It is often possible to buy a train ticket that includes bus travel at your destination. For further information visit the Plusbus website (🖳 plusbus.info). Alternatively, for details of taxi companies operating at railway stations throughout England visit 🖳 traintaxi.co.uk.

By coach   [see box opposite]

National Express is the principal coach (long-distance bus) operator in Britain. Coach travel is generally cheaper but takes longer than travel by train.

At the time of research the NX402 service to Marlborough, which is just 4 miles (6.5km) from Overton Hill and the start of the Ridgeway, was no longer

---

❏ RAIL SERVICES

Note: only direct services are included and not all stops are listed. Engineering works often happen at weekends and services then are provided by a rail replacement bus.

GWR (🖳 gwr.com)
● London Paddington to Bristol Temple Meads via Reading, Didcot Parkway, **Swindon**, Chippenham & Bath Spa, Mon-Sat 2-4/hr, Sun 1-2/hr
(Note: services from Swansea, Cardiff Central, Bristol Parkway, and Cheltenham Spa to London Paddington generally stop at Swindon.)
● London Paddington to Didcot Parkway via Maidenhead, Twyford, Reading, Tilehurst, Pangbourne, **Goring & Streatley** & Cholsey, daily 1/hr
● Twyford to Henley-on-Thames, Mon-Sat 1-2/hr, Sun 1/hr
● London Paddington to Exeter St David's via Maidenhead, Reading, Newbury, Pewsey & Taunton, Mon-Sat 13/day (7-8/day call at Newbury & Pewsey), Sun 10/day (4-5/day call at Newbury & Pewsey)
● Reading to Bedwyn via Newbury & Hungerford, Mon-Sat 1/hr, Sun 7-8/day

Chiltern Railways (🖳 chilternrailways.co.uk)
● London Marylebone to Aylesbury via High Wycombe, Saunderton & **Princes Risborough**, daily 1/hr
● London Marylebone to Banbury via High Wycombe & **Princes Risborough**, Mon-Fri approx 7/day, Sat & Sun 1/hr
● London Marylebone to Aylesbury via Amersham & **Wendover**, daily 2/hr

Southern (🖳 southernrailway.com) (part of Govia Thameslink Railway)
● Clapham Junction to Milton Keynes Central via West Brompton, Wembley Central, Watford Junction, Hemel Hempstead, Berkhamsted & **Tring**, Mon-Fri 1/hr, Sat & Sun 1/hr but to Watford Junction only

London Northwestern Railway (🖳 londonnorthwesternrailway.co.uk)
● London Euston to Cheddington via Watford Junction, Hemel Hempstead, Berkhamsted & **Tring**, Mon-Sat 2/hr to Tring plus 1/hr to Cheddington, Sun 1/hr
● London Euston to Northampton via Watford Junction, Hemel Hempstead, Berkhamsted, **Tring** & Milton Keynes Central, Mon-Sat 1/hr, Sun approx 1/hr

---

❏ **COACH SERVICES**

National Express
(☎ 0871 781 8181, lines open 8am-10pm daily, 💻 nationalexpress.com)
401   London Victoria Coach Station to **Swindon** via Heathrow Airport, 4/day
          (1/day continues to/starts from Bristol and 1/day to/from Frome)
707   Heathrow Airport to Birmingham via **Hemel Hempstead**, Luton Airport
          & Milton Keynes & Northampton, 3/day plus 2/day to Northampton
737   Oxford to **Stansted Airport** via High Wycombe, **Hemel Hempstead**,
          Luton Airport & Hatfield, 8/day

Oxford Bus (💻 airline.oxfordbus.co.uk)
theairline Oxford to Heathrow Airport via **Lewknor Turn (M40 J6)**, daily 1-2/hr
theairline Oxford to Gatwick Airport via **Lewknor Turn (M40 J6)**, daily 1/hr

Oxford Tube (operated by Stagecoach; 💻 oxfordtube.com)
          London to Oxford via **Lewknor Turn (M40 J6)**, daily (24hrs/day) 1-5/hr

Green Line (💻 arrivabus.co.uk/greenline)
748/758 London to **Hemel Hempstead**, 2-10/day

---

operating. However, National Express 401 services stop in Swindon from where you can take Stagecoach's 48/48A/80 or Salisbury Red's X5 bus to Marlborough (see box on pp50-1). From Marlborough take Swindon's Bus Company No 42 service (Mon-Sat only) to the West Kennett bus stop, just a few hundred metres from Overton Hill.

The nearest place to Ivinghoe Beacon at which National Express coaches stop is Hemel Hempstead (10 miles/16km) from where you can get a local bus to Tring and then to Ivinghoe (see box on pp50-1). You can buy National Express tickets online or through their app. **Green Line** also operates services to Hemel Hempstead from London Victoria.

Most of the **Oxford Tube** bus services between London and Oxford call at Lewknor, a good starting point for a walk to Princes Risborough or Wendover.

If you are planning to walk from Wantage, ask for a connector ticket from London rather than a single/return ticket as there will then be no additional charge for the journey from Oxford to Wantage on either Stagecoach Gold's S8 or S9 (see box on pp50-1). However, this can only be bought on the bus.

The Oxford Tube operates on a first-come-first-served basis and tickets can either be bought online, through their app, or on the bus (cash or contactless card).

By car
Even though it is easy to drive to both the start and end of the route, and indeed to many places in between, parking for more than a day is not easy, or necessarily safe, so unless someone you know will give you a lift it's probably easier and cheaper and certainly better for the environment to use public transport.

(cont'd on p52)

PLANNING YOUR WALK

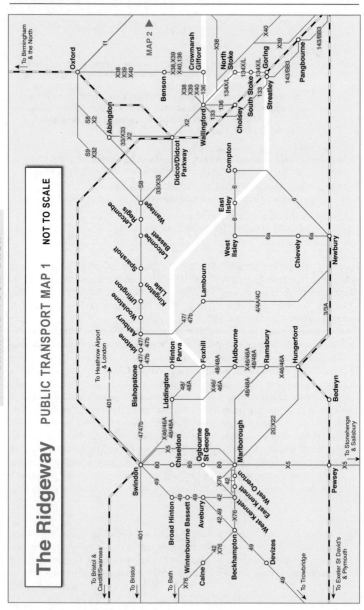

The Ridgeway PUBLIC TRANSPORT MAP 1   NOT TO SCALE

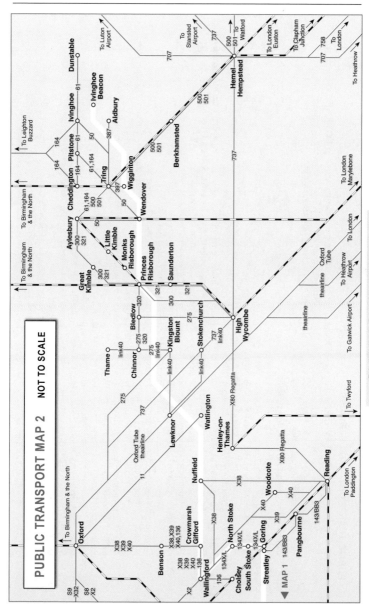

PLANNING YOUR WALK

❑ PUBLIC TRANSPORT – BUS SERVICES

Notes: The services listed below were correct at the time of research but may change, particularly because of COVID-19, so check before you travel.

Towns/villages on, or very near to, the Ridgeway and also the Marlborough to Avebury walk are highlighted.

Services are listed in chronological order.   Not all stops are listed.

No	Operator	Route and frequency details
3/3A	N&D	Newbury to Hungerford, Mon-Sat 5/day
4/4A/4C	N&D	Newbury to Lambourn, Mon-Sat 7/day
6	N&D	Newbury to **West Ilsley** via **Compton & East Ilsley**, Mon-Sat 4-5/day
6a	N&D	Newbury to **West Ilsley** via Chievely, Mon-Sat 1-2/day
11	TT/GA	Oxford to **Watlington**, Mon-Sat 10/day, Sun 4/day
20/X22	SBC	Hungerford to **Marlborough**, Mon-Fri 7/day, Sat 4/day (note: some services at Hungerford wait for the train to arrive)
42	SBC	Calne to Marlborough via Beckhampton, **Avebury**, **West Kennett**, **East Kennett**, & **West Overton**, Mon-Sat 6/day (note: for some services stops are request only so check in advance)
33/X33	TT/GA	Abingdon to **Wantage** via Didcot Parkway, Mon-Fri 11-12/day, Sat 10/day
46A/X46	S'coach	Swindon to Hungerford via **Liddington**, Aldbourne & Ramsbury, Mon-Fri 4/day, Sat 5/day
47/47b	GF	Swindon to Lambourn via **Bishopstone**, **Idstone & Ashbury**, Mon-Sat 5/day
48/48A	S'coach	Swindon to **Marlborough** via **Liddington**, **Foxhill**, Aldbourne & Ramsbury, Mon-Sat 5-6/day
49	S'coach	Swindon to Trowbridge (The Trans Wilts Express) via Broad Hinton, Winterbourne Bassett, **Avebury**, Beckhampton & Devizes, Mon-Fri approx 1/hr plus 2/day to Devizes, Sat 1/hr
50	RRT	Swindon to Devizes via Broad Hinton, Winterbourne Bassett, **Avebury** & Beckhampton, Sun 6/day
50	Redline	Aylesbury to RAF Halton via **Wendover**, Mon-Sat 2/hr (see also Redline)
55	RRT	Aylesbury to **Ivinghoe** via **Wendover** & **Tring**, Sun & Bank Hols other than Xmas 2-3/day
61	RedE	Aylesbury to Amersham via **Wendover**, Mon-Fri 6/day
80	S'coach	Aylesbury to Dunstable via **Tring**, Pitstone & **Ivinghoe**, Mon-Sat 4/day
133	GF	Swindon to **Marlborough** via Chiseldon & **Ogbourne St George**, Mon-Fri 7/day, Sat 5/day
134X/L	GF	**Wallingford** to **Goring** via **Streatley**, Mon-Fri 1-2/day
136	TT/GA	**Wallingford** to **Goring** via **North Stoke**, **South Stoke** & Cleeve, Mon-Fri 3-4/day
143/BB3	TT/GA	Cholsey to Benson via **Wallingford** & **Crowmarsh Gifford**, Mon-Fri 14/day, Sat 12/day
		Reading to **Goring** via Pangbourne & **Streatley**, Mon-Sat 1/day (also BB3 1/day in term time)

164	Redline	Aylesbury to **Ivinghoe** via **Tring, Pitstone,** Cheddington & Wilstone, Mon-Fri 2/day plus 5/day to Wilstone, Sat 4/day to Wilstone
275	RRT	High Wycombe to Oxford via Bledlow Ridge, **Chinnor, Kingston Blount** & Wheatley, Mon-Fri 2-3/day
300	ABB	Aylesbury to High Wycombe via Stoke Mandeville, Great Kimble & **Princes Risborough,** Mon-Sat 2-3/hr, Sun 1/hr
320	Redline	**Chinnor** to **Princes Risborough** via Bledlow, Mon-Fri 7-9/day (connects at P Risborough with trains to/from London)
321	Redline	High Wycombe to Aylesbury via Saunderton & **Princes Risborough,** Mon-Fri 4/day plus 3/day to Princes Risborough
387	RRT	**Tring** to **Aldbury,** Mon-Fri 7/day, Sat 5/day
397	RRT	**Tring** to **Wigginton,** Mon-Sat 4/day
500	ABB	Aylesbury to Watford via **Tring,** Berkhamsted & Hemel Hempstead, Mon-Sat 2-3/hr
501	RRT	Aylesbury to Watford via **Tring,** Berkhamsted & Hemel Hempstead, Sun 1/hr
link40	Car	High Wycombe to Thame via Stokenchurch, **Lewknor, Kingston Blount** & **Chinnor,** Mon-Sat 12/day, Sun 9/day
S8	S'coach	(Stagecoach Gold) Oxford to **Wantage** via Abingdon, daily 1/hr
S9	S'coach	(Stagecoach Gold) Oxford to **Wantage** via Cumnor, Mon-Fri 2/hr, Sat & Sun 1/hr
X2	TT/GA	Oxford to **Wallingford** via Abingdon & Didcot, Mon-Sat 2/hr, Sun 1/hr
X5	S Reds	Swindon to Salisbury via **Ogbourne St George** (Mon-Sat 1/day), **Marlborough** & Pewsey, Mon-Sat 1/hr
X32	TT/GA	Oxford to **Wantage,** Mon-Sat approx 1/hr
X38	TT/GA	(River Rapids) Reading to Oxford via Caversham, Henley-on-Thames, **Nuffield Common, Wallingford, Crowmarsh Gifford** & Benson, Mon-Fri 14/day, Sat 12/day
X39	TT/GA	(River Rapids) Reading to Oxford via Caversham, **Wallingford, Crowmarsh Gifford** & Benson, Mon-Sat approx 1/hr
X40	TT/GA	(River Rapids) Reading to Oxford via Caversham, Woodcote, **Wallingford, Crowmarsh Gifford** & Benson, daily approx 1/hr; NX40 operates on Fri evening (2/day; Wallingford to Oxford)
X76	SBC	Bath to **Marlborough** via Calne, Beckhampton & **West Kennett,** Mon-Fri 1/day
X80	Regatta Car	High Wycombe to Reading via Marlow & Henley-on-Thames, Mon-Sat 1/hr plus 1/hr to Marlow

Operator contact details: ABB (Arriva in Beds & Bucks; ▢ arrivabus.co.uk); **Car** (Carousel; ☎ 01494 450151, ▢ carouselbuses.co.uk); **Con** (Connect; W Berkshire Council Transport; ▢ westberks.gov.uk/transport); **GF** (Going Forward Buses; ▢ goingforwardbuses.com); **N&D** (Newbury & District; Reading Buses ☎ 0118 959 4000, ▢ reading-buses.co.uk); **Red** (Redline Buses; ☎ 01296 426786, ▢ redlinebuses.com); **RedE** (Red Eagle; ▢ redeagle.org.uk/bus-services); **RRT** (Red Rose Travel; ☎ 01296 747926, ▢ redrose travel.com); **S Reds** (Salisbury Reds; ☎ 01202 338420, ▢ salisburyreds.co.uk); **S'coach** (Stagecoach; ▢ www.stagecoachbus.com); **SBC** (Swindon's Bus Company; ▢ swindonbus.co.uk/services); **TT/GA** (Thames Travel/Go Ahead; ☎ 01865 785400, ▢ thames-travel.co.uk)

PLANNING YOUR WALK

(cont'd from p47) To reach the official start of the Ridgeway leave the M4 motorway at junction 15; from there it's a short drive down the A345 to Marlborough, then onto the A4 to the start at Overton Hill. You shouldn't, however, leave your car overnight in the small car parking area at Overton Hill so you should find somewhere to leave it in Marlborough, though even this could be tricky.

The Ivinghoe Beacon end of the Ridgeway is best reached from junction 11 (Dunstable) of the M40 or via Aylesbury along the A41. There is a National Trust car park for Ivinghoe Beacon about half a mile (1km) south of the B489 on the minor road to Ringshall, but, like at Overton Hill, don't plan to leave your car here overnight.

However, overall it's probably easier and cheaper and certainly better for the environment to use public transport.

LOCAL TRANSPORT

There are few useful train services along the Ridgeway so you will have to rely on the bus services. These, although extensive, aren't always frequent, especially on Sundays, and many had already been reduced due to council cutbacks before further reductions due to the COVID-19 pandemic.

In some areas buses connect the places you might need but at times trying to get from one place to another can involve travelling first to a larger town, then changing buses and continuing from there. Obviously this can be quite time consuming and if you don't want to end up paying for a taxi this is certainly one aspect of your trip that you will need to plan.

The public transport maps on pp48-9 give an overview of the most useful bus, coach and train routes. The bus services table on pp50-1 gives service numbers, the operator, route details (but not always all the stops) as well as the days and approximate frequency of services in both directions. Operator contact details are also provided. It is essential to check the latest details before travelling as services do change and also to ensure you know what time the last bus departs: check online, or you can pick up bus timetables for free at any of the tourist information centres along the route.

If the contact details in the box on p51 prove unsatisfactory, you can contact **traveline** (☎ 0871 200 2233, 🖥 traveline.info) which has public transport information for the whole of the UK; traveline also has an app. Alternatively contact the public transport department of the relevant county council (see box on p62).

MINIMUM IMPACT & OUTDOOR SAFETY

2

Minimum impact walking

ECONOMIC IMPACT

Support local businesses

Rural businesses and communities in Britain have been hit hard in recent years by a seemingly endless series of crises (most recently COVID-19). In light of the economic pressures that many businesses are under there is something you can do to help: buy local.

Look and ask for local produce to buy and eat. Not only does this cut down on the amount of pollution and congestion that the transportation of food creates (the so-called 'food miles'), but also ensures that you are supporting local farmers and producers; the very people who have moulded the countryside you have come to see and who are in the best position to protect it. If you can find local food which is also organic so much the better.

It's a fact of life that money spent at local level – perhaps in a market, or at the greengrocer, or in an independent pub – has a far greater impact for good on that community than the equivalent spent in a branch of a national chain store or restaurant. While no-one would advocate that walkers should boycott the larger supermarkets, which after all do provide local employment, it's worth remembering that businesses in rural communities rely heavily on visitors for their very existence. For these shops and post offices to stay in business they must be used.

ENVIRONMENTAL IMPACT

A walking holiday in itself is an environmentally friendly approach to tourism. The following are some ideas on how you can go a few steps further in helping to minimise your impact on the natural environment while walking the Ridgeway.

Use public transport whenever possible

By using local bus services you will help to keep them operating. Although bus routes along the Ridgeway aren't always convenient for walkers, if fewer people use them they are more likely to disappear altogether. Public transport is always preferable to using private cars as it benefits everyone: visitors, locals and the environment.

Never leave litter

Leaving litter shows a total disrespect for the natural world and others coming after you. As well as being unsightly, litter kills wildlife, pollutes the environment and can be dangerous to farm animals. If you've carried everything at the start of the day you can probably carry whatever remains until you reach a rubbish bin. Put all your rubbish in a biodegradable bag so you can dispose of it in a bin in the next village. It would be very helpful if you could pick up litter left by other people too.

Is it OK if it's biodegradable? Not really. Apple cores, banana skins, orange peel and the like are unsightly, encourage flies, ants and wasps and ruin a picnic spot for others. Using the excuse that they are natural and biodegradable just doesn't cut any ice. When was the last time you saw a banana tree in England?

The lasting impact of litter A piece of orange peel left on the ground takes six months to decompose, silver foil takes 18 months, a plastic bag 10 years, clothes 15 years and an aluminium can 85 years.

Erosion
Stay on the main trail The effect of your footsteps may seem minuscule but when they are multiplied by several thousand walkers each year they become rather more significant. Avoid taking shortcuts, widening the trail or taking more than one path; your boots will be followed by many others.

Consider walking out of season Maximum disturbance by walkers coincides with the time of year when nature wants to do most of its growth and repair. In high-use areas, like that along much of the eastern section of the Ridgeway, the trail never recovers. Walking at less busy times eases this pressure while also generating year-round income for the local economy. Not only that, but it may make the walk a more relaxing experience with fewer people on the path and less competition for accommodation.

Respect all wildlife
Care for all wildlife you come across along the Ridgeway: it has as much right to be there as you. Tempting as it may be to pick wild flowers, leave them so the next people who pass can enjoy them too. Don't break branches off or damage trees in any way. If you come across wildlife, keep your distance and don't watch for too long. Your presence can cause considerable stress, particularly if the adults are with young, or in winter when the weather is harsh and food is scarce. Young animals are rarely abandoned. If you come across young birds keep away so that their mother can return.

The code of the outdoor loo
'Going' in the outdoors is a lost art worth re-learning, for your sake and everyone else's. As more and more people discover the joys of the outdoors this is becoming an important issue.

In some parts of the world where visitor pressure is higher than in Britain walkers and climbers are required to pack out their excrement. This may become necessary here. Human excrement is not only offensive to our senses but, more importantly, can infect water sources.

Where to go Wherever possible use a toilet. Public toilets are marked on the trail maps in this guide and you will also find facilities in pubs and cafés along the Ridgeway though to use them you are likely to have to have bought something.

If you do have to go outdoors choose a site at least 30 metres away from running water and also away from any site of historic or archaeological interest. Carry a small trowel and dig a hole about 15cm (6") deep in which to bury your excrement. It decomposes quicker when in contact with the top layer of soil or leaf mould. Use a stick to stir loose soil into your deposit as well as this speeds up decomposition even more. Do not squash it under rocks as this slows down the composting process. If you have to use rocks to cover it make sure they are not in contact with your faeces.

Toilet paper and tampons Toilet paper takes a long time to decompose whether buried or not. It is easily dug up by animals and may then blow into water sources or onto the path. The best method for dealing with it is to pack it out. Put the used paper inside a paper bag which you then place inside a biodegradable bag (or two). Then simply empty the contents of the paper bag at the next toilet you come across and throw the bag away. You should also pack out tampons and sanitary towels in a similar way: they take years to decompose and may also be dug up and scattered about by animals.

Wild camping

Unfortunately, wild camping is not allowed along the Ridgeway, but it is generally tolerated if you leave no trace of yourself on the ground when you leave the next morning. Wild camping is an altogether more fulfilling experience than camping on a designated site. Living in the outdoors without any facilities provides a valuable lesson in simple, sustainable living where the results of all your actions, from going to the loo to washing your plates, can be seen.

If you do insist on wild camping on land off the Ridgeway path always ask the landowner for permission. Follow these suggestions for minimising your impact and encourage others to do likewise.

● **Be discreet** Camp alone or in small groups, spend only one night in each place and pitch your tent late and move off early.
● **Never light a fire** The deep burn caused by camp fires, no matter how small, damages the turf which can take years to recover. Cook on a camp stove instead.
● **Don't use soap or detergent** There is no need to use soap: even biodegradable soaps and detergents pollute streams. You won't be away from a shower for more than a day or so. Wash up without detergent: use a plastic or metal scourer, or failing that, a handful of fine pebbles or even some bracken or grass.
● **Leave no trace** Learn the skill of moving on without leaving any sign of having been there: no moved boulders, ripped up vegetation or dug drainage ditches. Make a final check of your campsite before departing: pick up any litter that you or anyone else has left, so leaving the place in a better state than you found it.

ACCESS

Britain is a crowded cluster of islands with few places where you can wander as you please. Most of the land is a patchwork of fields and agricultural land and the area around the Ridgeway is no different. However, there are countless public rights of way, in addition to the official Ridgeway path, that criss-cross the land; so, what happens if you feel a little more adventurous and want to explore the downs, woodland and hills that can be found around the Ridgeway?

Rights of way

As a designated **National Trail** the Ridgeway is a **public right of way**; this is either a footpath, a bridleway or a byway – the Ridgeway is made up of all of these. Rights of way are theoretically established because the owner has dedicated them to public use. However, very few rights of way are formally dedicated in this way. If members of the public have been using a path without interference for 20 years or more the law assumes the owner has intended to dedicate it as a right of way. If a path has been unused for 20 years it does not cease to exist; the guiding principle is 'once a highway, always a highway'.

❑ THE COUNTRYSIDE CODE

The Countryside Code, originally described in the 1950s as the Country Code, was revised and relaunched in 2004, in part because of the changes brought about by the CRoW Act (see p58); it was updated in 2012, 2014, 2016 and again in 2020 to include considerations regarding COVID-19. The Code seems like common sense but sadly some people still appear to have no understanding of how to treat the countryside they walk in. An adapted version of the 2020 Code – launched under the logo 'Respect. Protect. Enjoy.' – is given below:

Respect other people
● **Consider the local community and other people enjoying the outdoors** Be sensitive to the needs and wishes of those who live and work there. If, for example, farm animals are being moved or gathered keep out of the way and follow the farmer's directions. Being courteous and friendly to those you meet will ensure a healthy future for all based on partnership and co-operation.
● **Leave gates and property as you find them and follow paths unless wider access is available** A farmer normally closes gates to keep farm animals in, but may sometimes leave them open so the animals can reach food and water. Leave gates as you find them or follow instructions on signs. When in a group, make sure the last person knows how to leave the gates.

Follow paths unless wider access is available, such as on open country or registered common land (known as 'open access land'). Leave machinery and farm animals alone – if you think an animal is in distress try to alert the farmer instead.

Use gates or gaps in field boundaries if you can – climbing over walls, hedges and fences can damage them and increase the risk of farm animals escaping. On some of the side trips you may find the paths less accommodating. If you have to climb over a gate because you can't open it always do so at the hinged end. Also be careful not to disturb ruins and historic sites. Stick to the official Ridgeway path across arable/pasture land. Minimise erosion by not cutting corners or widening the path.

On a public right of way you have the right to 'pass and repass along the way' which includes stopping to rest or admire the view, or to consume refreshments. You can also take with you a 'natural accompaniment' which includes a dog but obviously could also be a horse on bridleways and byways. All 'natural accompaniments' must be kept under close control (see p196).

Farmers and land managers must ensure that paths are not blocked by crops or other vegetation, or otherwise obstructed, that the route is identifiable and the surface is restored soon after cultivation. If crops are growing over the path you have every right to walk or ride through them, following the line of the right of way as closely as possible. If you find a path blocked or impassable you should report it to the appropriate **highway authority**. Highway authorities are responsible for maintaining public rights of way. Along the Ridgeway the highway authorities are **Wiltshire Council**, **Swindon Borough Council**, **Oxfordshire County Council**, **West Berkshire Council**, **Buckinghamshire Council** and **Hertfordshire County Council** (see box on p62). The councils are also the surveying authorities with responsibility for maintaining the official definitive maps of the public rights of way.

● **Follow the path but give way to others when it is narrow** (unless they give way to you).

Protect the natural environment

● **Leave no trace of your visit and take all your litter home** Take special care not to damage, destroy or remove features such as rocks, plants and trees. Take your litter with you (see p54); litter and leftover food doesn't just spoil the beauty of the countryside, it can be dangerous to wildlife and farm animals.

● **Keep dogs under effective control** This means that you should keep your dog on a lead or keep it in sight at all times, be aware of what it's doing and be confident it will return to you promptly on command. Across farmland dogs should always be kept on a short lead. During lambing time they should not be taken with you at all.

Always clean up after your dog and get rid of the mess responsibly – 'bag it and bin it'. (See also pp196-7).

● **Don't have BBQs or fires** Fires can be as devastating to wildlife and habitats as they are to people and property – so be careful with naked flames and cigarettes at any time of the year.

Enjoy the outdoors

● **Plan ahead, check what facilities are open and be prepared** You're responsible for your own safety: be prepared for natural hazards, changes in the weather and other events. Wild animals, farm animals and horses can behave unpredictably if you get too close, especially if they're with their young – so give them plenty of space.

● **Follow advice and local signs and obey social distancing measures** In some areas temporary diversions are in place; take notice of these and other local trail advice as well as signs about social distancing. Walking on the Ridgeway is pretty much hazard-free but ensure you follow the simple guidelines outlined on pp58-60.

MINIMUM IMPACT & OUTDOOR SAFETY

Right to roam

The Countryside & Rights of Way Act 2000 (CRoW), or 'Right to Roam' as dubbed by walkers, gives the public access to areas of countryside, deemed to be uncultivated open country, in England and Wales – this essentially means moorland, heathland, downland and upland areas. Some land is covered by restrictions (ie high-impact activities such as driving a vehicle, cycling and horse-riding are not permitted) and some land is excluded (such as gardens, parks and cultivated land). Full details are given on the Natural England website (see box on p62).

With more freedom in the countryside comes a need for more responsibility from the walker. Remember that wild open country is still the workplace of farmers and home to all sorts of wildlife. Have respect for both and avoid disturbing domestic and wild animals.

Outdoor safety

AVOIDANCE OF HAZARDS

With good planning and preparation most hazards can be avoided. This information is just as important for those out on a day walk as for those walking the entire Ridgeway.

Ensure you have **suitable clothes** (see pp39-40) to keep you warm and dry whatever the conditions, and a spare change of inner clothes. A compass, whistle, torch and first-aid kit should be carried and are discussed further on p40. The **emergency signal** is six blasts on a whistle or six flashes with a torch.

Remember to take your **mobile phone** (and ensure it is fully charged); you can get a decent signal on nearly all the Ridgeway and not only will you be able to contact someone in an emergency, but the signal from your phone can be traced to pinpoint your location (see box below).

Take plenty of **food** with you for the day and at least one litre of **water** although more would be better, especially on the long western stretches. It is a good idea to fill up your bottle whenever you pass a water tap as they aren't very common. You will eat far more walking than you do normally so make sure you have enough for the day, as well as some high-energy snacks (chocolate, dried fruit, biscuits) in the bottom of your pack for an emergency.

> ❑ **DEALING WITH AN ACCIDENT**
> ● Use basic first aid to treat the injury to the best of your ability.
> ● Work out exactly where you are. The What3Words **app** (🖳 what3words.com) can pinpoint your location to a 3 sq m area – familiarise yourself with it before you go walking. If possible leave someone with the casualty while others go to get help. If there are only two people, you have a dilemma.
> ● If you decide to get help leave all spare clothing and food with the casualty.
> ● Telephone ☎ 999 and ask for the ambulance service.

Stay alert and **know exactly where you are** throughout the day. The easiest way to do this is to regularly check your position on the map. If visibility suddenly decreases with mist and cloud, or there is an accident, you will be able to make a sensible decision about what action to take based on your location.

If you choose to walk alone you must appreciate and be prepared for the increased risk. It's a good idea to leave word with someone about where you are going and remember to contact them when you have arrived safely.

WEATHER FORECASTS

The western section of the Ridgeway is particularly exposed. The difference in conditions between the villages below the Ridgeway and the path itself can be quite dramatic. You often only notice just how cold and windy it is when you stop for a few minutes.

You can get a localised 5-day forecast from ⌨ bbc.co.uk/weather, or install the BBC Weather app on your smartphone; just type in the name of the place for which you want information. Dark Sky (⌨ darksky.net/app) is another popular weather app, but is for iOS only. Alternatively check newspaper, TV, radio or one of the telephone forecasts before you set off. Plan the day accordingly and always anticipate that the weather may change.

HEALTH

Blisters
It is important to break in new boots before embarking on a long walk. Make sure the boots are comfortable and try to avoid getting them wet on the inside. Air your feet at lunchtime, keep them clean and change your socks regularly. If you feel any hot spots stop immediately and apply a few strips of zinc oxide tape and leave them on until the area is pain free or the tape starts to come off.

If you have left it too late and a blister has developed you should surround it with 'moleskin' or any other blister kit to protect it from abrasion. Popping it can lead to infection. If the skin is broken keep the area clean with antiseptic and cover with a non-adhesive dressing material held in place with tape.

Hypothermia
Also known as **exposure**, this occurs when the body can't generate enough heat to maintain its normal temperature, usually as a result of being wet, cold, unprotected from the wind, tired and hungry. It is usually more of a problem in upland areas. However, even on the Ridgeway in bad weather the body can be exposed to strong winds and driving rain making the risk a real one. The western stretches of the path are particularly exposed and there are few villages, making it difficult to get help should it be needed.

Hypothermia is easily avoided by wearing suitable clothing, carrying and consuming enough food and drink, being aware of the weather conditions and checking the morale of your companions. Early signs to watch for are feeling cold and tired with involuntary shivering. If this occurs, find some shelter as soon as possible and warm the person up with a hot drink and some chocolate or other high-energy food. If possible give them another warm layer of clothing and allow them to rest until feeling better.

If the patient's condition deteriorates, strange behaviour, slurring of speech and poor co-ordination will become apparent and they can quickly progress into unconsciousness, followed by coma and death. You should get the patient out of wind and rain quickly, improvising a shelter if necessary. Rapid restoration of bodily warmth is essential and is best achieved by bare-skin contact: someone should get into the same sleeping bag as the patient, both having stripped to their underwear, putting any spare clothing under or over them to build up heat. Send urgently for help.

Hyperthermia
Hyperthermia is the general name given to a variety of heat-related ailments. Not something you would normally associate with England, heat exhaustion and heatstroke are serious problems nonetheless. Symptoms of **heat exhaustion** include thirst, fatigue, giddiness, a rapid pulse, raised body temperature, low urine output and, if not treated, delirium and finally a coma. The best cure is to drink plenty of water.

Heatstroke is another matter altogether, and even more serious. A high body temperature and an absence of sweating are early indications, followed by symptoms similar to hypothermia (see p59) such as a lack of coordination, convulsions and coma. Death will follow if treatment is not instantly given. Sponge the victim down, wrap them in wet towels, fan them, and get help immediately.

Sunburn
It can easily happen even on overcast days and especially if you have a fair complexion. The only surefire way to avoid it is to stay wrapped up, but that's not really an option. What you must do, therefore, is to smother yourself in sunscreen with a minimum factor of 15 (30 is safer) and apply it regularly throughout the day. Don't forget your lips, nose, ears, the back of your neck if wearing a T-shirt, and even under your chin to protect against rays reflected up off the ground.

THE ENVIRONMENT & NATURE

At first glance, the Ridgeway path doesn't seem to be very distinctive. But when you look closer you see a wide variety of terrains and habitats from one end of the path to the other: grasslands, chalk downs, beech woodlands and a section along the banks of the River Thames. These varied environments are home to an equally diverse collection of animals, birds and plants. This book is not designed to be a comprehensive guide to all the wildlife you may encounter, but serves as an introduction to the flora and fauna the walker is likely to find along the Ridgeway.

Making that special effort to look out for wildlife and appreciating what you are seeing will enhance your enjoyment of the walk. To take it a step further is to understand a little more about the species you may encounter, appreciating how they interact with each other and learning a little about the conservation issues that are so pertinent today.

Conservation of the Ridgeway

NATURAL ENGLAND

The official responsibilities of Natural England are to 'enhance biodiversity and our landscapes and wildlife in rural, urban, coastal and marine areas; promote access, recreation and public well-being, and contribute to the way natural resources are managed, so they can be enjoyed now and for future generations'. Essentially this organisation: gives advice and information; designates **National Parks**, **Areas of Outstanding Natural Beauty (AONBs)** and **Sites of Special Scientific Interest (SSSIs)**; manages **National Nature Reserves (NNRs)** and enforces existing regulations. Natural England also manages England's **National Trails**: they provide most of the funding and resources for path maintenance and promote the conservation of wildlife, geology and wild places in England see also box on p63.

Although no part of the Ridgeway is inside a National Park, the route does lie within two pieces of land designated **AONBs** which are administered by the relevant local authorities. The western part of the path is in the 1730 sq km **North Wessex Downs AONB** that was created in 1972. It lies within the County Council boundaries of Wiltshire, Hampshire and Oxfordshire. The eastern part of the trail is included in the 833 sq km **Chilterns AONB** that was created in 1965 and lies within the County Council boundaries of Bedfordshire, Buckinghamshire, Hertfordshire and Oxfordshire.

There are over 220 **NNRs** in England and the course of the Ridgeway includes Fyfield Down NNR (see p98), just a couple of miles from the official start of the route, and Aston Rowant NNR (see Map 28, p164) near Watlington. These two areas are also **SSSIs** along with over 4100 others in England. Other SSSIs along the Ridgeway include White Horse Hill SSSI and Chinnor Chalk Pit SSSI. **Special Areas of Conservation** (SACs) are designated by the European Union's Habitats Directive and provide an extra tier of protection to the areas that they cover. Along the Ridgeway, Aston Rowant NNR and SSSI is also a SAC along with the Chilterns' beechwoods and Hackpen Hill (see p101). More information on NNRs, SSSIs and SACs can be found on the Natural England website (see box below).

There is no doubt that these designations play a vital role in safeguarding the land they cover for future generations. However, the very fact that we rely on these labels for protecting limited areas begs the question: what are we doing to the vast majority of land that remains relatively unprotected? Surely we should be aiming to protect the natural environment outside protected areas just as much as within them.

RIDGEWAY PARTNERSHIP

The Ridgeway Partnership took over the management, development and promotion of the Ridgeway in April 2015; before that Natural England oversaw a National Trails Management Group that administered both the Ridgeway and the Thames Path national trails. The main groups in The Ridgeway Partnership

---

❏ STATUTORY BODIES

- **Department for Environment, Food and Rural Affairs** (🖥 gov.uk/defra) Government ministry responsible for sustainable development in the countryside.
- **Natural England** (🖥 gov.uk/government/organisations/natural-england) See p61.
- **Historic England** (🖥 historicengland.org.uk) Created in April 2015 as a result of dividing the work originally done just by English Heritage (see opposite). Historic England is the government department responsible for looking after and promoting England's historic environment and is in charge of the listing system, giving grants and dealing with planning matters.
- **Forestry Commission** (🖥 gov.uk/government/organisations/forestry-commission) Government department for establishing and managing forests, including Hale Wood (see p182), for a variety of uses.
- **County/Borough Councils: Wiltshire** (🖥 wiltshire.gov.uk); **Oxfordshire** (🖥 oxfordshire.gov.uk); **Buckinghamshire** (🖥 buckinghamshire.gov.uk); **Hertfordshire** (🖥 hertfordshire.gov.uk); **Swindon** (🖥 swindon.gov.uk); **West Berkshire Council** (🖥 westberks.gov.uk).

❏ **NATIONAL TRAILS**

The Ridgeway is one of 15 National Trails (🖳 nationaltrail.co.uk) in England and Wales. These are Britain's flagship long-distance paths which grew out of the post-war desire to protect the country's special places, a movement which also gave birth to National Parks and AONBs (see p61). The first National Trail was the Pennine Way in 1965. Since then over 2500 miles (4000km) of walking routes have been designated.

are Oxfordshire Country Council, other local authorities (see box opposite), National Trust, North Wessex Downs AONB, Chilterns Conservation Board and other stakeholders, such as The Friends of the Ridgeway. The Partnership has set up a Strategic Links Project to identify the main routes used by walkers, cyclists and horse riders from the Ridgeway to local amenities; to do this they need the help of volunteers but also landowners and the Highway authorities, and of course feedback from anyone using the Ridgeway (see box on p199). Once linking routes have been identified any necessary improvement work will be carried out; general maintenance is done by the Ridgeway National Trails team.

CAMPAIGNING AND CONSERVATION ORGANISATIONS

The **Friends of the Ridgeway** (🖳 ridgewayfriends.org.uk) group focuses specifically on the trail and is particularly vocal on the subject of motorised vehicles using and damaging the tracks. They also have a volunteer scheme for people who wish to get actively involved in preserving the Ridgeway.

The **National Trust** (🖳 nationaltrust.org.uk) is a charity with over three million members which aims to protect, through ownership, threatened coastline, countryside, historic houses, castles, gardens and archaeological remains. The Trust manages land and sites along the Ridgeway including the sites in the Avebury area (see p85), the Uffington White Horse area (pp117-18) and the nearby Wayland's Smithy neolithic long barrow (p115). However, all these sites are actually owned by English Heritage.

Often seeming to overlap the work of the National Trust, **English Heritage** (🖳 english-heritage.org.uk) actually looks after, champions and advises the government on historic buildings and places, whereas the National Trust focuses more on country houses. However, in April 2015 English Heritage was divided into a new charitable trust that retains the name English Heritage and a non-departmental public body, Historic England (see box opposite). Most of the sites around Avebury (see p85) are English Heritage properties though some are actually managed by the National Trust.

The Wildlife Trusts (🖳 wildlifetrusts.org) is the umbrella organisation for the 47 wildlife trusts in the UK. Regional branches relevant to the Ridgeway are: **Wiltshire Wildlife Trust** (🖳 wiltshirewildlife.org); **Berks, Bucks & Oxon Wildlife Trust** (**BBOWT**; 🖳 bbowt.org.uk); **Hertfordshire & Middlesex Wildlife Trust** (**H&MWT**; 🖳 hertswildlifetrust.org.uk). Reserves include a 70-acre site (Oakley Hill, managed by BBOWT, Map 29), on Chinnor Hill, which has a mixture of open grassland and woodland comprising oak, ash and beech. Aldbury Nowers Nature Reserve (managed by H&MWT), see box on p192, has butterflies and wildflowers. Another reserve, Dancersend & Crong Meadow, is between Wendover and Hastoe.

The **Woodland Trust** (🖳 woodlandtrust.org.uk) aims to conserve, restore and re-establish native woodlands throughout the UK: it cares for over a thousand woods around the UK. The Ridgeway passes through one of their woods, Tring Park (p183), towards the end of the trail.

Butterfly Conservation (🖳 butterfly-conservation.org) was formed in 1968. They now have 32 branches throughout the British Isles and operate over 34 nature reserves and also sites where butterflies are likely to be found. The branches relevant to the Ridgeway are Wiltshire (🖳 wiltshire-butterflies.org.uk) and the Upper Thames (🖳 upperthames-butterflies.org.uk).

The **Royal Society for the Protection of Birds** (RSPB; 🖳 rspb.org.uk) is the largest voluntary conservation body in Europe focusing on providing a healthy environment for birds, with 200 reserves in the UK. Although the RSPB doesn't have any reserves directly on the Ridgeway they run projects on some areas of it. In particular they are involved in a scheme to encourage stone curlew to breed in the Wessex area.

Flora and fauna

FLOWERS

You'll be walking amongst many different species of wild flowers on the Ridgeway, though unless you keep an eye out it can be easy to miss some of them. Despite the trail being constantly exposed to wind and direct sunlight there will still be a wide selection of common flowers at any time between March and November though the biggest selection appears during the summer months. You'll also have the chance to see some of the more uncommon flowers native to chalk grassland. The best time for spotting these is during the summer months in the areas around Barbury Castle, Uffington Castle, the Pitstone Hills and Ivinghoe Beacon.

There will be plenty of **scentless mayweed** (*Tripleurospermum inodorum*), **common mouse-ear** (*Cerastium glomeratum*) and **common vetch** (*Vicia sativa*) at any time between April and November along most stretches of the Ridgeway. Another common flower is the **red campion** (*Silene dioica*), but this is found mainly in wooded areas and hedgerows. Despite its name, you'll recognise it by the profusion of shocking pink flowers it produces. A common flower with an even more misleading name is the **black medick** (*Medicago lupulina*) that grows mainly on grassland and has yellow flowers. **Herb Robert** (*Geranium robertianum*) also flowers throughout the spring, summer and early autumn. It has attractive pink and white flowers and is found in shady, often rocky areas.

Common Vetch
Vicia sativa

Herb-Robert
Geranium robertianum

Red Campion
Silene dioica

Lousewort
Pedicularis sylvatica

Meadow Cranesbill
Geranium pratense

Common Dog Violet
Viola riviniana

Common Knapweed
Centaurea nigra

Violet
Viola riviniana

Old Man's Beard
Clematis vitalba

Early Purple Orchid
Orchis mascula

Spotted Orchid
Dactylorhiza fuchsii

Pyramidal Orchid
Anacamptis pyramidalis

Gorse
Ulex europaeus

Meadow Buttercup
Ranunculis acris

Marsh Marigold (Kingcup)
Caltha palustris

Bird's-foot trefoil
Lotus corniculatus

St John's Wort
Hypericum perforatum

Tormentil
Potentilla erecta

Primrose

Cowslip
Primula veris

Honeysuckle
Lonicera periclymemum

Common Ragwort

Yarrow
Achillea millefolium

Hogweed
Heracleum sphondylium

Rowan (tree)
Sorbus aucuparia

Dog Rose
Rosa canina

Forget-me-not
Myosotis arvensis

Scarlet Pimpernel
Anagallis arvensis

Self-heal
Prunella vulgaris

Germander Speedwell
Veronica chamaedrys

Ramsons (Wild Garlic)
Allium ursinum

Bluebell
Hyacinthoides non-scripta

Ox-eye Daisy
Leucanthemum vulgare

Foxglove
Digitalis purpurea

Rosebay Willowherb
Epilobium angustifolium

Viper's Bugloss
Echium vulgare

Peacock
Inachis io

Small Tortoiseshell

Common Blue
Polyommatus icarus

Small Garden/Cabbage White
Pieris rapae

Large Garden/Cabbage White
Pieris brassicae

Chalkhill Blue
Lysandra coridon

Painted Lady
Cynthia cadui

Small Copper
Lycaena phlaeas

Small Heath
Coenonympha pamphilus

Red Admiral *Vanessa atalanta*

White Admiral
Limenitis camilla

Meadow Brown
Maniola jurtina

In the spring, flowers such as **greater stitchwort** (*stellaria holostea*) and **dovesfoot cranesbill** (*Geranium molle*) are common in the hedgerows while the distinctive **cowslip** (*Primula veris*) with its clusters of yellow, funnel-shaped flowers is widespread in more open areas. The **common dog** and **heath dog violets** (*Viola riviniana, V. canina*) can be found in shady, open woodlands during the spring while another violet-coloured flower, the **common field speedwell** (*Veronica persica*), prefers cultivated land.

During the late spring and summer months, the variety of flowers along the Ridgeway is at its best. An aptly named example is the **traveller's joy** or **old man's beard** (*Clematis vitalba*) that climbs over hedgerows and displays dense clumps of white, feathery flowers with a strong scent. Another climber you are likely to see is the large-leafed, white-flowered **white bryony** (*Bryonia dioica*). Summer is also when you can see the striking flowers of the **common mallow** (*Malva sylvestris*) that can grow to 150cm high. The yellow, star-shaped flowers of the medicinal **St John's wort** (*Hypericum perforatum*) can be spotted in wooded areas and is so named as it flowers around St John's Day, 24th June.

Upright hedge parsley (*Torilis japonica*) is common along the hedgerows and on the edges of woodland whereas the similar-looking **wild parsnip** (*Pastinaca sativa*) grows mainly on grassland. **Wild carrot** (*Daucus carota*) can sometimes be seen in open grassy areas, distinguished by its large dome-shaped clusters of white flowers. Large **oxeye daisies** (*Leucanthemum vulgare*) are difficult to miss and you may also see **silverweed** (*Potentilla anserina*) along the trail showing grey/silver sharply toothed leaves and yellow flowers.

Flowers that grow only on chalk grassland areas of the Ridgeway include **devil's-bit scabious** (*Scabiosa pratensis*) that can flower as late as October, **squinancywort** (*Asperula cynanchica*) that has slender stems bearing pale-pink and white flowers and **viper's bugloss** (*Echium vulgare*) with its tall thick stem and purple funnel-shaped flowers. This type of chalky ground also plays host to various orchids including the **common spotted** (*Dactylorhiza fuchsii*) that has pale leaves spotted with crimson and the **fragrant** (*Gymnadenia conopsea)* and **pyramidal** (*Anacamptis pyramidalis*), both with reddish petals but with the pyramidal variety being darker.

BUTTERFLIES

The chalk downlands along the Ridgeway provide a habitat in which many species of butterfly can flourish. Indeed, near the end of the trail, just before Ivinghoe Beacon, is **Aldbury Nowers** (see box on p192), a nature reserve and the home of over 30 species of butterfly. Given that the UK can boast only 59 species in total, that's a remarkable figure! Among their number are such rarities as **Essex skippers**, **marbled whites**, **green hairstreaks**, **brown argus** and the moth-like **grizzled and dingy skippers**.

The most common species seen during the summer along the Ridgeway is the **meadow brown** (*Maniola jurtina*), overall a dusty brown colour, but with orange patches on its forewings, inside which are black eye-spots. This is one of the most common butterflies in Europe, as well as on the Ridgeway.

THE ENVIRONMENT & NATURE

Also likely to be flitting around at this time is the **small heath** (*Coenonympha pamphilus*), recognisable by its dull-orange wings edged with grey; it has black eye-spots on the underside of its forewings.

You'll probably see some **large white** (*Pieris brassicae*) and **small white** (*Pieris rapae*) butterflies too. These are both essentially white with dark-grey wing tips. On the large white, both male and female have two black eye-spots on the underside of the forewings, but only the female has them on the upper side. On the small white, both sexes have two black eye-spots on the underside of their forewings, but on the upperside, the female has two small spots and the male only a single spot.

There are several different kinds of blue butterfly that you may see on the chalklands. The most likely is the **common blue** (*Polyommatus icarus*). The male is violet-blue with a fine black edging to its wings; the female is actually brown though has a row of red spots along her wings which are edged with black. Less common is the **chalkhill blue** (*Lysandra coridon*); the male is altogether duller than the common blue but has more extensive black and white edging around the wings. The female is dark brown and has the same wing edging.

There are usually some **small copper** (*Lycaena phlaeas*) butterflies around that are distinctive despite their size. The forewings are bright orange with heavy black spots and black fringing whereas the hindwings are predominantly black with a thick band of bright orange edging at the bottom.

Two common day-flying moths are the **five-spot burnet** (*Zygaena trifolii*) and **six-spot burnet** (*Zygaena filipendulae*). Each has very dark wings, patterned with five or six orange/red spots.

TREES

You'll see few trees along the western half of the Ridgeway. Most of those you do see have been planted by man over the centuries to serve a specific purpose, eg coppices, windbreaks and plantations. Though many of these are no longer maintained you can still see evidence of them if you look. The eastern half of the Ridgeway is often wooded, usually with beech.

Coppices are areas of woodland, usually oak, hazel or elm, managed by man through the periodic cutting of the trees right back to the ground; multiple fast-growing shoots then appear from the cut trees and are harvested. Many coppices were fenced to keep animals out and often the fence sat on a raised earth ridge that you can still see around many disused coppiced areas. Coppices were an important supply of wood until the mid 1800s after which demand declined. However, most coppices were still maintained and today some are being fully used once more to supply wood for charcoal, greenwood furniture and craft items.

Windbreaks, such as hedges, serve multiple purposes. They give livestock a place to shelter from the wind and also provide shade. They also prevent soil erosion and provide a habitat for varied wildlife such as birds, insects, rabbits and pheasants. With the correct maintenance a hedge can last indefinitely and they are an extremely effective way of containing animals. Despite fences pro-

THE ENVIRONMENT & NATURE

viding none of these benefits, they have often been a more popular choice with farmers who want to maximise their field size or change the layout of their fields. To a small extent, hedges are starting to make a comeback as their full benefits are realised and you'll see some recently planted hedges along parts of the Ridgeway.

Plantations were most common between 1600 and 1900; popular species included oak, beech, elm and ash. It was intended that when the trees were mature they would be used for ship-building, furniture-making and other tasks. Many plantations did provide wood for these purposes, like the beech plantations on the eastern section of the Ridgeway, but others, especially the oak plantations, which took years to mature, were never used owing to the availability of cheap coal and imported timber being sourced from around the British Empire. These unused plantations form some of what are now considered traditional woodland.

During World War I there was a timber shortage that led to large conifer plantations being started. However, these weren't ready for cutting during World War II and this meant that large tracts of private woodland had to be felled. After World War I the increased need for food led to the felling of plantations and removal of hedges to increase the size of available farmland.

Today the creation of new plantations has virtually stopped. Many of the conifer plantations, started between the wars, have matured and been felled though there are still many which are managed for their timber. In a country where so many of the ancient forests have long since disappeared, plantations are now as near as some of us can get to the real thing.

MAMMALS

You could walk the length of the Ridgeway and come to the conclusion that there isn't much wildlife on the route. Obviously walking in a group and making unnecessary noise will dramatically reduce your chances of seeing anything, but if you take some time to look carefully and become aware of your surroundings you are likely to see much more than just the back end of a rabbit diving into the undergrowth. You can be fairly certain that the wildlife you are looking for will have seen you well before you see it and will often be making its escape by the time you do. You'll have to be either very patient or very quick if you want to get photographs.

As a brief 'checklist', depending on the time of year, you can expect to see the following animals along the Ridgeway: deer, foxes, rabbits, hares, stoats, weasels, grey squirrels and perhaps even a badger.

The biggest wild animal you will see along the Ridgeway is the deer. There are two different species in this region: the **fallow deer** (*Dama dama*) and the **roe deer** (*Capreolus capreolus*). They have basically the same lifestyle, usually living in woodland but sometimes on open land with plenty of hedges and copses for cover. Both species are most likely to be seen in the early morning and early evening when they are feeding. The easiest way to tell them apart, if you are close enough, is by their size. The adult roe deer grows to about 60cm high at the shoulder while the fallow deer can be up to 90cm at the shoulder. Male fallow deer have large, flat antlers unlike the roe deer whose antlers are spiky. The rutting season for fallow deer is July and August; this is when the males fight each other both for females and territory. You are most likely to see deer in the open during these months. At other times of the year you might be able to spot one or two of them together against a hedge on the edge of a field or at the perimeter of a clearing in the woods.

The much-maligned **fox** (*Vulpes vulpes*) inhabits woods and farmland. Despite relentless persecution it is a born survivor, even having adapted to life in cities where they are quite tolerant of human presence. They aren't exclusively nocturnal and in areas where they feel less threatened they are quite likely to be active during the day. Although they can be seen year-round, sightings of foxes are usually brief and at a distance, perhaps as one crosses a field.

Among other denizens of woods and farmland are a number of common but shy mammals. One of the most difficult to see is the **badger** (*Meles meles*), a sociable animal with a distinctive black-and-white-striped muzzle. Badgers live in family groups of around ten in large underground setts, coming out to root for worms on the pastureland after sunset, though they will eat practically anything. Some setts can be in use for well over a hundred years if left undisturbed by humans. They do sometimes emerge during daylight hours and the best time for spotting them is between May and September. Unfortunately, the most common sight of badgers is as a bloody mess on the road; they are one of the most frequent animal road casualties.

The animal you are most likely to see on the Ridgeway is the **rabbit** (*Oryctolagus cuniculus*). In fact, at numerous places, especially on the trail near the aptly named Warren Farm just before Streatley, you'll find it hard to miss them. You can see them at all times of the year when they come out during the day and at night to find food such as grass and farm crops. Despite the fact that they won't hang around after they have detected your presence, you can still get a good look at them.

Like rabbits, **hares** (*Lepus capensis*) also feed on grass and farm crops and although they live above ground and like open countryside they are far harder to spot. They generally keep well hidden during the day, except for the months of March and April when you might see them dashing around fields or getting involved in 'boxing matches' with other hares. This isn't, as you might presume, an exclusively male preserve as mixed boxing has also been witnessed. If you are hoping to get a photo of a hare be aware that they can run at speeds up to 40mph/65kph!

The carnivorous **stoat** (*Mustela erminea*) and its smaller cousin the **weasel** (*Mustela nivalis*) are common along the Ridgeway and can be seen year-round but just as with the hares you'll have to be quick if you want to see more than the tail-end of one. They can be difficult to tell apart, especially if you only get a glimpse, but the weasel is noticeably smaller than the stoat. Weasels eat mice, shrews and birds' eggs but owing to their size stoats can tackle larger prey such as adult rabbits and farm birds. This has led to their persecution by farmers who lose poultry to them. Weasels and stoats are by nature very inquisitive so just because they dart for cover as you approach doesn't mean they might not poke their head out for another look just after you have passed.

The **grey squirrel** (*Sciurus carolinensis*) was introduced to Britain from North America in the late 19th century and its outstanding success in colonising the country is very much to the detriment of other native species including songbirds and, most famously, the red squirrel. Grey squirrels inhabit woodlands, parks and gardens and are a common sight from January to June during their breeding season. You might also see them during the autumn on the woodland floor, burying nuts to keep themselves supplied throughout the winter.

At dusk during the summer months **bats** can be seen hunting for moths and flying insects along hedgerows, over rivers and around street lamps. As the weather gets colder they will hibernate though can sometimes still be seen on warmer evenings. Bats have had a bad press thanks to Dracula and countless other horror stories but anyone who has seen one up close knows them to be harmless and delightful little creatures. As for their blood-sucking fame, the matchbox-sized species in Britain would not even be able to break your skin with their teeth let alone suck your blood. Their reputation is improving all the time thanks to the work of the many bat conservation groups around the country and all fourteen species found in Britain are protected by law. The most numerous species is the **common pipistrelle bat** (*Pipistrellus pipistrellus*).

Some other small but fairly common species which can be found in the grassland and hedgerows on the Ridgeway include the **hedgehog** (*Erinaceus europaeus*) and a variety of **voles**, **mice** and **shrews**.

BIRDS

The two halves of the Ridgeway provide distinctly different environments for birds. On the whole the western half, up to Streatley, is exposed with few trees while the eastern half is mostly wooded. Both sections provide ample opportunity for bird spotting with the western section providing the most variety. Early mornings and early evenings are generally the best times for spotting birds.

The western half

One of the most common birds on the open downs is the **skylark** (*Alauda arvensis*). Its dull brown plumage with a darker stripe doesn't make it the most distinctive of birds but when in flight you can recognise it by the white edges of the outer tail feathers. It nests on the ground in a hollow and makes little attempt to conceal its eggs.

SKYLARK
L: 185MM/7.25"

The **corn bunting** (*Emberiza calandra*) can often be heard singing its sharp jangly song along the path. It doesn't look dissimilar to the skylark though it has no white edging on its tail feathers and its beak is shorter and more rounded. You are also likely to see some **yellowhammers** (*Emberiza citrinella*) among the hedgerows and bushes along the path. Although the young birds only have a yellow head, as they grow older the entire body takes on a yellow base colour. Their song is a single repetitive note with a higher note to finish.

Another common sight on this section is the **meadow pipit** (*Anthus pratensis*). Its light brown plumage, blending into buff on its underside, is marked with darker brown bars all over. You can often see it hopping quickly along the ground where it nests but it conceals its home well with thick brambles.

YELLOWHAMMER
L: 160MM/6.25"

LAPWING/PEEWIT
L: 320MM/12.5"

The **lapwing** (*Vanellus vanellus*) with its long legs, short bill and distinctive long headcrest feeds on arable farmland. Sadly, this attractive bird is declining in numbers. The name comes from its lilting flight, frequently changing direction with its large rounded wings. It's also identified by a white belly, black and white head, black throat patch and distinctive dark green wings.

There are also several larger birds that you might see on the Ridgeway. The **buzzard** (*Buteo buteo*) is the most common and can often be seen hovering in the sky, looking for prey such as mice, rabbits and snakes. It has a deep brown plumage with a rounded black and brown banded tail. The **kestrel** (*Falco tinnunculus*) can also be seen hovering above the ground, hunting for prey. Both the male and female are of a reddish brown colour, though the male has a blueish head. Their wings are broad and flat and widely spread when hovering.

BARN OWL
L: 340MM/13.5"

You might also be lucky enough to see an owl, even in the daytime. The **barn owl** (*Tyto alba*) is normally nocturnal, but when it has young, or if it is desperate for food, it will hunt during the day. The back of the owl is a sandy brown colour with grey spots while the front is white with brown spots. The white face is heart-shaped, set with deep, dark eyes. Its legs are covered with dense, short white feathers. If you can see one of these birds perched where you can get a good look at it you really have been fortunate.

Pheasants (*Phasianus colchicus*) are common around hedgerows and bushes; they can often be spotted in open fields when feeding. The male can be seen strutting around, showing off his long brown and black striped tail and colourful neck and head. The females are buff and brown all over with a shorter tail than the males. You can usually get a good look at these birds as they aren't particularly shy which might go some way to explaining why they are also the most popular game bird in England.

Other game birds you may see in the fields along the western part of the Ridgeway include the partridge and the quail. The **partridge** (*Perdix perdix*) is often seen in pairs during the spring and summer. Although there are many colour variations in its plumage, it is often light grey with brown bars and its head is usually brown. This bird feeds mainly on insects and seeds. The **quail** (*Coturnix coturnix*) feeds on similar fare, though it is much smaller than the partridge, at half the size. It is only found in England during the late spring and summer and resembles a partridge but its colouring is reddish-tan with dashes of cream and black. It's not easily spotted as it often hides in grass when disturbed.

CURLEW
L: 600MM/24"

If you are very lucky, you might see a **stone curlew**, but realistically, the chances are very low. This long-legged summer visitor nests on the ground and its colouring of light brown with dark brown and cream streaks camouflages it well in such an environment. Its large yellow eyes are ideal for spotting any far-off danger from which it is more inclined to hide rather than take flight.

RED KITE
L: 650MM/25"

The eastern half

Common birds seen in the woodlands of the eastern section of the Ridgeway include the **nuthatch** (*Sitta europaea*) which can often be seen clinging to tree trunks looking for insects. It's a distinctive small bird with a blue back, white throat and chestnut-coloured underside. The nuthatch nest will often be in a hole in a tree trunk. If the hole is too big, the nuthatch will partially block it with mud, thus making it quite easy to spot.

Various species of tit also live in the woodlands with the **great tit** (*Parus major*) being the largest and one of the most common. It has a black and white head, green back, blue and white wings and a yellow underside. Other tits seen in the woodlands include the **long-tailed tit** (*Aegithalos caudatus*) which is black and white with a long black tail with white edging and the **coal tit** (*Parus ater*), another black and white specimen found in more open areas of woodland.

The number of **red kites** in the Chilterns is increasing owing to reintroduction programmes run by Natural England and the RSPB and there is a good chance that you will see one or more. Their large size – adults have a wingspan of around 1.8m – make them easy to spot and their long forked red tail makes them easy to identify. They have reddish brown bodies with darker wings which also have large patches of white, visible when they are in flight.

SWALLOW
L: 190MM/7¹/₂"

HOUSE MARTIN
L: 140MM/5¹/₂"

Blackbirds (*Turdus merula*) appear all along the Ridgeway and are unmistakable as the males are jet-black with orange beaks. The females are the same size but have brown bodies, graduating to black at the tail, and brown beaks.

If you, by chance, spot a **jay** (*Garrulus glandarius*) before it spots you and flies off, you are doing well. They are members of the crow family but are notoriously shy. Their plumage is a brownish-red overall with the top of the head white with black dashes. The tail is black with dark blue flashes.

Swallows (*Hirundo rustica*), **house martins** (*Delichon urbica*) and **swifts** (*Apus apus*) love to swoop low over water to drink or take flies. The swift cannot perch like the swallow and martin: its legs are mere hooks and it is unable to walk.

You should be able to see woodpeckers during your walk and will certainly hear them hammering away at tree trunks. The most common is the **great-spotted woodpecker** (*Dendrocopos major*) which has mainly black and white plumage enhanced by red patches on the back of its head and on its lower underside. Where the woods are on the edge of open country, you can find **green woodpeckers** (*Picus viridis*). The lifestyle of this bird is similar to that of the great-spotted woodpecker. Its striking green body, white underside and red head with black dashes make this a very attractive bird. The woodpecker bores into trees, not only to find insects and their larvae but also to hollow them out to make a nest.

SWIFT
L: 200MM/8"

Marlborough

Marlborough is the nearest town to the start of the Ridgeway. It has all the shops and services you might need before setting off and boasts a large array of pubs, cafés and restaurants for you to enjoy. Convenient bus links to Avebury, near to the start/end of the Ridgeway, also make this a useful place to base yourself at the beginning or end of your walk.

Although there is evidence of human activity in the area dating back to around 3700BC, the first mention of the town is in the Domesday Book of 1087. A royal charter was granted by King John in 1204 that allowed the town to hold markets on Wednesdays and Saturdays, a practice that remains to this day. In 1653 a devastating fire destroyed around 250 houses in Marlborough and it was decreed that from then on no house in the town could have a thatched roof. The long-term prosperity of the town was assured by its position on the old coach road between London and Bristol; the town still has an air of affluence, perhaps owing in part to the presence of the exclusive Marlborough College, founded in 1843.

SERVICES

The town's shops and services are concentrated along the High St and include a **post office** (Mon-Fri 9am-5.30pm, Sat 9am-12.30pm) in the **One Stop** convenience store (☎ 01672 515792; **fb**; daily 6am-10pm) and various branches of **banks**, all with **ATMs**. There is also a **chemist** (Boots; ☎ 01672 512351, 🖳 boots.com; Mon & Thur-Sat 8.45am-5.30pm, Tue & Wed from 9am, Sun 10am-4pm) and a Waitrose **supermarket** (☎ 01672 513337, 🖳 waitrose.com; Mon-Thur & Sat 7.30am-8pm, Fri to 9pm, Sun 10am-4pm) on the High St. On Wednesdays and Saturdays there is a **market** on the High St.

The **tourist information point** (TIP; ☎ 01672 512487, 🖳 marlborough-tc.gov.uk/visitors; Mon-Thur 10am-4pm, Fri to 2pm), in the Town Council Building at 5 High St, has a variety of leaflets about the area; in 2021 they also hope to have a self-service point in the car park where people can pick leaflets up when the TIP is closed. **White Horse Bookshop** (☎ 01672 512071, 🖳 whitehorsebooks.co.uk; Mon-Sat 10am-5pm) has a good selection of books about the local area.

For outdoor equipment and supplies try **Landmark** (☎ 01672 515000, 🖳 landmarkstores.com; Mon-Fri 10am-4.30pm, Sat 9.30am-5pm, Sun 10.30am-4.30pm). They have a good range of outdoor clothing and accessories in case you have forgotten something. **The Marlborough Bike Company** (☎ 01672 515156, 🖳 marlboroughbike.co.uk; Mon-Sat 9am-5.30pm) can repair your bike. There are free public **toilets** in the car park by the river.

TRANSPORT

[See pp48-51] There are regular **bus** services to Marlborough. Stagecoach's Nos 48/48A and 80 operate from Swindon; their No 80 goes to Ogbourne St George. Salisbury Red's No X5 calls here en route between Swindon and Salisbury. Swindon's No 20/X20 & X22 services operate to Hungerford, their No 42 to Calne and their No X76 to Bath.

Taxi firms include Arrow (☎ 01672 515567, email bookings preferred: 🖳 bookings@arrow-cars.co.uk) and Marlborough Taxis (☎ 01672 512786), though the bus services are good so you shouldn't need them.

WHERE TO STAY

On the High St the rather grand-looking *Castle & Ball Hotel* (☎ 01672 515201, 🖳 greenekinginns.co.uk; 1S/27D/4T/2Tr/3Qd, all en suite; ▼; WI-FI; 🐕) dates back to the 15th century. B&B costs vary according to season/demand etc but range between £32.50pp and £70pp (sgl from £55, sgl occ room rate).

The Merlin (☎ 01672 512151, 🖳 merlinrooms@gmail.com, online booking through 🖳 booking.com; 2S/1T/5D/1Qd, all en suite; ▼; WI-FI) is in the large, cream-coloured Georgian building and shares an entrance with the Pizza Express restaurant (see Where to eat). Rates start from £40pp (sgl/sgl occ from £70); note that breakfast is not available here. At the time of research they were considering closing between October and February.

Several pubs in town also offer accommodation. *The Bear* (☎ 01672 512134, 🖳 thebearmarlborough.com; 8D all en suite; WI-FI) charges around £27.50-32.50pp (sgl occ room rate). At the time of research they were not offering the rooms (2D/1Tr/1Qd) with shared facilities but this may change.

Around the corner from The Bear is *The Lamb Inn* (☎ 01672 512668, 🖳 thelambinnmarlborough.com; 5D/1T/1Qd, all en suite; WI-FI; 🐕) that has light, airy rooms for £40-45pp (sgl occ from £60).

At the other end of the High St is *The Marlborough* (☎ 01672 515011, 🖳 themarlboroughgroup.co.uk; 4D/1Tr, all en suite; WI-FI; 🐕); the building dates

---

SYMBOLS USED IN TEXT

▼ Bathtub in, or for, at least one room   WI-FI means wi-fi is available

Ⓛ packed lunch available if requested in advance

🐕 Dogs allowed but subject to prior arrangement for accommodation (see p197)

fb signifies places that have a Facebook page (for latest opening hours)

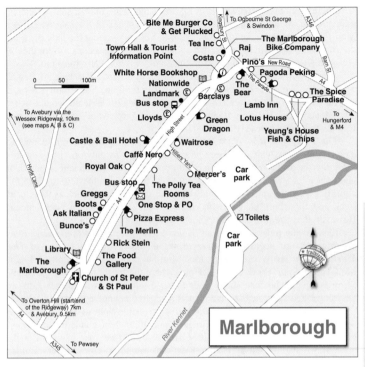

Marlborough

from the 15th century, but it offers rather stylish rooms for £30-90pp (sgl occ room rate). Another option, though it was closed at the time of writing, is **Green Dragon** (☎ 01672 514847, 🖳 greendragonmarlborough.co.uk; 3D/1T/1Qd, all en suite; ☞; WI-FI; 🐾; £40-45pp (sgl occ from £55).

WHERE TO EAT AND DRINK

For breakfast or lunch you could try **Bunce's** (☎ 01672 513515, 🖳 bunces bakehouse.co.uk; Thur-Mon 9am-3pm, food served until 2pm), where you'll find a small but interesting range of breakfast buns, chicken sandwiches and salads to go with their selection of teas and coffees. At the time of research they were only doing takeaway.

   The Food Gallery (☎ 01672 514069, 🖳 thefoodgallery.co.uk; Mon-Fri 8am-4pm, Sat 8.30am-4pm, Sun 9.30am-4pm) lies across the High St. They take great pride in the quality of their coffee and produce some excellent eat-in or takeaway sandwiches (£3.40-4.50).

   There's also a branch of the national sandwich/snack chain **Greggs** (☎ 01672 516681; Mon-Sat 7am-3pm, Sun 8am-3pm).

There are more **coffee shops** in Marlborough than you can shake a cinnamon stick at, including a branch of *Caffè Nero* (☎ 01672 516188; WI-FI; 🐕; Mon-Fri 7.30am-6pm, Sat to 6.30pm, Sun to 5.30pm) – about the only place on the High St, other than the pubs, that allows dogs. Where there's a Nero there's always a *Costa* (🖥 costa.co.uk; Mon-Sat 8am-5pm, Sun 9am-4pm) too.

Away from the chains, in Hilliers Yard you'll find *Mercer's* (☎ 01672 511377; **fb**; Wed-Fri 9.30am-5.30pm, Sat 9am-5.30pm, Sun 10am-4.30pm), and on Kingsbury St there's *Tea Inc* (☎ 01672 514129, 🖥 teainc.co.uk; WI-FI; 🐕; Mon, Wed-Fri & Sun 10am-4pm, Sat 9am-5pm) where you can choose from over 80 different teas!

The Polly Tea Rooms (☎ 01672 512146, 🖥 thepollytearooms.com; **fb**; daily 10am-4pm), which has been here since 1932, was only providing a takeaway service at the time of writing, but hopefully that will change as it was a good place for a cooked breakfast (from £5.95 for eggs on toast up to £7.95 for a full English); they also have plenty of home-made lunches, such as their local steak and Ramsbury ale pie with chips & peas (£9.95), and a vegan menu. However, they are probably best known for their cream teas (£8.50).

Most of the **pubs** on the High St serve food both at lunchtime and in the evening and are licensed to serve drinks all day. You could head to *The Marlborough* (see Where to stay; food Mon-Sat noon-2.30pm, Sun to 3.30pm, Mon-Thur 6-9pm, Fri & Sat to 9.30pm) where the food on the ever-changing menu is several notches above your average pub grub, with dishes such as teriyaki glazed salmon (£16) and always a vegetarian and vegan dish.

The *Royal Oak* (☎ 01672 512064, 🖥 greeneking-pubs.co.uk; WI-FI; 🐕; food daily noon-9pm), owned by Greene King, offers their standard menu; most of the main courses are around £10. *Castle & Ball Hotel* (see p74; food daily noon-9pm), also owned by Greene King, unsurprisingly offers a very similar menu to the Royal Oak. Continuing on the pub crawl you might like to visit *The Bear* (see p74; food Thur-Sat noon-3pm & 5.30-9pm) for Arkell's beers and Kitchen Sisters burgers (including veggie burgers!) or *Green Dragon* (food Mon-Fri daily 11am-9pm) to try some locally brewed 6X from the Wadworth brewery. At *The Lamb Inn* (see p74; food daily noon-2.30pm) you can also try Wadworth beer straight from the wood.

Rick Stein (☎ 01841 532700, 🖥 rickstein.com/restaurants/rick-stein-marlborough; Mon-Fri 9am-9.30pm, Sat 8.30am-9.30pm, Sun to 8pm) focuses on Cornish seafood with mains from £10.95 to £44.95, but offers only one vegetarian option. There are two- and three-course set menus for £20.95 and £25.95. They also have a good breakfast menu (£4.50-12.95).

On Kingbury St is the ever popular Indian restaurant, *Raj* (☎ 01672 515661, 🖥 rajindiancuisine.co.uk; daily 5.30-11pm), and it is always busy, though at the time of research were only offering takeaway or delivery. They have the usual extensive menu with plenty of vegetarian options. Most main dishes cost £8.50-9.50. On Sunday they have a buffet for £8.95.

A short walk up the hill from the High St leads to *Bite Me Burger Co* and *Get Plucked* (☎ 01672 514776, 🖥 bitemeburger.com / 🖥 getplucked.co.uk; 🐕; Mon

& Tue 3-9.30pm, Wed-Sun noon-9.30pm), in the same building. The burgers are made from aged Galician beef, though there are duck and vegan options too. At Get Plucked chicken burgers include an option with kimchi and gochujang sauce for £10.

If you just want a takeaway you could head to one of three places next to each other on The Parade: *Spice Paradise* (☎ 01672 519959, 🖳 spiceparadise online.com; Wed-Mon 5-11.30pm); *Yeung's House Fish & Chips* (☎ 01672 515654; Mon-Sat noon-2pm & 5-10pm); and *Lotus House* (☎ 01672 512715; daily 5-10.30pm) which cooks Chinese food for takeaway only. Alternatively, a minute or so back up the hill is *Pagoda Peking* (☎ 01672 512886, 🖳 pagoda peking.co.uk; Mon-Sat 5-9pm); it's a pretty standard Peking Chinese restaurant with a lengthy menu and reasonable prices (£6.80 for vegetable chow mein); takeaway is available here too.

For **Italian food** head to *Pino's* (☎ 01672 512969, 🖳 pinosristorante.co.uk; Mon-Sat noon-2.30pm, daily 5.30pm to late), a family-owned restaurant serving risotto, pasta and pizzas, including a Gamberoni Siciliana (garlic-marinated prawns, fresh chilli & rocket leaves on a mozzarella & tomato base) for £12.95. Booking is advised to eat in but takeaway is available. Another option is *Pizza Express* (☎ 01672 519229, 🖳 pizzaexpress.com/marlborough; Mon-Wed 11.30am-10pm, Thur-Sat to 11pm, Sun noon-10pm), at *The Merlin* (see p74), which has a sunny courtyard and the usual selection of pizza and pasta. And on the other side of the High St, *Ask Italian* (☎ 01672 288022, 🖳 askitalian.co.uk/ restaurant/marlborough; Sun-Wed 11.30am-9.30pm, Thur to 10pm, Fri & Sat to 11pm) has a more interesting selection and the menu changes regularly; they also offer takeaway.

MARLBOROUGH TO AVEBURY WALK
[MAP A pp78-9, MAP B pp80-1, MAP C pp82-3]

[See pp95-6 for notes on using the route guide and maps] If you're spending time around the beginning of the Ridgeway, the chances are you'll need to get to Avebury from Marlborough, or vice versa, at some point. You could always take a bus, but as these only run about every two hours you might prefer to walk, which is also far more interesting.

The route in fact follows the course of the Wessex Ridgeway (see p198) and is an easy 6 miles/9.5km across the Marlborough Downs with the only mildly strenuous section occurring at the Avebury end of the walk; and the only potentially difficult section when it comes to route-finding occurs on the outskirts of Marlborough. Although most of this route is very exposed to the elements, the conditions underfoot are generally excellent, consisting mainly of hard gravel tracks.

From Marlborough, where the High St joins Hyde Lane, to The Red Lion at Avebury (or vice versa) it'll take 2-3 hours.

Marlborough to Avebury The starting point in Marlborough is **Hyde Lane** which runs up the side of The Marlborough (hotel). *(cont'd on p80)*

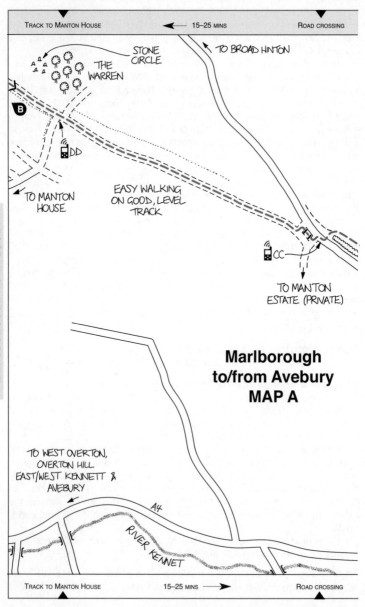

TRACK TO MANTON HOUSE   ← 15–25 MINS   ROAD CROSSING

TO BROAD HINTON

STONE CIRCLE

THE WARREN

B

DD

TO MANTON HOUSE

EASY WALKING ON GOOD, LEVEL TRACK

CC

TO MANTON ESTATE (PRIVATE)

Marlborough to/from Avebury MAP A

TO WEST OVERTON, OVERTON HILL EAST/WEST KENNETT & AVEBURY

A4

RIVER KENNET

TRACK TO MANTON HOUSE   15–25 MINS →   ROAD CROSSING

MARLBOROUGH TO AVEBURY

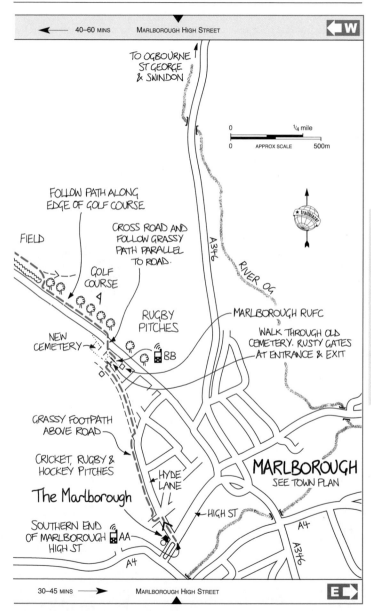

TO OGBOURNE
ST GEORGE
& SWINDON

0   ¼ mile
0   APPROX SCALE   500m

★ trailblazer

FOLLOW PATH ALONG
EDGE OF GOLF COURSE

FIELD

CROSS ROAD AND
FOLLOW GRASSY
PATH PARALLEL
TO ROAD.

A346

RIVER OG

GOLF
COURSE

RUGBY
PITCHES

MARLBOROUGH RUFC

NEW
CEMETERY

WALK THROUGH OLD
CEMETERY. RUSTY GATES
AT ENTRANCE & EXIT

BB

GRASSY FOOTPATH
ABOVE ROAD

CRICKET, RUGBY &
HOCKEY PITCHES

HYDE
LANE

MARLBOROUGH
SEE TOWN PLAN

The Marlborough

HIGH ST

SOUTHERN END
OF MARLBOROUGH
HIGH ST

AA

A4

A4

A346

(cont'd from p77) As the road bends right you follow a track leading to two **cemeteries** (Map A), the first and oldest of which you pass through to reach a lane beyond which, on the other side, are some rugby pitches. The path takes you alongside this lane as it borders a golf course, before you cross back to its southern side and forsake it altogether by the driveway for **Manton Estate** where a well-established stable and stud has been operating since the 19th century.

The path is clear from here as you join a well-made gravel track. **Gallops** parallel the track for long stretches; indeed, you'll notice plenty of evidence of the racehorse business (see box on p108); if you're lucky you could see some thoroughbreds being exercised. When walking on the edge of the grassy gallops instead of on the gravel track you'll notice just how soft and springy the ground is; this is one of the main reasons that this area is so favourable for training racehorses. At one point on this stretch, if you look across the fields to your right just after The Warren (a copse), you may be able to make out the top of a **stone circle**. The stones themselves are rather unimpressive when compared to the giants of Avebury, and there is no (official) footpath to reach them, but this glimpse nevertheless provides you with a tantalising taste of the delights that await both at the end of this walk and on the Ridgeway itself.

Leaving the gallops behind, and having passed an **underground reservoir** to the right of the path which looks rather anomalous in this landscape, you soon enter the weird but wonderful world of **Fyfield Down National Nature Reserve (NNR)**. To most people it's just another attractive area for a stroll, but for geologists it's one of the most important sites in Britain. The sides and

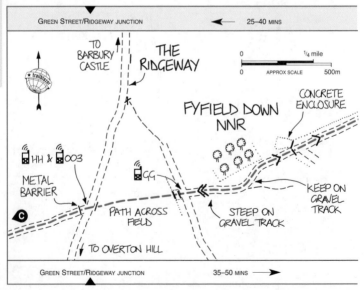

bottom of the valley in the reserve are littered with **sarsen stones** – the very same kind of stones that were used to build Avebury and many of the more recent buildings in the vicinity. Some of these sarsens are also home to rare mosses and lichens. There is something of a fantasy-world feel to this place, as if you might pass a wandering hobbit or see an elf resting on a sarsen.

This NNR takes you all the way to the Ridgeway trail itself; turn left to reach the beginning or right to start the trail just under two miles in. To reach Avebury, cross over the Ridgeway and drop down the track opposite, **Green Street** (Map C) – also known as **Herepath**, an Anglo-Saxon road meaning 'army road'; this snakes its way into the centre of Avebury and *The Red Lion*, the perfect place to enjoy a well-earned drink!

Avebury to Marlborough Start your walk at the *The Red Lion* in the centre of Avebury. Head up **Green Street** (Map C) – also known as **Herepath**, an Anglo-Saxon road meaning 'army road'. At the junction with the Ridgeway you need to cross straight over to the gate into **Fyfield Down National Nature Reserve (NNR)** and walk straight across the field to a set of two gates either side of some gallops. Once through these you are into the NNR proper where the path starts to descend into the valley. For geologists, this is one of the most important sites in Britain. The sides and bottom of the valley are littered with **sarsen stones** – the very same kind of stones that were used to build Avebury and many of the more recent buildings in the vicinity. Some of these sarsens are also home to rare mosses and lichens. *(cont'd on p84)*

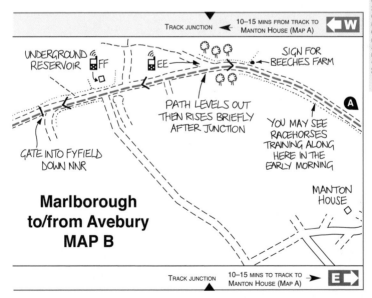

TRACK JUNCTION ← 10–15 MINS FROM TRACK TO MANTON HOUSE (MAP A) — W

UNDERGROUND RESERVOIR FF

EE →

SIGN FOR BEECHES FARM

A

PATH LEVELS OUT THEN RISES BRIEFLY AFTER JUNCTION

YOU MAY SEE RACEHORSES TRAINING ALONG HERE IN THE EARLY MORNING

GATE INTO FYFIELD DOWN NNR

MANTON HOUSE

Marlborough to/from Avebury MAP B

TRACK JUNCTION 10–15 MINS TO TRACK TO MANTON HOUSE (MAP A) → E

MARLBOROUGH TO AVEBURY

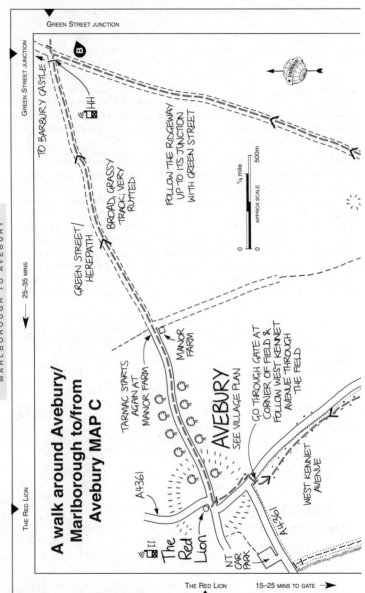

MARLBOROUGH TO AVEBURY

GREEN STREET JUNCTION

GREEN STREET JUNCTION

TO BARBURY CASTLE

HH

GREEN STREET/ HEREPATH

BROAD, GRASSY TRACK; VERY RUTTED

FOLLOW THE RIDGEWAY UP TO ITS JUNCTION WITH GREEN STREET

B

APPROX SCALE

0 — 500m
0 — ¼ mile

TARMAC STARTS AGAIN AT MANOR FARM

MANOR FARM

AVEBURY
SEE VILLAGE PLAN

GO THROUGH GATE AT CORNER OF FIELD & FOLLOW WEST KENNET AVENUE THROUGH THE FIELD

WEST KENNET AVENUE

A4361

The Red Lion

II

NT CAR PARK

A4361

A walk around Avebury/ Marlborough to/from Avebury MAP C

25–35 MINS

THE RED LION

THE RED LION

15–25 MINS TO GATE →

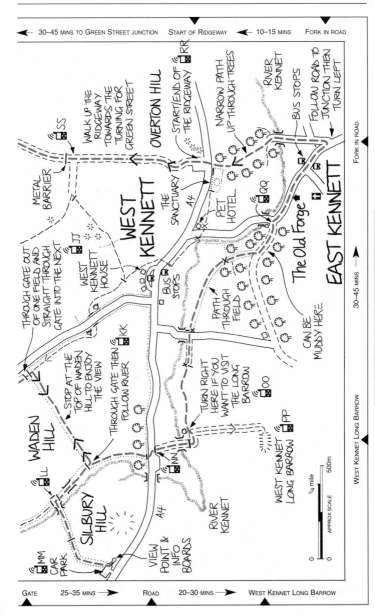

30–45 MINS TO GREEN STREET JUNCTION START OF RIDGEWAY 10–15 MINS FORK IN ROAD

FORK IN ROAD

WALK UP THE RIDGEWAY TOWARDS THE TURNING FOR GREEN STREET

OVERTON HILL

START/END OF THE RIDGEWAY

NARROW PATH UP THROUGH TREES

RIVER KENNET

BUS STOPS

FOLLOW ROAD TO JUNCTION THEN TURN LEFT

SS

METAL BARRIER

WEST KENNETT

THE SANCTUARY

A4

PET HOTEL

QQ

The Old Forge

EAST KENNETT

JJ

WEST KENNETT HOUSE

THROUGH GATE OUT OF ONE FIELD AND STRAIGHT THROUGH GATE INTO THE NEXT

BUS STOPS

PATH THROUGH FIELD

CAN BE MUDDY HERE

30–45 MINS

STOP AT THE TOP OF WADEN HILL TO ENJOY THE VIEW

KK

THROUGH GATE THEN FOLLOW RIVER

TURN RIGHT HERE IF YOU WANT TO VISIT THE LONG BARROW

OO

WADEN HILL

WEST KENNET LONG BARROW

PP

LL

SILBURY HILL

NN

MM CAR PARK

VIEW POINT & INFO BOARDS

A4

RIVER KENNET

¼ mile   500m

APPROX SCALE

0   0

GATE   25–35 MINS   ROAD   20–30 MINS   WEST KENNET LONG BARROW

(cont'd from p81) There is something of a fantasy-world feel to this place, as if you might pass a wandering hobbit or see an elf resting on a sarsen.

The track meanders along, passing by a concrete enclosure used for cattle before leaving the NNR via a gate. It's high and exposed along here with good views to the south. The track is hard, but in good condition for all weathers.

You'll pass by an **underground reservoir** (Map B) to the left of the path and about half a mile after this the track bends right. Some way off the track, by **The Warren** (Map A), a copse, you can see a small stone circle – it's not quite on the same scale as the one at Avebury and there is no (official) footpath to reach it for a closer look. Shortly after here, just past where the track goes off right to Manton House, the track is paralleled by **gallops**. In the early morning you can see race-horses being exercised along here. You'll realise why this area is so favourable for training horses if you leave the gravel track and walk on the gallops – the ground is soft and springy. It's a lot easier on your feet than the hard track.

At the end of the track, and gallops, you join the road at the driveway to **Manton Estate**. Cross this road and enter the field, turning right to follow the hedge along its edge. As the path curves off left around the edge of the field, you should take the obvious right turn to follow the path between the road and the golf course. Cross the road when you see the two **cemeteries** on the other side. Ignore the older first one and walk through the gates of the second, newer, cemetery. At the other end, exit through the gates and turn right, onto the track. Follow this to where it joins the road (**Hyde Lane**) and continue straight ahead, down the hill, to the southern end of Marlborough High St where you'll emerge by the side of The Marlborough.

❑ CROP CIRCLES

If you are in the Wiltshire area, particularly around Avebury, during the summer months you have a good chance of seeing a crop circle. It's usually free to go into the field to have a look inside the formation but as you'll be just one of many doing this they get damaged very quickly. It's not often easy to get good photographs of crop circles because although they are generally on hillsides, the gradient isn't steep enough to present a clear view of the pattern. However, nearly every formation that appears in Wiltshire will have an aerial photograph taken of it and these are easily found on the internet. Websites such as 🖥 cropcircleconnector.com often have photos of crop circles within a day of them first being reported.

The appearance of crop circles in Wiltshire certainly dates back as far as the early 1980s and some farmers say they noticed them earlier than that. In the 1990s, when the more elaborate designs started to appear, the media became interested. However, within a few years much of the media interest faded, though the circles continue to appear. Theories abound as to how the circles are created, though people have comprehensively demonstrated how to make complex designs in just a few hours. You can take your pick of the theories out there, some more 'out there' than others. Are they created by a 'plasma vortex', UFOs, the presence of ley lines, or something completely different that no one has even thought of yet?

If it all gets a bit confusing, unwind with a pint of Crop Circle, a beer produced by Hop Back Brewery (see box on p22) and available in some local pubs.

Avebury and around

AVEBURY

This small village, spread around one of the most important Neolithic sites (see box on pp88-9) in Europe, attracts thousands of visitors every year, but for all that, it's still essentially a quiet and unassuming place. Most tourists are here for just a couple of hours on a whistle-stop coach tour and those day-trippers who arrive by car are usually gone by mid afternoon, too. It's remarkable how you can walk just a few minutes away from the throngs of visitors around the stone circle and be on your own in the countryside. Another remarkable thing about this place, that's impossible to miss, is how the busy A4361 road from Beckhampton to Swindon zigzags straight through the stone circle itself. It really couldn't be any less subtle.

It is well worth spending as much time as you can in and around Avebury. There is so much to see and the walking is easy – an ideal warm-up for the Ridgeway proper or a great way to relax after walking it. Not only is there the stone circle, but the Great Barn and museums, West Kennet Avenue, Silbury Hill, West Kennet Long Barrow, the Sanctuary and Windmill Hill. And if you're really lucky you might even see a crop circle (see box opposite)! A useful website for information about the sights is 🖳 avebury-web.co.uk.

The **Alexander Keiller Museum** (🖳 english-heritage.org.uk; daily Easter-Oct 10am-6pm, Nov-Easter 10am-4pm) is spread over two locations: one ticket (£4.40/2.20 for adults/children, £4.90/2.50 inc Gift Aid; free for members of English Heritage and National Trust) admits you to both galleries. The **Barn Gallery** is in the magnificent late 17th-century Great Barn, and **Stables Gallery** is a few minutes' walk away. This museum was started in 1935 to gather together archaeological finds from Avebury and the surrounding area dating back 6000 years. A visit is recommended as it really helps to put the surviving monuments in and around the village in context.

Close to the Stables Gallery, but closed at the time of writing, is **Avebury Manor and Gardens** (☎ 01672 539250, 🖳 nationaltrust.org.uk/avebury; Easter-Oct daily 11am-5pm; £9.50/4.50 adults/children, £10.50/5 inc Gift Aid; free for NT members). There was originally a Benedictine Priory on this site dating back to the 13th century, but the current buildings date from the 16th century with renovations made by a Colonel Jenner in the early 20th century.

The immaculate gardens, with their box hedges and medieval walls, are open to the public, as is most of the Manor House including the Tudor and Georgian dining rooms. Unusually, you are allowed to sit on many of the chairs, lie on many of the beds and touch many of the exhibits in the Manor. There is also a *tea room* here but the opening times vary.

Services

The **post office** in the small car park on the High St, opposite the shop, operates limited hours (Mon 9am-noon, Wed-Fri 2-5pm). The **village shop** (☎ 01672 539200; daily 10am-4pm) stocks a selection of groceries including fresh pies and pasties; vegan and gluten-free options are available.

There is no longer a tourist information centre, though the **National Trust Shop** (daily Apr-Oct 10am-5.30pm, Nov-Mar 11am-4pm), closed at the time of writing, close to the Great Barn has some tourist information leaflets. They also have a good range of postcards and souvenirs.

The Henge Shop (☎ 01672 539229; daily late Mar to late Oct 9.30am-5.30pm, rest of year to 5pm) is a large souvenir shop that sells some interesting Avebury paraphernalia as well as shelf upon shelf of generic tourist tat.

The National Trust **car park** (open 10am-5pm), just outside the village, costs £7 per day (£4 after 3pm), but is free to National Trust and English Heritage members.

There are frequent **bus** services to Swindon (Stagecoach's No 49) and services about every two hours to Marlborough (Swindon's No 42); see pp48-51 for further details. For a **taxi**, call one of the firms in Marlborough, see p74.

Where to stay

B&B options in Avebury village are expensive and even if you can afford to stay here you should book well ahead to secure a room.

There are, however, a couple of cheaper options just outside the village, at *No 6 Beckhampton Road* (☎ 01672 539588, 🖳 angelaraiymont@btinternet .com; 1D en suite; WI-FI; ⓛ). The friendly proprietor charges from £35pp (sgl occ £60). At the time of research she hadn't opened but was expecting to by 2021. She is happy to cater for all dietary needs if requested in advance. You could walk here from the village as it's only about half a mile (1km) along the A4361 towards Beckhampton though there isn't a pavement all the way. The B&B is in the line of cottages on the main road at the top of the hill. A quieter and safer but less straightforward route would be to follow the High St to its western end and then take the series of paths to **Trusloe hamlet** and cut through to the B&B. Alternatively, you could get a bus (Stagecoach's No 49, see pp48-51): the first bus stop out of Avebury village is more or less opposite the B&B.

Nearby in **Avebury Trusloe** is *Avebury Life B&B* (☎ 01672 539644, 🖳 aveburylife.com; 1D en suite, 1T private bathroom; WI-FI; ⓛ) which charges from £44.50pp (sgl occ discount if not busy) and serves a vegetarian breakfast.

In the centre of Avebury village is *Silbury House* (☎ 01672 539356, 🖳 sil buryhouse.co.uk; 1D/1T both private facilities; 🖤; WI-FI; 🐾) which charges from £60pp (sgl occ room rate). Both rooms have a fridge and a breakfast pack is put in that. Also in the centre and just up the High St is *Avebury Lodge* (☎ 01672 539023, 🖳 aveburylodge.co.uk; 1D private bathroom, 1Tr en suite; 🖤; WI-FI; ⓛ); they charge from £97.50pp (sgl occ £155). The food is vegetarian or vegan and, where possible, organic.

In addition there is the accommodation listed on **Airbnb** (see pp20-1), including one pretty close to the centre of the village.

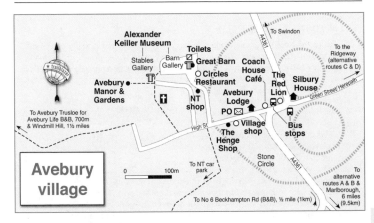

Where to eat and drink

National Trust's *Circles Restaurant* (🖥 nationaltrust.org.uk/avebury/features/ circles-restaurant; daily 11am-4pm) is in a good location next to the Great Barn. At the time of writing, they were only providing a takeaway service for their tea, coffee, cold drinks, cakes, sandwiches, ice-creams and snacks. Note dogs are not allowed inside though there are tables outside. They also run the *Coach House Café* (🖥 nationaltrust.org.uk/avebury/features/coach-house-cafe; weekends, holidays and occasional weekdays 11am-5pm) in the village centre which serves a range of drinks, sandwiches and pasties. However, at the time of writing it was closed.

The Red Lion (☎ 01672 539266, 🖥 greeneking-pubs.co.uk/pubs/wilt shire/red-lion; WI-FI; food daily 11am-9pm) is right in the centre of the stone circle and is also the only pub in the village. The building dates back to the early 17th century but it was only in the early 18th century that it became a pub. Since then the original building has been enlarged. Naturally, the place has its own ghost – a murdered lady – who might or might not put in an appearance depending on how long you've spent at the bar. The pub is busier at lunchtimes than in the evening and food-wise it offers the standard Greene King pub menu with burgers, steaks, pies and 'pub classics' from £9.99 to £16.99. Note that the pub's car park is free to customers; it's the most central parking in the village.

WEST OVERTON   [see map p93]

This village is about a mile/1.6km from the start of the Ridgeway. On the A4 at the main turning for the village is *The Bell* (☎ 01672 861099, 🖥 thebellwest overton.co.uk; WI-FI; 🐾 on lead; Wed-Sat, bar noon-3pm & 6-10.30pm, Sun noon-6pm, **food** Wed-Sat noon-2pm & 6-9pm, Sun noon-3pm), which has a consistently good reputation for its food. Main courses (£15-25) include a range of fresh fish from Cornwall, though there's only one vegetarian option. They also serve around three locally brewed real ales. *(cont'd on p90)*

❏ AVEBURY STONE CIRCLE

A visit to the Neolithic stone circle complex at Avebury is undoubtedly one of the highlights of the Ridgeway. This is one of the largest stone circles in the world though it's often overshadowed by the more famous Stonehenge, about 24 miles away. Although most tourists are here for just a couple of hours, it would be easy to spend a day or two investigating Avebury and the surrounding monuments.

The immense task of constructing this site spanned about 500 years, starting around 2500BC. The irregularly shaped stones come from the Marlborough Downs, a few miles from where they were set up in the henge, and were transported here with great effort though it's still unclear why. There are several clear solar alignments within the formation but an overall theory about the purpose and usage of the stone circle remains elusive. If you are in need of an answer, you'll find plenty of ideas out there, with many entering the realms of fantasy, but none of which can comprehensively explain this huge site.

Starting from the outside and working in, there is a roughly circular earth bank about 400 metres in diameter immediately dropping down into a deep ditch. Lining the other side of this ditch is the main stone circle. It is highly significant that the earth bank is on the outside of the ditch as this means that the site cannot have been defensive in nature, unlike all the later hill forts which have the ditch outside the bank and therefore are defensive. The alignment of outer bank and inner ditch is what defines a 'henge', though there is one exception to this of course – Stonehenge itself!

The **Outer Circle**, the main stone circle, once consisted of nearly 100 stones, but today just 30 are standing. There are two main reasons for the disappearance of the stones: some were pulled over and buried in pits during the 14th century and others were broken up and used as building materials for houses in the village in the late 17th and 18th centuries. Most of the stones standing today were unearthed during excavations and re-erected. The two smaller **inner circles** (Northern and Southern) are both about 100 metres in diameter. Like the outer circle, many of the stones that once formed these circles are now missing and have been replaced by concrete markers.

Two of the best-known stones in the outer circle are the 'Swindon Stone' and the 'Barber Surgeon Stone'. The **'Swindon Stone'**, roughly square in shape, is one of the largest and marks the northern entrance to the circle. It weighs in at an estimated 60 tonnes and is one of the only stones never to have fallen.

The **'Barber Surgeon Stone'**, towards the south of the outer circle, is so named because a skeleton was found under it during excavations in the 1930s. The story goes that, during the 14th century when many of the stones were pulled over and buried one unfortunate man happened to be in the wrong place and was squashed. When Alexander Keiller excavated this stone the man's skeleton was found underneath it, along with a pouch containing scissors and some coins. Research indicated this unfortunate individual was probably an itinerant craftsman who performed many roles including that of a barber and a surgeon.

What you can see today is the result of immense excavation work and restoration projects, mainly led by Alexander Keiller during the 1920s and 1930s; up till then, the site had suffered centuries of deliberate damage and neglect. Keiller relied heavily on the previous work of two antiquarians, John Aubrey and William Stukeley,

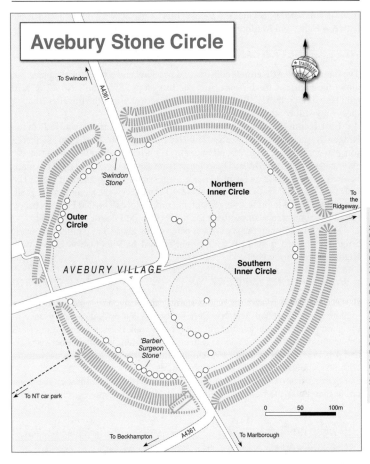

to interpret the remains of the stone circle. Aubrey was the first person to study Avebury in detail and record what he found. His main findings were written up in 1690 and proved an invaluable resource for William Stukeley who, in the 18th century, drew maps of the entire complex of stones and also wrote extensively about his findings. As the period following Aubrey's and Stukeley's work was one of the most destructive in Avebury's history, had it not been for their surviving records much of Keiller's work, and indeed even modern archaeology in the Avebury area, would have proved an impossible task.

There is no entrance fee to the circle, mainly because it would be impractical to enforce such a scheme; hence it is open for visitors all day, every day.

(cont'd from p87)   Swindon's No 42 **bus** stops at West Overton en route between Calne and Marlborough; see pp48-51 for further details.

WEST KENNETT & EAST KENNETT   [see Map C pp82-3 & map p93]

The hamlet of **West Kennett** consists of a pet hotel and a few houses spread out along the main A4 road. Apart from the **bus** stops (Swindon's No 42 & X76 stop here, see pp48-51), there is nothing of practical use to the traveller (though there may still be an **Airbnb** property, see pp20-1).

East Kennett, a very picturesque village, provides the closest B&B to the Ridgeway, though very little else. *The Old Forge* (☎ 01672 861686, 🖳 theold forge-avebury.co.uk; 1Qd/2D, all en suite, 1D private bathroom; 🛏; WI-FI; Ⓛ; 🐾) really is a lovely B&B. They charge from £50pp (sgl occ £90). This place is often busy so book as far in advance as possible. For an evening meal, The Bell (see p87) at West Overton is about 10 minutes' walk along a quiet road. However, subject to prior arrangement, the proprietor at The Old Forge is happy to provide a meal in your room on the nights The Bell doesn't serve food.

From East Kennett the start of the path is only about half a mile/1km away. Should you need a shop, it's a straightforward half-hour stroll along West Kennet Avenue to Avebury.

A WALK AROUND AVEBURY   [MAP C pp82-3]

If you have some spare time before starting the Ridgeway, you might like to explore the area around Avebury. Detailed below is a walk designed to take in the main attractions outside the village. As this walk is circular and starts from the centre of Avebury, you can do it in either direction. It will take between 2½ and 4 hours. It's about 6 miles/9.5km and the walking is generally easy going with just a couple of mildly tiring uphill stints.

Starting from **The Red Lion** follow the main road south through the stone circle then enter the field and follow **West Kennet Avenue** (see box below).

MARLBOROUGH TO AVEBURY

❑ WEST KENNET AVENUE   (see map pp82-3)

West Kennet Avenue dates from about 2400BC and runs south from the henge at Avebury to The Sanctuary, a distance of about 1½ miles/2.5km. The course of the avenue was originally marked by two parallel rows of around one hundred sarsen stones, though today only the first 750 metres of the avenue is lined with them.

These stones were excavated and re-erected by Maud Cunnington in 1912 and by Alexander Keiller in the 1930s. As with the henge at Avebury, concrete markers replace stones that have disappeared or been destroyed. Despite various sources of evidence – the 18th-century records of William Stukeley and excavations in both the 20th century and in 2002 – the exact course of the avenue is still a subject of debate. There is a second avenue of stones at Avebury, leading away from the henge to the west. This was first noticed by William Stukeley in the 18th century, but no longer shows above ground and was only rediscovered following excavations in 1999. It is called Beckhampton Avenue because it heads out towards the long stones at Beckhampton.

❏ WEST KENNET LONG BARROW

Even if you don't plan to do the whole walk around Avebury (see opposite) you should make the effort to go up to West Kennet Long Barrow, located on a ridge about a mile from Silbury Hill. At 100 metres long it's one of the largest Neolithic burial mounds in the country and dates back to 3600BC, nearly a thousand years before Wayland's Smithy (see box on p115). It's thought that this long barrow was used for around a thousand years before it was filled in with earth and sealed with the huge sarsen stones that stand across the entrance. During several excavations, the last in 1955-6, the remains of 45 people of all ages were discovered in the various chambers.

The main advantage this site has over Wayland's Smithy is that you can actually enter this long barrow and walk into all five of the burial chambers, but don't expect the underground passage to take you along the entire length of the long barrow – it only extends about ten metres into the mound. There is no entrance fee for the long barrow and it is open all the time. Take a torch, though.

When you reach the **gates** at the end of the field follow the fence line up **Waden Hill** from the top of which you get very good views of Silbury Hill.

At the bottom of the hill you have a choice, the route you take depending on how close you want to get to Silbury Hill. For most, the distant view of Silbury Hill from here is enough, and they should turn left to cross the A4 and head towards West Kennet Long Barrow. However, if you want a closer look, you should turn right and follow the River Kennet to the junction where you need to take the left turn and go over the bridge – straight ahead leads back to Avebury, if you are already tired. After turning left you will skirt around **Silbury Hill** (see box on p92), eventually arriving at a car park. Here you can get a closer view of the Hill from a special viewing area. You are not allowed to walk any nearer. That said, the road does in fact pass much closer if you do want that closer look – though this does involve a rather unpleasant schlep along the A4. You must then look for a turning on the other side of the road which leads up to **West Kennet Long Barrow** (see box above). The climb up is a bit tiring but will get you in good shape for the Ridgeway.

❏ THE SANCTUARY

Opposite the official start of the Ridgeway is The Sanctuary. It's not one of the more memorable relics in the Avebury area, but is worth a visit nonetheless. It consists of various concentric circles marked out with small concrete posts in the ground.

This was the site of a circular wooden building, possibly a temple, dating back as far as 2500BC. The smaller circle marks out the boundary of the original building while the larger ones suggest that the structure was considerably and repeatedly expanded over the course of the next thousand years. Eventually the wooden buildings were replaced by two stone circles, noted by John Aubrey in 1648, and these were connected to Avebury by a stone avenue (West Kennet Avenue), parts of which you can still follow. The views from here over to Silbury Hill and West Kennet Long Barrow are particularly good.

❑ SILBURY HILL

Despite the enormity of this hill it's often neglected in favour of the stone circle up the road. But do make the effort to come here as it's only at this closer proximity that you can start to understand the almost super-human effort that must have been required to build this structure.

The history of the hill dates back to around 2600BC when construction started. The first phase created a stepped structure. The steps were then filled in with chalk and after that earth was shaped over the steps to create a smooth face. You can still see one of these steps near the top of the hill but it's only clear when viewed from the eastern side. The top of the mound was left flat, but not level, and is 39m high and 30m wide. The base is perfectly round with a diameter of 167m. Just to really impress you, the hill contains around a quarter of a million cubic metres of chalk.

Why was it built? No one really knows, but there have been some earnest efforts to find out. The first of these was in 1776 when a shaft was dug from the summit down to the base. Nothing was found apart from construction materials. In 1849 another approach was tried, this time digging a tunnel from the base to the centre. Again, nothing was found. Yet another investigation took place in the late 1960s but the new tunnel into the base, again, revealed no evidence to point to Silbury Hill's raison d'être.

The hill was previously open to the public but slippages of the top soil were detected and any more human trampling would have only accelerated this deterioration. In 2000 a large hole also opened up on the summit, owing to a collapse of the shaft dug in 1776. It was infilled with polystyrene blocks and then covered with chalk. Investigations by English Heritage around the base of Silbury Hill in 2007 discovered evidence of a Roman settlement and later in the same year a major task was undertaken to stabilise the hill. Tunnels which had previously been dug into the hillside were filled with hundreds of tonnes of chalk to prevent any more collapses. As this work was sealing up the tunnels for good, English Heritage also took the opportunity to undertake one final archaeological survey in a bid to finally understand why the hill was built. Although they ultimately didn't come any closer to finding an answer to the question, the stabilisation work on the hill was carried out successfully.

Naturally, various theories regarding Silbury Hill's purpose have been developed to fill the vacuum, among them that it was a solar observatory or was symbolic of a Mother Goddess, but none really explains why such a gargantuan effort was made to build something so seemingly purposeless.

After visiting the Long Barrow and admiring the views you should retrace your steps to the path junction where you need to take a right turn, heading for **East Kennett** village. This is an idyllic place; take a few minutes to look at the church and wander past the attractive village houses before you get to the fork in the road. At this point you should follow the other lane, almost doubling back on yourself. This lane turns into a path and you cross the River Kennet once more, heading up to **The Sanctuary** (see box on p91) by the side of the A4. When you feel you have soaked up the atmosphere of this place you should cross the road to the official start of the Ridgeway and make your way up the hill to the junction with **Green Street/Herepath**. Turn left onto this track and follow it down to the Red Lion at Avebury. It's a handy place to finish for obvious reasons.

GETTING TO AND FROM OVERTON HILL   [See map below]

Anyone who has walked the Ridgeway will agree that even though it is a national trail the official start at Overton Hill, by the side of the A4 road, is rather lacking in atmosphere. Avebury is, of course, the obvious place to which it should be relocated. So, until it is changed, here are four routes that link Avebury and the Ridgeway. **Route A** goes via the stones of West Kennet Avenue, so you still get to experience the Ridgeway in its entirety. Thanks to a couple of permissive paths, you don't need to walk along any pavement-less roads either. **Routes B and C** connect with the Ridgeway at the same point, 700m from the car park at Overton Hill, but they follow different paths. Route B goes via West Kennet Avenue and four intriguing tree-covered tumuli; this is my favourite route. Route C uses Green Street/Herepath, turning at Manor Farm. **Route D** goes straight up Green Street/Herepath; by taking this route you actually miss out 1.8 miles/2.7km of the Ridgeway.

E ➜ Route A ((1.7 miles/2.75km, 35-50 mins; see also Map C, pp82-3) This is the longest route. Walk out of the village along West Kennet Avenue and when

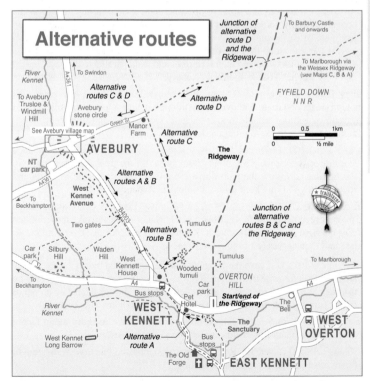

this peters out go through two gates. Keep walking parallel to the road until you reach a gate onto the road, by a couple of minor stones. Cross the road directly to another gate and follow the path along the edge of the field to another gate* (note: this is the same gate that is marked with an asterisk in the route text below). Go through it and straight ahead, following the edge of another field. You'll reach a gap in the hedge where you should cross the A4 to a gate down some steps directly opposite. Follow the path left, through the field to a stile in the far corner. Go over this, and also over the stile directly across the road. Follow the path across the field to a gate into the Sanctuary. Walk through the Sanctuary to a gate onto the A4. The Ridgeway starts in the car park across the road; be careful crossing this – it's fast and visibility isn't good.

←W Route A This is the longest route. From Overton Hill, cross the road into The Sanctuary. Be careful crossing this road – it's fast and visibility isn't good. Once in the Sanctuary, bear right and cross the stile at the far end of the enclosure then walk straight across the field on a clear path to reach a stile onto the road. Cross straight over to another stile and, once over it, follow the path across the field, towards a gate in the hedge. This leads up some steps to the A4 road. Cross here and directly opposite enter a field through a gap in the hedge and follow the path along its edge, to your left. When you reach a gate* (see note in eastbound route A above) go through it and straight ahead, following the path along the edge of the field to a gate onto the B4003 road. Cross directly to another gate and then turn right and walk parallel to the road, reaching West Kennet Avenue and then Avebury.

E → Route B (1.6 miles/2.5km, 30-45 mins) Follow Route A to gate* (see note in eastbound route A above); once through it, take a left up the hill and past a group of wooded tumuli to another gate. Go through and turn right. About 200m along this track you join the Ridgeway.

←W Route B Leave the Ridgeway at the signposted byway where a track leads directly to some trees about 200m away. By the trees there is a gate. Go through it and follow the path down the hill to gate* (see note in eastbound route A above). From here follow Route A to Avebury.

E → Route C (1.7 miles/2.75km, 35-50 mins) Leave Avebury along Green Street/Herepath. Follow this until you reach Manor Farm and take the track that turns off right, immediately after it. Keep on this path for just over a mile as it rises and then curves left to join the Ridgeway.

← W Route C Leave the Ridgeway at the signposted byway where a track leads directly to some trees about 200m away. Ignore the gate here, but stay on the track as it curves right and starts to descend. You'll reach a junction at Manor Farm. Turn left onto Green Street/Herepath and follow this into Avebury.

E → Route D (1.5 miles/2.4km, 30-45 mins) Leave Avebury along Green Street/Herepath and follow this straight up to the Ridgeway.

← W Route D Leave the Ridgeway at the signposted junction. Walk straight down this track until you reach Avebury.

ROUTE GUIDE & MAPS

5

Using this guide

This route guide has been divided according to logical start and stop points. However, these are not intended to be strict daily stages since people walk at different speeds and have different interests. The maps can be used to plan how far to walk each day. The route summaries describe the trail between significant places and are written as if walking the path both from west to east and east to west.

To enable you to plan your own itinerary practical information is presented clearly on the trail maps. This includes walking times for both directions, all places to stay, camp and eat, as well as shops where you can buy supplies. Further service details are given in the text under the entry for each place.

For a condensed overview of this information see **Itineraries** on p32 & p34 and the **town and village facilities tables** on p33 & p35.

For **overview maps** and **altitude profiles** see the colour pages at the end of the book.

TRAIL MAPS

[see map key p199]

Direction
(See pp30-1 for the pros and cons of walking **west to east** or **east to west**.) In the text and maps that follow look for the **E →** symbol which indicates information for those walking **east from Avebury and Overton Hill to Ivinghoe Beacon** and the **← W** symbol with shaded text (also on the maps) for those walking **west from Ivinghoe Beacon to Overton Hill and Avebury**.

Scale and walking times
The trail maps are to a scale of 1:20,000 (1cm = 200m; 3¹/₈ inches = one mile). Walking times are given along the side of each map and the arrow shows the direction to which the time refers. Black triangles indicate the points between which the times have been taken. **See box on p96 about walking times**.

The time-bars are a tool and are not there to judge your walking ability. There are so many variables that affect walking speed, from the weather conditions to how many beers you drank the previous evening. After the first hour or two of walking you will be able to see how your speed relates to the timings on the maps.

> **❏ IMPORTANT NOTE – WALKING TIMES**
> Unless otherwise specified, **all times in this book refer only to the time spent walking**. You should add 20-30% to allow for rests, photos, checking the map, drinking water etc, not to mention time simply to stop and stare. When planning the day's hike count on 5-7 hours' actual walking.

Up or down?
Other than when on a track or bridleway the trail is shown as a red dotted line. An arrow across the trail indicates the slope; two arrows show that it is steep. Note that the arrow points towards the higher part of the trail. If, for example, you are walking from A (at 80m) to B (at 200m) and the trail between the two is short and steep it would be shown thus: A— — — >> — — — B. Reversed arrow heads indicate a downward gradient.

Other features
Other features are marked on the map only when they are pertinent to navigation. To avoid clutter, not all features are marked all the time.

ACCOMMODATION

[See also box on pp20-1] Apart from in large towns where some selection of places has been necessary, almost everywhere to stay that is within easy reach of the trail is marked. Details of each place are given in the accompanying text. The number and type of rooms is given after each entry: **S** = Single, **T** = Twin room, **D** = Double room, **Tr** = Triple room and **Qd** = Quad. Note that most of the triple/quad rooms have a double bed and one/two single beds (or bunk beds); thus for a group of three or four, two people would have to share the double bed, but it also means that the room can be used as a double or twin. See also pp18-21.

    Rates quoted for B&B-style accommodation are **per person (pp) based on two people sharing a room** for a one-night stay; rates may well be discounted for longer stays. Where a **single room (sgl)** is available, the rate for that is quoted if different from the rate per person. The rate for **single occupancy (sgl occ)** of a double/twin may be higher and the per person rate for three/four sharing a triple/quad may be lower.

    Unless specified, rates are for bed and breakfast. At some places the only option is a **room rate**; this will be the same whether one or two people (or more if permissible) use the room. In tourist towns, particularly, you can expect to pay extra at weekends (whereas in the few places on this route that cater to business people the rate is likely to be higher during the week). Note that a few places accept only a two-night stay, particularly at weekends and in the main season.

    Rooms either have **en suite** (bath or shower) facilities, or a **private** or **shared** bathroom or shower room, often just outside the bedroom. The text notes if a bath (☛) is available for those who prefer a relaxed soak at the end of the day.

The text also indicates whether the premises have: **wi-fi** (WI-FI); if a **packed lunch** (Ⓛ) can be prepared, subject to prior arrangement; and if **dogs** (🐾 – see also p29 and pp196-7) are welcome, again subject to prior arrangement, either in at least one room (many places have only one room suitable for dogs), or at campsites. The policy on charging for dogs varies; some places make an additional charge per day or per stay, while others may require a refundable deposit against any potential damage or mess.

The Ridgeway route guide

E ▶ FROM AVEBURY If you're doing this walk in an **easterly direction** (from west to east starting in Overton Hill to Ivinghoe Beacon) follow the maps in an ascending order (from 1 to 39) and the text as below, looking for the **E➜ symbol** on overview text and on map borders.

◀ W FROM IVINGHOE BE If you're walking in a **westerly direction** (Ivinghoe Beacon to Overton Hill) follow the maps in a descending order (from 39 to 1) and the text with a **red background**, looking for the **◀W symbol** on overview text and on map borders. **Turn to p194 to start your walk in this direction**.

E➜ OVERTON HILL TO FOXHILL   [MAPS 1-8]

This first **16½-mile/26.5km (6¾-8½hrs)** stage of the Ridgeway includes many interesting sights but most of them are before Ogbourne St George. By comparison, thereafter, it can seem a bit of a slog in parts, especially the last section from Liddington Hill to Foxhill.

The full length of this stage will leave you tired after your first day but you'll have to push on to Bishopstone to find accommodation (a further 1.2 miles/2km). Alternatively you could stay at Ogbourne St George which is only 9 miles/14.5km from the start of the Ridgeway. It would make an easy first day's walking and would also allow time to investigate Fyfield Down National Nature Reserve and take a long break at Barbury Castle.

❏ **TUMULI**

Especially on the western half of the Ridgeway, and in particular on the first 15 miles of it, you will see many tumuli – burial mounds dating from around 4500 to 4000 years ago which now just look like raised grassy humps. In fact there are three right next to the start/end of the Ridgeway (see Map 1, p99) and you'll see a couple more around 10 minutes along the path. Sometimes they are planted over with trees, so if you see an isolated bunch of trees in the middle of a field, this could suggest a tumulus underneath.

They are generally marked on Ordnance Survey maps, though not all features marked as tumuli are necessarily burial mounds. They could be just, as yet, unidentified lumps on the landscape.

Overton Hill There are several ways to start or end your walk along the Ridgeway (map p93) that are all more interesting than the official one. It just depends how serious you are about following every step of the real path. The official, but rather uninspiring, start/end point is Overton Hill (Map 1), at the side of the Beckhampton to Marlborough road (the A4). Use Alternative route A between here and Avebury.

Green Street/Fyfield Down junction In clear weather there are excellent views west from here (Map 1) to the obelisk monument on Cherhill Hill, 5 miles/8km away. It was built on an Iron Age hill fort in 1845/6 in memory of Sir William Petty, the 17th-century economist. **Windmill Hill** (see box below), 2½ miles/4km to the west, is another easily spotted landmark.

This junction is also linked to Avebury by Alternative route D on one side and a gate into **Fyfield Down NNR** (see p62) on the other. Up here it's exposed to the elements with few trees or bushes to shelter you though the broad, grassy track provides good going underfoot. This area is popular with both walkers and cyclists.

❏ **WINDMILL HILL**

This 20-acre site forms the largest of the 66 known Neolithic causewayed enclosures in Britain, with evidence of activity here dating from about 3700BC. A causewayed enclosure is a piece of land, usually oval in shape, bounded by one or more segmented banks or ditches. Windmill Hill has three such series of banks and ditches, with the outermost series being by far the most substantial. These sites represent the earliest examples of artificially enclosing an open area in Britain.

The findings of excavations by Rev HGO Kendall and Alexander Keiller, that took place here in the 1920s, not only established Neolithic causewayed enclosures as a distinct class, but also granted Windmill Hill its status as the most important one in Britain. The site even lent its name to 'Windmill Hill Ware', a distinctive type of pottery found at this and other similar sites in Britain.

From the 1920s onwards, the theory was that Neolithic people had lived in 'pit dwellings' – in the ditches of the enclosure – owing to the large quantity of animal bones and pottery found there. Keiller's findings from the 1920s were not properly written up at the time and it wasn't until 1965 that a summary of the excavations was published. This led to renewed excavations on the site and by the late 1960s the theory of 'pit dwellings' had totally lost favour. Although we now know that this was not a site of permanent settlement it is still unclear exactly what its purpose was. We can presume that ceremonies and feasts took place here, but the size of the enclosure would suggest a more substantial use. Several round burial mounds on Windmill Hill have also been excavated but these have been dated to the Bronze Age.

Despite the significance of Windmill Hill to archaeologists, a casual visit can prove disappointing. Apart from the views of the surrounding countryside there really isn't much to see on the hill itself as large sections of the banks and ditches have been ploughed into farmland. It's certainly far less visually dramatic than an Iron Age hill fort like Barbury Castle, only 5 miles/8km along the Ridgeway from Avebury.

If you want to visit Windmill Hill you should walk to the western end of Avebury High St and follow the signposts from there; it's about 2 miles (3km) from the village.

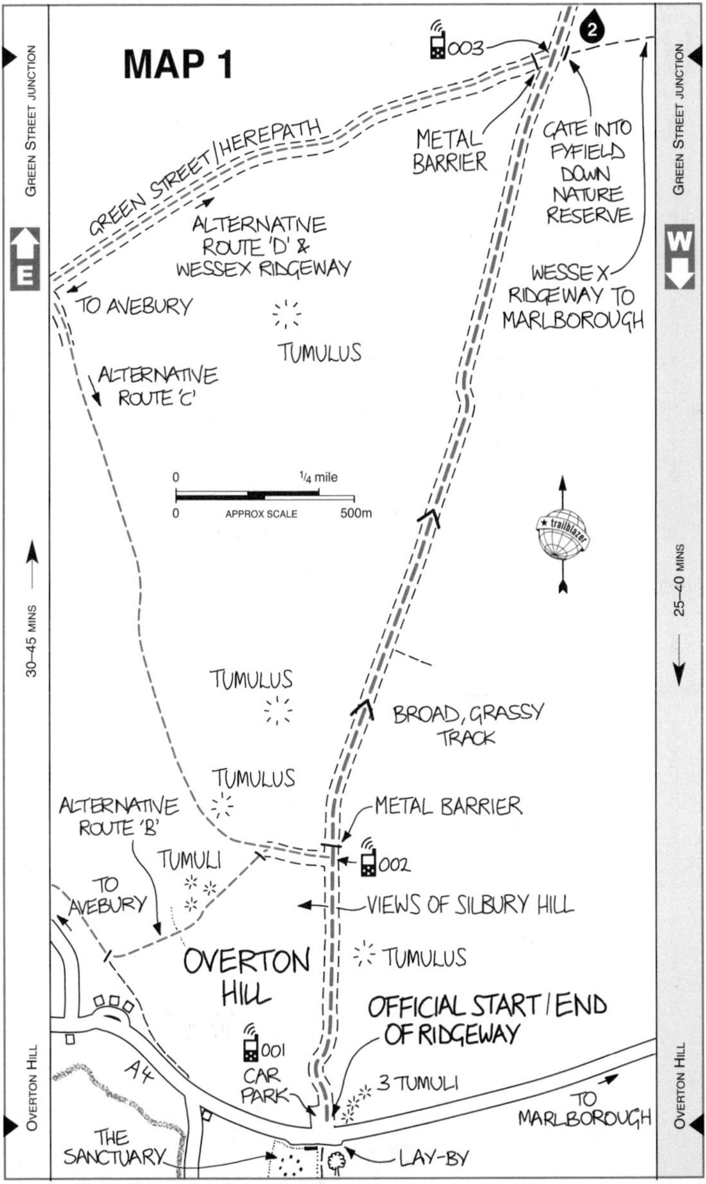

MAP 1

GREEN STREET/HEREPATH

ALTERNATIVE ROUTE 'D' & WESSEX RIDGEWAY

TO AVEBURY

ALTERNATIVE ROUTE 'C'

TUMULUS

003

METAL BARRIER

GATE INTO FYFIELD DOWN NATURE RESERVE

WESSEX RIDGEWAY TO MARLBOROUGH

2

E

W

0   ¼ mile
0   500m
APPROX SCALE

30-45 MINS

25-40 MINS

TUMULUS

TUMULUS

BROAD, GRASSY TRACK

ALTERNATIVE ROUTE 'B'

TUMULI

TO AVEBURY

METAL BARRIER

002

VIEWS OF SILBURY HILL

TUMULUS

OVERTON HILL

OFFICIAL START/END OF RIDGEWAY

001 CAR PARK

3 TUMULI

TO MARLBOROUGH

OVERTON HILL

OVERTON HILL

A4

THE SANCTUARY

LAY-BY

ROUTE GUIDE AND MAPS

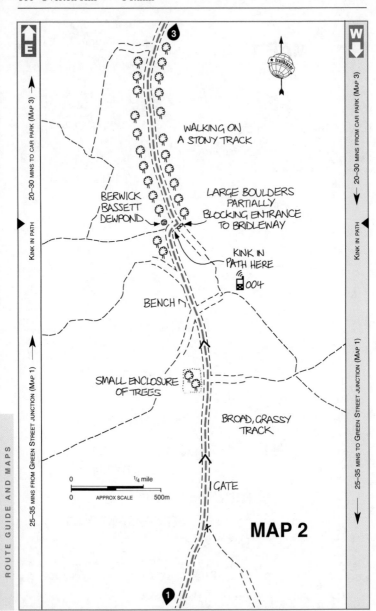

Hackpen White Horse When you get to the junction where the Broad Hinton to Marlborough road crosses the Ridgeway (Map 3) you'll have the opportunity to see the Hackpen White Horse (see box on p118) cut into the chalk of the hillside. You can't see it from the track as you are above it so you'll need to make a slight diversion. It is not an ancient White Horse – this one was cut into **Hackpen Hill** in 1838 – so don't feel the steep detour is obligatory,

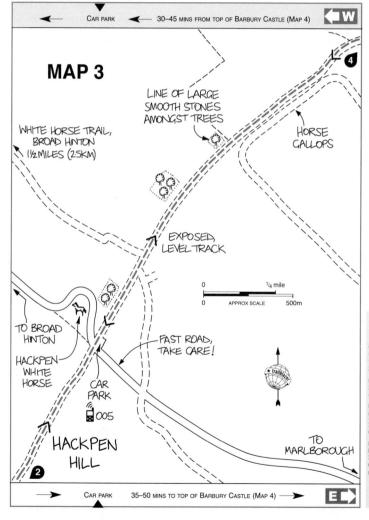

MAP 3

← CAR PARK ← 30–45 MINS FROM TOP OF BARBURY CASTLE (MAP 4) ◄W

LINE OF LARGE SMOOTH STONES AMONGST TREES

HORSE GALLOPS

WHITE HORSE TRAIL, BROAD HINTON 1½ MILES (2.5KM)

EXPOSED, LEVEL TRACK

0 ¼ mile
0 APPROX SCALE 500m

TO BROAD HINTON

HACKPEN WHITE HORSE

FAST ROAD, TAKE CARE!

★ trailblazer

CAR PARK
📱005

HACKPEN HILL

TO MARLBOROUGH

→ CAR PARK 35–50 MINS TO TOP OF BARBURY CASTLE (MAP 4) → E►

ROUTE GUIDE AND MAPS

especially as the original white horse at White Horse Hill is far more impressive. This section of the Ridgeway path is also part of the **White Horse Trail** (see box on p118).

Barbury Castle In addition to Barbury Castle (Map 4) there are two more Iron Age forts on the Ridgeway (Liddington Castle, p108, and Uffington Castle, p117), but this is the only one that the path cuts directly through. The 11-acre fort is ringed by double ramparts and deep grassy ditches with entrances at both ends through which the Ridgeway passes. Some Iron Age finds from the castle

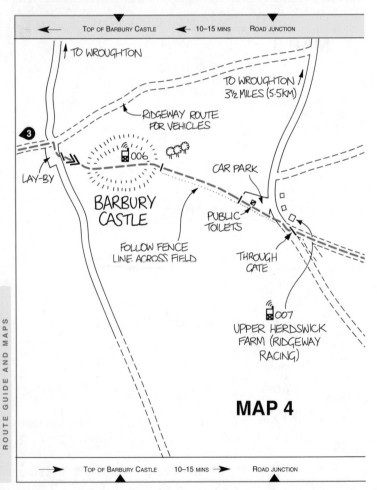

are on display at Wiltshire Museum (⌨ wiltshiremuseum.org.uk), in Devizes. The castle's defensive position is indisputable and this guaranteed its importance long after the Iron Age finished. In fact the name 'Barbury' is thought to come from the Old English name, 'Bera', after the Saxon chief who controlled the castle around AD550. Even as late as World War II it was being used as a potentially defensive position by allied troops.

The views from up here on a clear day are fantastic and it's a popular place at weekends with walkers, cyclists and horseriders. The White Horse Kite

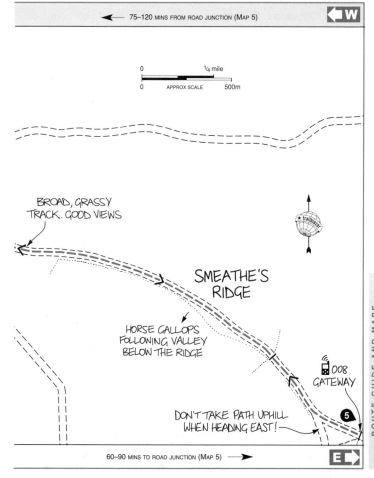

75–120 MINS FROM ROAD JUNCTION (MAP 5)

W

0   ¼ mile
0   APPROX SCALE   500m

BROAD, GRASSY
TRACK. GOOD VIEWS

★ trailblazer

SMEATHE'S
RIDGE

HORSE GALLOPS
FOLLOWING VALLEY
BELOW THE RIDGE

008
GATEWAY

5

DON'T TAKE PATH UPHILL
WHEN HEADING EAST!

60–90 MINS TO ROAD JUNCTION (MAP 5)

E

Flyers (🖳 whkf.org.uk) also use this place for their club meets. You might wonder how all the people manage to get up here but when you get to the other side of the castle you'll understand. There you'll find a large car park, picnic tables, public **toilets** and the road north to Wroughton, 3½ miles/5.5km away.

Smeathe's Ridge When the weather is good the walking on Smeathe's Ridge (Map 4) makes for some of the most enjoyable parts of this stage; the soft grass underfoot means walking is easy and the views are superb. It's a popular area with cyclists who will often whizz past, but there's plenty of room on the wide expanse of the ridge.

Visiting Ogbourne St George Although the official path skirts round Ogbourne St George (Map 5) on shady farm tracks you can follow the signposted footpath, about half a mile/1km, into this attractive village if you want to stop here.

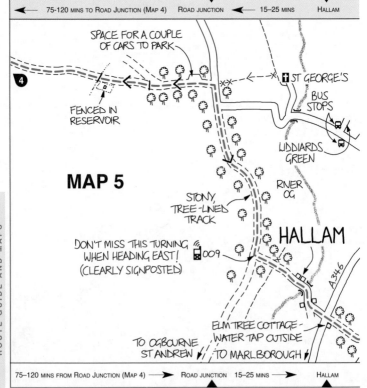

OGBOURNE ST GEORGE [MAP 5]

The name of this village refers to the river Og (Map 5) and the name of its church, St George's. A mile/1.5km or so south of here is the village of Ogbourne St Andrew, named in the same way. Ogbourne St George is a pretty-enough village but unless you are planning to stay the night, there really isn't much point making the detour, especially as there aren't any shops.

Ogbourne is a stop on Stagecoach's No 80 **bus** service which operates between Swindon and Marlborough. Salisbury Red's X5 (Swindon to Salisbury) stops on the main A346 road just outside the village. See pp48-51 for further details.

If you need a **taxi**, call one of the firms in Marlborough, see p74.

Where to stay, eat and drink

Wherever you stay, arranging to have a packed lunch is useful, as there is no shop in the village.

The Sanctuary (☎ 01672 841473, ☎ 07850 325344, 🖳 the-sanctuary.biz; 2D or 1T both en suite, 1Tr private facilities; ▼; WI-FI; (L); 🐴) is a well-run, friendly **B&B** that's used to walkers. They serve good breakfasts and B&B costs £41-42.50pp (sgl occ £74-80). They welcome dogs in return for a donation to their favourite canine

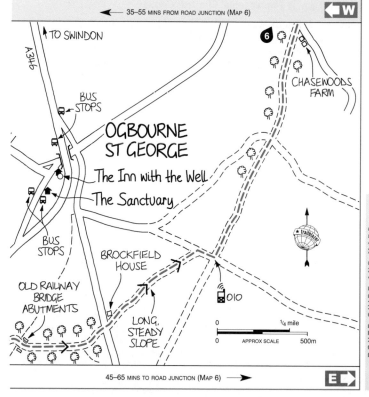

charity (£5 to Black Retriever X Rescue), but be aware that they also have chickens and sometimes they may be in their garden. Luggage transfer is available subject to prior arrangement.

The only place for **food** in the evenings is *The Inn with the Well* (☎ 01672 841445, 🖳 theinnwiththewell.co .uk; 3D/2T/1Tr, all en suite; ☛; WI-FI; Ⓛ; 🐾); it is a deservedly popular place with both locals and people travelling from the surrounding area. The bar opens at 4pm (Mon-Sat, generally Sun also May-Sep) and they serve real ales straight from the barrel; their varied menu (**food** Mon-Sat 6-8pm) includes some hearty pub food and tasty vegan curries. **B&B** costs from £47.50pp (sgl occ £85).

Do remember to check on **Airbnb** (see pp20-1); at the time of writing there was one in a modern annex of an old farmhouse but there may be more by the time you are here.

Hallam This village (Map 5) must contain one of the most picturesque collections of cottages anywhere and is so perfect it's almost twee.

On this stage, apart from the few buildings at Barbury Castle, this is the most heavily built-up area you will pass through. You get occasional glimpses of Ogbourne St George through the trees to the north as you walk through the hamlet. There is a **water tap** at Elm Tree Cottage.

Midland & South Western Junction (M&SWJ) Railway On the stony, tree-lined track a few hundred metres from Hallam you will pass between the hefty **stone abutments** of an old railway bridge which was once the route of the M&SWJ Railway (Map 5). This section opened in the 1880s but has long since disappeared. It linked Swindon and Chiseldon, to the north, with Marlborough, to the south. The route has been developed into the Chiseldon & Marlborough Railway Path and is popular but often muddy. Following this railway path north is a good way to get to Ogbourne St George.

Snap When you arrive at the crossroads with the **reservoir** (Map 6) on the corner that looks like a fortified concrete bunker, there is the opportunity to visit the former village of Snap. A small farming community existed on this site for

---

❏ **SIGNPOSTS ON THE RIDGEWAY**

The Ridgeway is one of the most comprehensively signposted long-distance trails in the country. At nearly every junction on the path there is a dedicated and distinctive black 'Ridgeway' signpost (see photo on p17), not only to keep you going in the right direction, but also to inform you of other options.

At a glance these waymarkers look to be made in the traditional manner from wood that has been treated with creosote, but in fact the material used is Plaswood. This is an environmentally friendly plastic material made from 30% consumer waste and 70% from other waste sources. It is strong, durable and impervious to water so it will not rot or splinter as wood does. This also means that it is maintenance free.

You will see many traditional wooden signs along the Ridgeway in various states of decay but the Plaswood signs will remain looking the same as the day they were set into the ground for years to come. Some have been there for more than 15 years already. Plaswood is now used for many other products, often as a substitute for wood in outdoor areas. Items such as benches, planters, walkways and street furniture are all being constructed from the material.

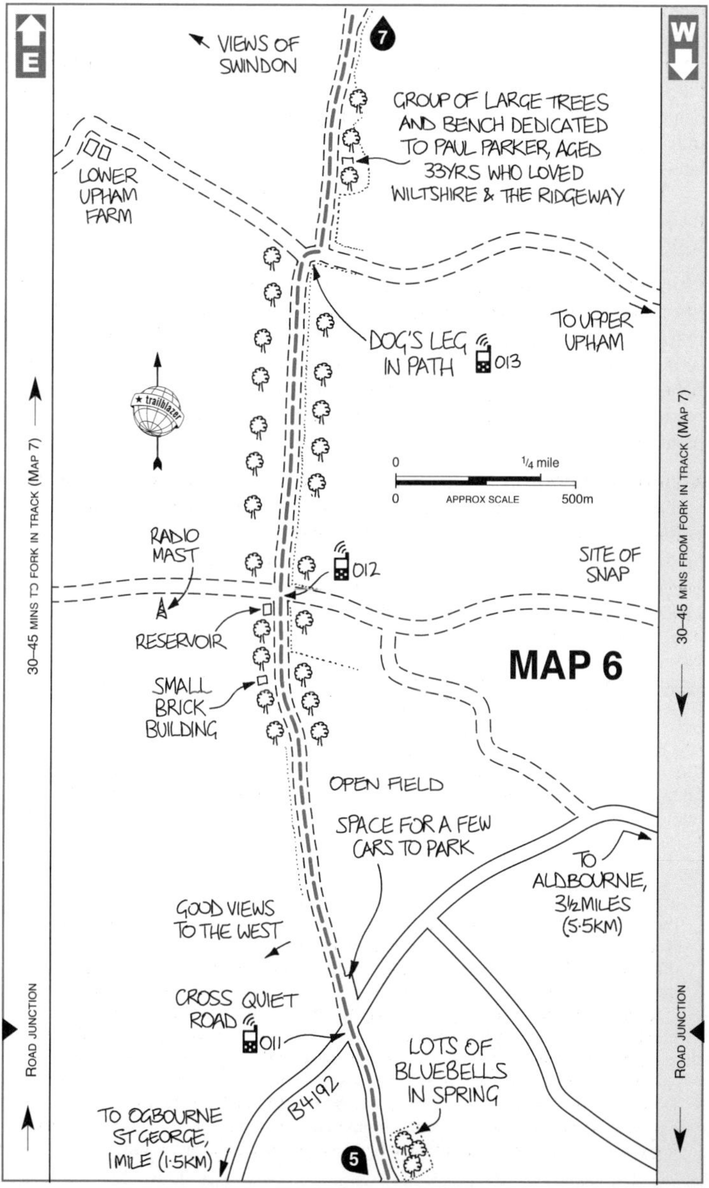

VIEWS OF SWINDON

GROUP OF LARGE TREES AND BENCH DEDICATED TO PAUL PARKER, AGED 33YRS WHO LOVED WILTSHIRE & THE RIDGEWAY

LOWER UPHAM FARM

7

DOG'S LEG IN PATH 013

TO UPPER UPHAM

★ trailblazer

0   ¼ mile
0   APPROX SCALE   500m

RADIO MAST

 012

SITE OF SNAP

RESERVOIR

SMALL BRICK BUILDING

MAP 6

30–45 MINS TO FORK IN TRACK (MAP 7)

30–45 MINS FROM FORK IN TRACK (MAP 7)

OPEN FIELD

SPACE FOR A FEW CARS TO PARK

TO ALDBOURNE, 3½ MILES (5·5KM)

GOOD VIEWS TO THE WEST

CROSS QUIET ROAD 011

LOTS OF BLUEBELLS IN SPRING

B4192

TO OGBOURNE ST GEORGE, 1MILE (1·5KM)

5

ROAD JUNCTION

ROAD JUNCTION

ROUTE GUIDE AND MAPS

hundreds of years until the late 19th century when farming became less economically viable owing to cheap imports and spare land was bought up by wealthy local landowners for use as sheep-grazing. Most of the population left the village to find work elsewhere and by the early 20th century the village was empty. To get there follow the track heading east from the path for about half a mile/1km. Since being abandoned, the village has all but disappeared into the landscape, so unless you have plenty of time…

The 'Snap crossroads' is worth noting because just a short way down the track heading west is the **radio mast** that you'll probably have seen by now, whichever direction you're heading in.

Liddington Castle From Liddington Castle (Map 7) there are views of the M4 to the north-east and also the radio mast near the 'Snap crossroads' directly to the south. The Ridgeway does not actually go through Liddington Castle so if you'd like to visit follow the signpost that directs you along the fence line rather than going directly to the castle; it's about 500m. The trig point on top of the castle displays a height of 277m and the hill is a popular launch site for paragliders.

Visiting Liddington At the bottom of Liddington Hill, on the fast B4192, you'll have the possibility of walking to Liddington; though it is only worth going if you want to eat, drink, stay, or to get a bus. To get there simply continue down the B4192 for about half a mile (1km), crossing the M4 en route.

LIDDINGTON [see map p110]
The Village Inn (☎ 01793 790314, 🖳 vil lageinn-liddington.co.uk; 1D/1T, shared bathroom; 🍺; WI-FI; Ⓛ; 🐾) provides a friendly focus for the village and is usually busy. This creeper-clad inn, originally called The Bell, was built in the late 19th century. Their rooms were renovated for summer 2020 and cost from £25pp (sgl occ room rate). Breakfast is extra (approx £10pp).

Their excellent **food** (Wed-Sat noon-2pm, Tue-Sat 6-9pm, Sun noon-3pm) keeps the place full, particularly at weekends. The bar is open from 6pm on Tuesday, but closes at 4pm on Sundays and is closed on Mondays.

The other B&B option in the village is *Meadowbank House B&B* (☎ 01793 791401, 🖳 meadowbankhouse.com; 1D en

ROUTE GUIDE AND MAPS

❏ **RACEHORSES**

From virtually the start of the Ridgeway up until past East Ilsley you are likely to see racehorses. They won't be on the path itself, but will be training along the gallops that often run parallel to the path, sometimes with brushwood hurdles set up on them. As you may have noticed, the ground here is soft and springy and very open which makes it ideal for racehorse training. The early morning is the best time to see the small groups of horses being put through their paces with their trainers. When the Ridgeway is right next to the gallops you can feel the power of the horses as they thunder by.

When you are at Barbury Castle you can look down onto the Marlborough Downs and see Barbury Castle racecourse, but it's the Lambourn Downs area, further east, that is really famous as a centre for racehorse training. There are around 50 racing yards around Lambourn which train up to 2000 horses at any one time.

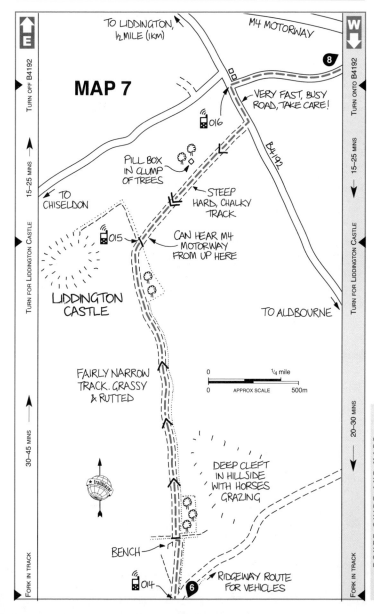

TO LIDDINGTON, ½ MILE (1km)

M4 MOTORWAY

MAP 7

8

VERY FAST, BUSY ROAD, TAKE CARE!

016

B4192

PILL BOX IN CLUMP OF TREES

STEEP HARD, CHALKY TRACK

TO CHISELDON

015

CAN HEAR M4 MOTORWAY FROM UP HERE

LIDDINGTON CASTLE

TO ALDBOURNE

FAIRLY NARROW TRACK. GRASSY & RUTTED

0   ¼ mile

0   500m
APPROX SCALE

trailblazer

DEEP CLEFT IN HILLSIDE WITH HORSES GRAZING

BENCH

014

6

RIDGEWAY ROUTE FOR VEHICLES

TURN OFF B4192 — 15–25 MINS — TURN FOR LIDDINGTON CASTLE — 30–45 MINS — FORK IN TRACK

TURN ONTO B4192 — 15–25 MINS — TURN FOR LIDDINGTON CASTLE — 20–30 MINS — FORK IN TRACK

ROUTE GUIDE AND MAPS

suite/2D share bathroom; 🛏; WI-FI; (Ⓛ); it is a supremely comfy place with B&B for £42.50-47.50pp (sgl occ from £60); guests have access to a sitting room and a drying room. The doubles that share a bathroom are only both let if booked by a family/group. The house lies less than a mile from the path on Medbourne Lane, near the B4192. They are happy to pick up from the B4192 (and drop off the next day) if arranged in advance – they will also take guests to a local pub if the Village Inn is closed, and if a two-night stay is booked they will take you to where you want to start walking.

There are two **bus** stops in the village. Stagecoach's Nos 46A & 48A services stop by The Village Inn and their Nos X46 & X48 (Swindon to Hungerford & Swindon to Marlborough) call at Spinney Close.

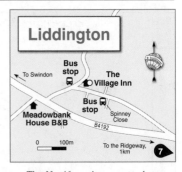

The No 46 services operate between Swindon and Hungerford & the No 48 between Swindon and Marlborough. See pp48-51 for further details of these bus services.

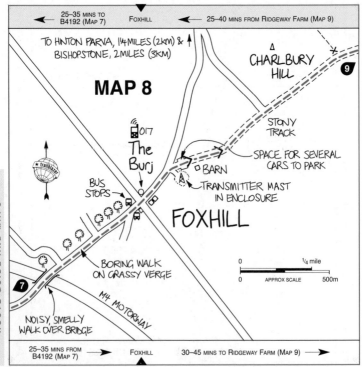

Bridge over the M4 After enduring a stretch of road walking you must cross the bridge over the M4 (Map 8). You'll be surprised just how noisy and smelly it is; although the fumes disappear quickly when you reach the other side, the noise will stay with you all the way to Foxhill at the end of this stage. There is still about 700m of walking to go after the bridge but it's all on a neat grassy verge.

Foxhill The crossroads at Foxhill are dominated by ***The Burj*** (☎ 01793 791888, 💻 theburj.co.uk; WI-FI; 🐾; Mon-Thur 5-9pm, Fri-Sun 4-9pm), an Indian restaurant. This place used to be Shepherds Rest pub, a most welcoming stop during a Ridgeway walk. Since the closure of this pub, there is now no pub directly on the western half of the Ridgeway. Anyway, The Burj does cook some very tasty food from an extensive menu, has plenty of interesting vegetarian options and a vegan menu too. Main courses cost £8.50-15 but they also have a set menu for £25pp. Whilst COVID-19 is an issue they prefer bookings, but they do accept walk-ins, and when things have settled down they hope to open at lunchtime again.

Stagecoach's Nos 48/48A **buses** call here; see pp48-51 for further details.

W← FOXHILL TO OVERTON HILL [MAPS 8-1]

[Route section begins on Map 8, opposite] This final **16½-mile/26.5km (5½-8¼hrs)** stage of the Ridgeway contains some interesting sights, especially if you choose to finish at Avebury.

It is a bit of a dull start up to crossing the **M4 motorway** and getting up to **Liddington Castle** (Map 7), but from there on there is some great walking with expansive views across the countryside. You only pass through one village on this stage – **Hallam** (Map 5) – after which is the fantastic walk along **Smeathe's Ridge** to reach **Barbury Castle**. From there on it's easy walking on good tracks with more excellent views. There are several ways to finish the Ridgeway and all involve walking downhill on the final stretch – something you might be grateful for as this is a tiring day.

E→ FOXHILL TO COURT HILL (& WANTAGE) [MAPS 8-13]

This second stage of the Ridgeway totals **11½ miles/18.5km (3¾-5½hrs)** (plus 2 miles/3km to reach Wantage). On the whole the walking is easy along very broad grassy tracks and although there are a few ascents, they're not too draining. This is also the most remote section of the Ridgeway and is completely exposed to the elements with little shelter available. If it rains there is little you can do but continue walking and get very wet. But on a sunny day in spring it's quite delightful.

After leaving Foxhill, you'll pass a turning for **Bishopstone** (map p113) before arriving at the crossroads on **Idstone Hill** (Map 10) where there is an intermittent water tap. When you arrive at the **B4000 road crossing** you can turn off to **Ashbury** (Map 10). However, the day's first major point of interest is **Wayland's Smithy** (Map 10) which you should take some time to investigate.

This is shortly followed by the turn for **Woolstone** (off Map 11) before you reach the fantastic **Uffington Castle** and **White Horse** (Map 11). There's also the option to visit Uffington village (map p119) from here.

On the far side of Kingston Hill there is an **important junction** (Map 12) where you can leave the Ridgeway to visit **Sparsholt** (off Map 12) and two accommodation options at **Sparsholt Firs** (Map 12) are nearby.

Not much further along the path, to the north, is the **Devil's Punchbowl** (Map 12) followed some time later by the iron-age **Segsbury Camp** (Map 13), where you can turn off the trail to visit **Letcombe Regis** (map p123). The end of the stage at Court Hill is just over half a mile further on.

Above Foxhill Looking to the west you can gaze upon the ever-spreading town of Swindon. Closer by, several hundred metres north of the Ridgeway, is the trig point on **Charlbury Hill** (Map 8) which would be a pleasant spot for lunch. Down in the valley, parallel to the Ridgeway, lie the villages of Hinton Parva, Bishopstone, Idstone and Ashbury. Paths run down off the Ridgeway to these villages and many people from the surrounding area bring their dogs up here for exercise.

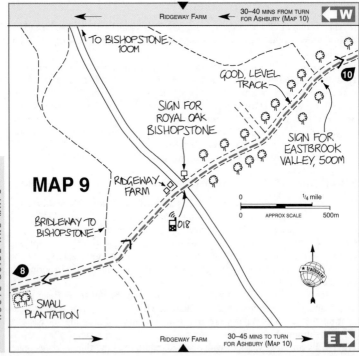

ROUTE GUIDE AND MAPS

Visiting Bishopstone There are several ways from the Ridgeway to Bishopstone, but the best is to take the turn at **Ridgeway Farm** (on Map 9) along the narrow surfaced road. From this turning it's about half a mile/1km.

BISHOPSTONE

Although this is a fairly large village, facilities for the walker are a little thin on the ground. There is no shop or post office but there are some great places to stay and the pub serves delicious food. It's an attractive place for a wander, especially by the village pond and on the shady short-cut paths around the village. However, like some of the other settlements on this stretch, it's only worth coming all the way down off the Ridgeway if you plan to stay or eat here.

Going Forward's No 47/47b **bus** passes through on its way between Swindon, Ashbury and Lambourn; see pp48-51 for further details.

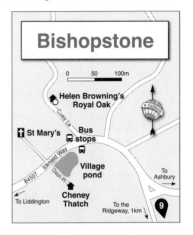

Where to stay and eat

Helen Browning's Royal Oak (☎ 01793 790481, 🖳 helenbrowningsorganic.co.uk/ royal-oak; WI-FI; 🐾), in a grand building set on a quiet lane, has been here for about 200 years and is well worth stopping off at. They serve Arkell's ales, amongst others, and have an excellent restaurant (booking is recommended) serving a regularly changing selection of organic **food** (daily 8-10am, Mon-Fri noon-2.30pm & 5.30-8.30pm, Sat & Sun noon-3pm & 5.30-8pm); much of the meat served comes from their own organic farm. They have also opened a very stylish 12-bed **hotel** (9D/3D or T, all en suite; WI-FI; ⓛ; 🐾) with rooms for £47.50-80pp (sgl occ room rate).

Cheney Thatch (☎ 01793 790508; 2D, both with private bathroom; ➷; WI-FI; ⓛ; 🐾) is a 400-year-old cottage hidden away at the end of the lane by the village pond (look for a sign 'Oxon Place leading to The City') and is a very popular place for B&B. The lady has been running the show for years and provides first-rate accommodation and also a swimming pool. You'll need to book well ahead as this place has many admirers and is beloved by some of the walking companies. B&B costs from £35pp (sgl occ £60).

Idstone Hill At the crossroads with the barn on Idstone Hill (Map 10) there is a track heading north, down to the hamlet of **Idstone** (half a mile/1km) where Going Forward's No 47 **bus** service stops; see pp48-51 for details. From this junction to Bishopstone, via Idstone, it's a little over 1¼ miles/2km.

There is also a **water tap** (though the supply is intermittent) by the barn a few metres down the Idstone Hill turning.

B4000 road crossing You're likely to hear the noise of the B4000 road a good few minutes before you reach it. It comes up Ashbury Hill from Shrivenham and Ashbury, to the north, to cross the Ridgeway and continues south to the Lambourn villages. From this crossing (Map 10) it is about half a mile/1km down to the village of Ashbury.

ASHBURY   [see Map 10]

This is another delightful village in the string of settlements running parallel to the Ridgeway. The centre of Ashbury – spiritually, if not geographically – is **Ashbury Tea**

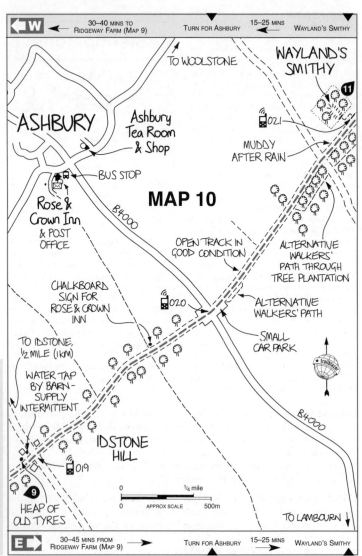

← W ← 30–40 MINS TO RIDGEWAY FARM (MAP 9)   TURN FOR ASHBURY   15–25 MINS ← WAYLAND'S SMITHY

TO WOOLSTONE

WAYLAND'S SMITHY

11

□021

ASHBURY

Ashbury Tea Room & Shop

MUDDY AFTER RAIN

BUS STOP

MAP 10

Rose & Crown Inn & POST OFFICE

B4000

ALTERNATIVE WALKERS' PATH THROUGH TREE PLANTATION

OPEN TRACK IN GOOD CONDITION

CHALKBOARD SIGN FOR ROSE & CROWN INN

□020

ALTERNATIVE WALKERS' PATH

SMALL CAR PARK

TO IDSTONE, ½ MILE (1KM)

★ trailblazer

WATER TAP BY BARN – SUPPLY INTERMITTENT

B4000

IDSTONE HILL

□019

0   ¼ mile

9

0   500m
APPROX SCALE

HEAP OF OLD TYRES

TO LAMBOURN ↓

E ► 30–45 MINS FROM RIDGEWAY FARM (MAP 9) →   TURN FOR ASHBURY   15–25 MINS → WAYLAND'S SMITHY

Room & Shop (☎ 01793 710068, 🖳 ash
buryshop.co.uk; WI-FI; 🐾 garden area only;
Tue-Sat 11am-2pm but they hope to return
to their standard hours of 7.30am-4.30pm)
serving good coffee and cakes as well as
homemade sandwiches, but not lunches as
such. Their shop stocks a good range of
general produce. Note that they always
close for their annual summer holiday in
the last week of August (and between
Christmas and the New Year).

There is also a **post office** (Wed & Fri
9.30-11am) in the *Rose & Crown Inn* (☎
01793 378354, 🖳 roseandcrownatashbury
.co.uk; 1S/1D/4D or T/1Qd, all en suite;

🍺; WI-FI; ⓛ; 🐾), occupies a commanding
position in the centre of the village. Rates
start from £40pp (sgl/sgl occ £65). At the
time of writing the pub was closed on
Sundays from about 6pm and all day on
Mondays. **Food** (Tue-Sat noon-2pm & 6-
9pm, Sun noon-3pm) is available and the
menu has a wide range of main courses
(£12-18) and always includes vegetarian/
pescatarian options. This is a popular place
for Ridgeway walkers to stay and they are
always made to feel welcome.

Going Forward's No 47/47B **bus** passes through on its way between Swindon and
Lambourn; see pp48-51 for further details.

Wayland's Smithy Look out for the (short) signposted path to Wayland's
Smithy (Map 10; see box below) from the closed-in track that the Ridgeway follows in this area. There is something a little eerie about this place, especially
when you're on your own here on a misty morning. It isn't, and never really
was, a smithy (blacksmith's/forge).

Visiting Woolstone Woolstone can be reached by taking the signposted track
down the hill at the crossroads which also leads to the car park for Uffington
Castle and White Horse (Map 11). It's about 1¼ miles/2km to the village, but
it's steep downhill so may feel more like double that on the way back up.

WOOLSTONE [off Map 11, pp116-17]

This is a very small, picturesque village at
the foot of the steep Uffington Hill. There
are many attractive buildings and the only
place offering food and accommodation is
one of the most enchanting buildings of all,
The White Horse (☎ 01367 820726, 🖳
whitehorsewoolstone.co.uk; 4D/2T, all en
suite; 🍺; WI-FI; ⓛ; 🐾). It is an attractive

16th-century coaching inn situated in the
'centre' of the village that's generally open
all day. The comfortable **accommodation**
is in the more modern building next to the
pub and costs from £45pp (sgl occ £75).
The menu (**food** Mon-Sat noon-2.30pm &
6-9pm, Sun noon-3pm) includes standard
pub dishes and in the summer months their

❑ WAYLAND'S SMITHY

This is a Neolithic long barrow. It was built in stages but was started around 3590BC
as a burial place for members of the important ruling families in this area. The barrow itself is set in a small fenced wood and the entrance passageway that leads to the
burial chamber is flanked by four huge sarsen stones. It's not possible to go far into
the underground chambers, but nevertheless it's still an impressive construction when
viewed just from the outside.

The name of this long barrow dates from a couple of thousand years after it was
built and comes from 'Wayland', the Saxon god of smiths. Apparently he made the
shoes for the Uffington White Horse and will even shoe your horse for you if you
leave it here, overnight, with some payment – cash only.

delicious pizzas (Thur & Sun 4-9pm; £11-13) are cooked in their wood-fired pizza oven. Booking is recommended but if that's not possible they may be able to offer take-away food.

No buses stop here. However, should you require transportation Faringdon Cars (☎ 01367 243838, 🖳 faringdoncars.co.uk) operates a **taxi** service in this area.

Uffington Castle and White Horse Heading east it's a steep climb up White Horse Hill on a good track to Uffington Castle; this is the toughest climb of this section but it doesn't last for long so count yourself lucky. You are even luckier if you're heading west, down the steep slope.

The National Trust area around this hill contains not only the aforementioned Uffington Castle and Uffington White Horse but also **The Manger**, a

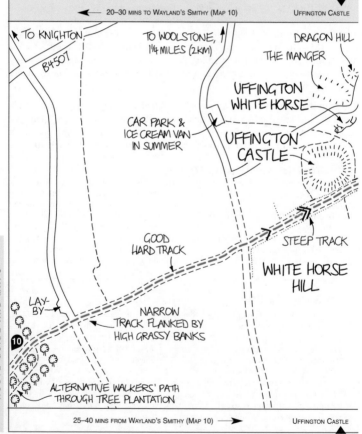

25–40 MINS FROM WAYLAND'S SMITHY (MAP 10) ⟶   UFFINGTON CASTLE

stunning coombe, lined with terraces, best viewed from the White Horse itself, and the perfectly formed, flat-topped **Dragon Hill**, just north of the White Horse, where St George battled with and slew the dragon.

Uffington Castle is a large Iron Age hill fort whose setting is certainly no less dramatic than that of Barbury Castle (see p102), though it's seven metres lower and only two-thirds its size. The double banks and ditches are still steep and well defined and the views from up here are magnificent.

Uffington White Horse lies on the side of the hill to the north of the castle and although it really is spectacular this is certainly not the best place from which to view it. In fact it's very difficult to get a good view of the horse from the ground. Short of hiring a helicopter, the better views are from down in the

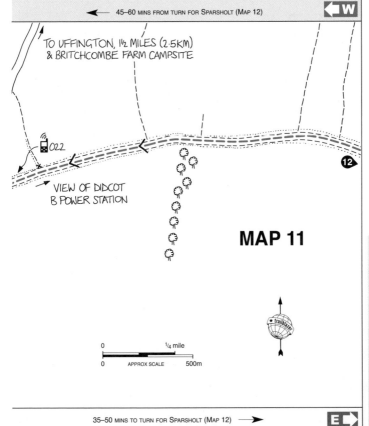

45–60 MINS FROM TURN FOR SPARSHOLT (MAP 12)

W

TO UFFINGTON, 1½ MILES (2.5KM)
& BRITCHCOMBE FARM CAMPSITE

022

12

VIEW OF DIDCOT
B POWER STATION

MAP 11

0   ¼ mile
0   APPROX SCALE   500m

trailblazer

35–50 MINS TO TURN FOR SPARSHOLT (MAP 12)

E

ROUTE GUIDE AND MAPS

valley: a steep descent and a very disappointing walk back up. If you don't think you can manage it, don't worry – even from down there the views are frustratingly incomplete. Perhaps remember to drive along the B4507 (the road running parallel to the Ridgeway along here) another time for views of the horse. Despite this, the **White Horse Hill area** really is one of the highlights of the Ridgeway trail so do take some time out to relax here and enjoy it.

At the time of writing ***Britchcombe Farm*** (🖥 britchcombefarm.co.uk; over 70 pitches; 🐾 on a lead; all year) was on the market so if you are camping check ahead before arriving. The current owner allows open fires in designated spots and sells firewood but of course things may change if there is a new owner. However, the location is hard to beat.

❏ WHITE HORSES

The **Uffington White Horse** (see Map 11) is the one that inspired them all. Scientists now think, after much debate, that it was first cut into the hillside around 800BC. It's over 100 metres long and superbly suggests the form of a horse rather than simply defining its outline. It's a mystery how the creators of the horse could cut it so well, given that the whole horse is only properly viewable from around a mile/1.5km away in the valley. Without a shadow of a doubt, Uffington White Horse is the best of the lot, but there are various other white horses scattered around the countryside near here. None of them is nearly as ancient and they don't even get close to the fluid beauty of the Uffington horse. Further west on the Ridgeway is another example at Hackpen Hill (Map 3) that was cut into the hillside in 1838.

The oldest and one of the most visible of all the modern horses is the **Westbury White Horse**. This was cut in 1778 but at some point in the 1950s it was concreted over. The concrete was then painted white. Owing to some unsightly deterioration and discolouration in the concrete, the horse was given another coating of concrete and paint in 1995. The logic was that concrete is easier to maintain. Using that logic maybe there should be concrete over the Ridgeway, too?

Cherhill White Horse is on a hill of the same name that is south of the A4 near Cherhill village, 3¾ miles/6km west of Avebury. This horse is one of the older ones in the area having been cut into the hillside in 1780. It was fully restored in 2002 and is easily visible from the A4.

There are other **white horses**: between Milk Hill and Walkers Hill, close to the village of Alton Barnes, about 3¾ miles/6km due south of Avebury is a good specimen; it was cut in 1812 and cleaned up in 2002. There is a further example of a well cared for horse near Broad Town on a north-west-facing slope. This horse is about 3 miles/5km north-west of the Hackpen Hill horse, though it's unclear when it was cut – probably in the 1860s. On Pewsey Hill, just south of the village of Pewsey, about 4¼ miles/7km south of Marlborough, is a well-groomed 1937 white horse.

The youngest white horse in the area is on Roundway Hill in Devizes, about 7½ miles/12km south-west of Avebury. It was created for the millennium and is unusual in that it faces to the right. There was a much older white horse close by here but it has long since disappeared.

There is now a recognised **White Horse Trail** that follows a roughly circular route and visits all the white horses in Wiltshire. The trail is around 90 miles/145km long and illustrated guides can be bought from tourist information centres in the area.

For further information visit 🖥 wiltshirewhitehorses.org.uk.

UFFINGTON

It's a bit of a trek to get to Uffington from the Ridgeway, and certainly a strenuous start to the day if walking back up to the trail, but there's a good place to stay in a decent pub, a shop with a post office, and even a museum.

Tom Brown's School Museum (🖥 museum.uffington.net; closed at the time of writing, but normal hours are Easter-end Oct, weekends & Bank Hols only 2-5pm; free) is logically located in the classroom featured in the 1857 novel *Tom Brown's School Days* by Thomas Hughes. Exhibits centre on local history and archaeology.

The **Post Office and Stores** (☎ 01367 820977; Mon-Sat 7am-5.30pm, Sun 8am-2pm; post office daily but opens one hour later than the shop) is well stocked with groceries and general supplies.

The only permanent option for eating and sleeping in the village is at *The Fox & Hounds* (☎ 01367 820680, 🖥 uffingtonpub .co.uk; WI-FI; 🐾; bar Mon-Sat 11am-11pm, Sun noon-10.30pm; **food** Tue-Fri noon-2pm & 6-9pm, Sat noon-3pm & 6-9pm,

Sun noon-3pm), near the cottage where John Betjeman lived. It's not often that you find a village pub with such accommodating opening hours and as such there is little excuse to pass it by. Being a freehouse, there is a good selection of real ales; there may be some that you might not have tried before. The menu is full of hearty pub grub

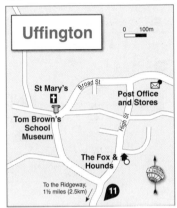

❏ MORRIS DANCING

If you hang around the pubs along the Ridgeway for long enough during the summer, you are likely to see some Morris dancing. Essentially the Morris teams (or sides) are performing traditional country dances and will often be accompanied by musicians. Each group of Morris men has its own particular outfit: embroidered smocks, waistcoats, decorated hats, neckerchiefs and clusters of bells abound. Depending on the dance they might also be waving handkerchiefs or hitting sticks together, sometimes with great force.

It is thought that these dances, often named after the villages where they were originally performed (such as Adderbury, Bampton, Ducklington or Stanton Harcourt), have also been influenced by traditional European dances. It's fairly safe to say that they were performed as long as 500 years ago, though many traditions died out in the 18th and 19th centuries.

The beginning of the 20th century saw a concerted effort to record the dances and music before they disappeared forever and the 21st century in particular has seen an increased interest in performing the traditions.

Morris groups based in the Ridgeway area include the White Horse Morris Men (🖥 whitehorsemorris.org.uk) and Icknield Way Morris Men (🖥 icknieldwaymorris men.org.uk), the latter being one of the more active.

Many of the village pubs along the western half of the Ridgeway are popular venues for Morris dancers including the Fox & Hounds at Uffington, Royal Oak at Bishopstone, the Rose & Crown at Ashbury, and The Bell at Aldworth to name a few.

which should satisfy the hungry walker. Mains start at £10.50 rising to £22.50 for the rib-eye steak and there is a vegetarian option. In their conservatory you can both eat and have views of the White Horse. They also have four **rooms** (1T/2Tr/1Qd, all en suite; WI-FI; Ⓛ; 🐾); rates are from £47.50pp (sgl occ room rate). The Icknield Way Morris Men (see box on p119) perform here several times a year.

There are often several accommodation options on Airbnb.

No buses stop at Uffington but Go Green Taxis (see p127) will operate here.

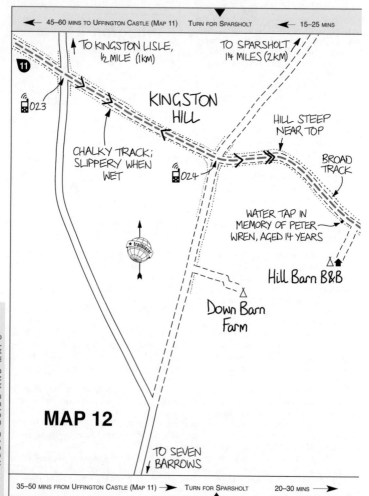

Important junction At the foot of the eastern side of **Kingston Hill** (Map 12) you will reach a **track crossroads** that is an important junction: take the track heading north for Sparsholt (see p122), a 1½-mile/2.5km walk away. Follow the track to the main road, turn right onto the road and follow it for 500m before turning left into the quiet village. Note, you can also reach Sparsholt via the road from Sparsholt Firs (Map 12), but this route requires more road walking.

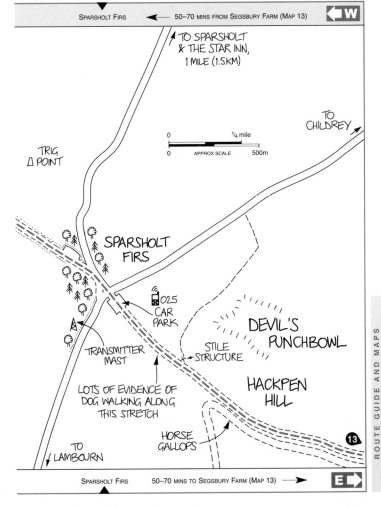

The track heading south from the junction leads to Down Barn Farm (also see below), about half a mile/1km away. The turning is marked as a byway though there is no sign for Down Barn Farm; the farm itself is not visible from here as it's round a corner and in a dip.

This track also leads to **Seven Barrows** (🖳 bbowt.org.uk/nature-reserves/ seven-barrows), a group of seven Neolithic burial mounds. There's nothing particularly dramatic about this place, but it's a nice spot, easily accessible and free to enter at any time. It's about two miles from the Ridgeway.

SPARSHOLT FIRS [MAP 12, pp120-1]

For a unique experience you might like to stay at *Down Barn Farm* (mob ☎ 0779 983 3115, 🖳 pennydownbarnfarm@gmail .com). This place really is out on its own, set on a grassland farm that rears organic pigs and cattle. You might occasionally hear the cows mooing or the cock crowing but that's about it at this haven of peace and quiet. There are several pitches for **campers** (🏕; £10pp inc shower; available all year), but it is exposed up here. Campers can use the toilet and a sink. Depending on the COVID-19 situation **B&B** (1T en suite, 1D/1T shared bathroom if both rooms let; ♥; limited WI-FI; Ⓛ; 🏕) may be available and rates are £37.50-50pp (sgl occ from £50). **Booking is**

essential, even if you are camping. If arranged in advance, but also depending on COVID, the owner can prepare evening meals (£15-20pp for three courses) and breakfast for campers (£10), which is just as well as the next nearest place offering food is a good couple of miles (3km) away.

Booking is also recommended for *Hill Barn B&B* (☎ 07885 368918, 🖳 hillbarn bedandbreakfast.co.uk; 1D/1T, both en suite; ♥; WI-FI; Ⓛ; 🏕). B&B costs from £42.50pp (sgl occ £60). You can also **camp** here for £7.50pp. The welcome is very friendly, there are drying facilities and evening meals are available by prior arrangement.

Water tap Right on the Ridgeway, and close to the turning for Hill Barn B&B (see above) is a water tap. This could prove very welcome on this isolated and exposed section of the path. There is a dedication on the tap to Peter Wren, aged 14 years.

SPARSHOLT   [off MAP 12]

The Star Inn (☎ 01235 751873, 🖳 the starsparsholt.co.uk; 4D/2T/1Tr, all en suite; ♥; WI-FI; Ⓛ; 🏕) is a very inviting 17th-century country inn with well-kept accommodation in a converted barn; **B&B** costs from £47.50pp (sgl occ room rate) – room only from £85 (sgl occ £75). Their menu (**food** Mon-Sat noon-2.30pm & 6-9pm, Sun noon-3.30pm) has some interesting mains (£14-22) including a poached duck egg

with purple sprouting broccoli, hazelnuts, warm new potato salad and a wild garlic hollandaise. They are also open for breakfast (Mon-Fri 7.30-9.30am, Sat & Sun 8-10am).

There is no shop or post office in the village and no buses stop here either. However, Faringdon Cars (☎ 01367 243838, 🖳 faringdoncars.co.uk) operates a **taxi** service in this area.

Devil's Punchbowl North of **Hackpen Hill** (Map 12) the valley drops away very steeply giving excellent views of the Devil's Punchbowl. You can get

❑ **IMPORTANT NOTE – WALKING TIMES**

All times in this book refer only to the time spent walking. You will need to add 20-30% to allow for rests, photography, checking the map, drinking water etc.

closer to the punchbowl by taking the path that branches left from the track where there is a stile structure marking the path junction. Although this should be a path, it seems to run straight through a planted field with no visible trail.

Segsbury Camp On reaching **Segsbury Farm** (Map 13), there is a 100-metre track heading north to Segsbury Camp: this is also called **Letcombe Castle**. It's more than double the size of Barbury Castle but far less popular; you'll usually have the place to yourself. Like Barbury Castle (see p102), this was an Iron Age hill fort and evidence of roundhouses were found during excavations in the 1990s. It was just around here that I once passed a nun on the track. She had walked from St Mary's Convent in Wantage, around three miles/5km away. You might also have some unlikely encounters on the Ridgeway – owls or deer, for instance, but meeting a nun up here must now be added to the list.

If you want to visit **Letcombe Regis** take the track north through Segsbury Camp. This isn't the only way to the village – you could follow the road past Court Hill Centre – but it's the most convenient. You'll also have the bonus of passing through Segsbury Camp on your way. From Court Hill Centre, it's about 1¼ miles/2km to the centre of the village.

LETCOMBE REGIS

This village, another in the chain of 'spring line' settlements below the Wessex Downs, dates back well over a thousand years although the 'Regis' part of the name was only added during the reign of Richard II (1377-99). However, the regal connections date from well before then as it was the property of King Stephen in the 12th century and there was a royal hunting lodge here in the 13th and 14th centuries.

The oldest remaining building in the village is the church, St Andrew's, parts of which date back to the 12th century though some of the houses don't look as if they are a great deal younger.

Letcombe Regis and its neighbour, Letcombe Bassett, are known for the watercress beds that covered the land between them though 'Regis' is also home to four racing stables, which generate considerably more income.

There aren't any shops or services, nor do any buses stop here, but nevertheless it would make a convenient and enjoyable overnight stop. Faringdon Cars (see Sparsholt opposite) operates a **taxi** service in this area should your legs be tired.

Where to stay, eat and drink

The Greyhound Inn (☎ 01235 771969, 🖳 thegreyhoundletcombe.co.uk; 5D/3D or T, all en suite; ➤; WI-FI; Ⓛ; 🐾) is a Georgian-style, traditional country inn with some lovely rooms (£52.50-72.50pp, sgl occ room rate) some of which can sleep additional children, but not more than two adults. Breakfast is served (Mon-Fri 7.30-9.30am, Sat & Sun 8-10am) but non-residents must pre-book. They also serve superior **food** (Mon-Fri noon-2.30pm & 6-9pm, Sat noon-2.30pm & 6-9.30pm, Sun noon-4pm & 6-8pm) and booking is recommended; the menu may include such delights as

Letcombe Regis

0   100m   To Wantage

Quince Cottage

The Greyhound Inn

St Andrew's

To the Ridgeway via Court Hill Rd, 2.5km

To Letcombe Bassett

13

13

To the Ridgeway via Segsbury Camp, 2.5km

ROUTE GUIDE AND MAPS

whole baked plaice, baby potatoes, sam-
phire, golden cherry tomatoes & chive butter sauce (£18), or slow-roasted aubergine
with tamarind, roasted onion & white bean
purée (£16).

Nearby is *Quince Cottage* (☎ 01235
763652, 🖳 quincebandb.com; 1S/1D/1Tr,

private facilities; 🍽; WI-FI; ⓛ), a charming
18th-century thatched cottage that charges
from £45pp (sgl/sgl occ £50). This is a great
place to stay and you are assured a friendly
welcome. An excellent cooked breakfast is
also served. Book well ahead as this place is
deservedly popular with walkers!

Court Hill At the foot of Court Hill, the Ridgeway crosses the main A338 road
coming from Wantage in the north and Hungerford in the south. The town of
Wantage (see pp126-9) has plenty of shops, banks and other services and is just
over 1½ miles/2.5km away.

Court Hill Centre is about 500 metres along this road, and although (other
than the tea rooms) it wasn't open at the time of writing, it is still worth checking. *Court Hill Centre* (☎ 01235 760253, 🖳 courthill.org.uk; 45 beds; open all
year) has accommodation in a **bunkhouse**: there are family (4-bed bunk rooms)
and dormitory rooms. Breakfast, packed lunches and an evening meal are available but all must be ordered in advance. Alternatively, there is a decent self-
catering kitchen. A limited number of **camping pitches** (🐾 on lead) is also
available. Campers have access to a toilet 24hrs a day and use of the other facil-

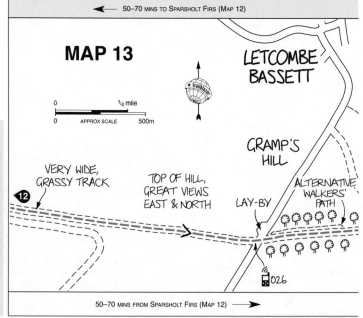

50–70 MINS TO SPARSHOLT FIRS (MAP 12)

MAP 13

LETCOMBE
BASSETT

0   ¼ mile
0   APPROX SCALE   500m

GRAMP'S
HILL

VERY WIDE,
GRASSY TRACK

TOP OF HILL,
GREAT VIEWS
EAST & NORTH

ALTERNATIVE
WALKERS'
PATH

LAY-BY

12

📱026

50–70 MINS FROM SPARSHOLT FIRS (MAP 12) →

ities during opening hours. Advance booking for both the bunkhouse and the campsite is recommended, as the bunkhouse in particular is often booked by groups on a sole occupancy basis.

If you're just passing by and not staying the night, you could always stop off at **Barn Tea Rooms** (daily 10.30am-4pm) where you'll find teas, coffees and cold drinks along with cakes, light lunches and ice-creams; they also do a very tasty fishfinger sandwich.

W ← COURT HILL (& WANTAGE) TO FOXHILL   [MAPS 13-8]

[Route section begins on Map 13, below] This penultimate stage of the Ridgeway totals **11½ miles/18.5km (3½-5¼hrs)** plus 2 miles/3km from Wantage to Court Hill. On the whole the walking is easy along very broad grassy tracks. Soon after starting at Court Hill you will pass by **Segsbury Camp**, an Iron Age Hill fort, where there is a turn for **Letcombe Regis**, before heading into the most isolated and exposed section of the Ridgeway. Due to this, in good weather it's one of the most enjoyable sections of the path, and in bad weather it has to rank as one of the worst.

The first point of interest is **Devil's Punchbowl** (Map 12) to the north of the path. There is an important junction near **Sparsholt Firs** (both Map 12)

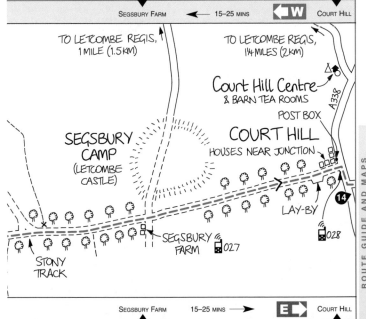

SEGSBURY FARM ← 15–25 MINS ◀W COURT HILL

TO LETCOMBE REGIS, 1 MILE (1.5KM)

TO LETCOMBE REGIS, 1¼ MILES (2KM)

A338

Court Hill Centre & BARN TEA ROOMS

POST BOX

SEGSBURY CAMP (LETCOMBE CASTLE)

COURT HILL

HOUSES NEAR JUNCTION

14

LAY-BY

SEGSBURY FARM   027

028

STONY TRACK

SEGSBURY FARM   15–25 MINS →   E▷ COURT HILL

which has options for visiting **Sparsholt** (off Map 12) and two nearby accommodation options.

Apart from a couple of road crossings, the walking is uninterrupted and the views are fantastic. You're not going to meet many other people along here, until you reach **Uffington Castle** and **White Horse** (Map 11). From here you can leave the Ridgeway to visit **Uffington** (map p119) while the path ahead becomes less exposed and, on the whole, fairly level. There's a turn for **Woolstone** (off Map 11) shortly before you reach the path to **Wayland's Smithy** (Map 10). Take some time to investigate this place before continuing the easy walking to the B4000 road crossing where you can leave the Ridgeway to visit **Ashbury** (Map 10).

At the crossroads on **Idstone Hill** (Map 10) there is an intermittent water tap and at the next crossroads is a turn for **Bishopstone** (map p113). After here it's an easy walk down to the end of the stage at **Foxhill** (Map 10).

[Next route overview on p111]

WANTAGE

Despite the lengthy walk from the Ridgeway and limited accommodation options, Wantage is a good place to stop and recharge your batteries. The town is famous as the birthplace of King Alfred the Great (849-99), the only Anglo-Saxon ruler who was not defeated by the Vikings. You can see his statue in the centre of Market Place.

Wantage has a compact centre with most of the shops, restaurants and pubs within a minute's walk of Market Place.

Vale & Downland Museum (☎ 01235 771447, 🖳 valeanddownlandmuseum.co .uk; Mon-Sat 9.30am-4pm, Sun 1.30-4pm; free but donations appreciated) is well worth a visit if you have some free time. There is a permanent historical exhibition and art gallery; the exhibition concentrates on the history of the town and features plenty of artefacts from King Alfred's time to the present. Part of the museum is housed in an 18th-century barn that was moved from a nearby village and rebuilt here; there is also a gift shop, visitor information point (see below) and a **café** (see Where to eat and drink).

Services

The **visitor information point** (☎ 01235 760176; same hours as museum) at the museum (see above) has lots of free information about local attractions.

For online information about Wantage visit 🖳 wantage.com.

There are branches of plenty of **banks** (such as TSB, Barclays & Nationwide), all with **ATMs**, around Market Place. You'll also find a Boots **chemist** (☎ 01235 765227, 🖳 boots.com; Mon-Sat 9am-5.30pm, Sun 10am-4pm) and a McColl's **convenience store** (☎ 01235 769164, 🖳 mccolls.co.uk; Mon-Sat 6am-9pm, Sun from 7am) on Market Place and a large Waitrose **supermarket** (☎ 01235 772313, 🖳 waitrose.com; Mon-Thur & Sat 8am-8pm, Fri to 9pm, Sun 10am-4pm) just a few steps away. There's a market every Wednesday and Saturday on Market Place and a **farmers' market** joins it on the last Saturday of the month.

The **post office** (Mon-Sat 9am-5.30pm) is in the Costcutter shop (☎ 01235 763134; Mon-Sat 5am-11pm, Sun 6am-11pm).

If you need **bike repairs** you should head to Ridgeway Cycles (☎ 01235 764445, 🖳 ridgewaycycles.com; Mon-Fri 9am-5.30pm, Sat to 5pm), on Newbury St.

There are free public **toilets** at the entrance to the pay and display car park (Mon-Fri 8am-6.30pm, Sun 10am-4pm).

Transport

Buses stop on Market Place and include services to: Oxford (Stagecoach's S8, S9 & Thames Travel's X32); Abingdon/Didcot (Thames Travel's No 33/X33 &

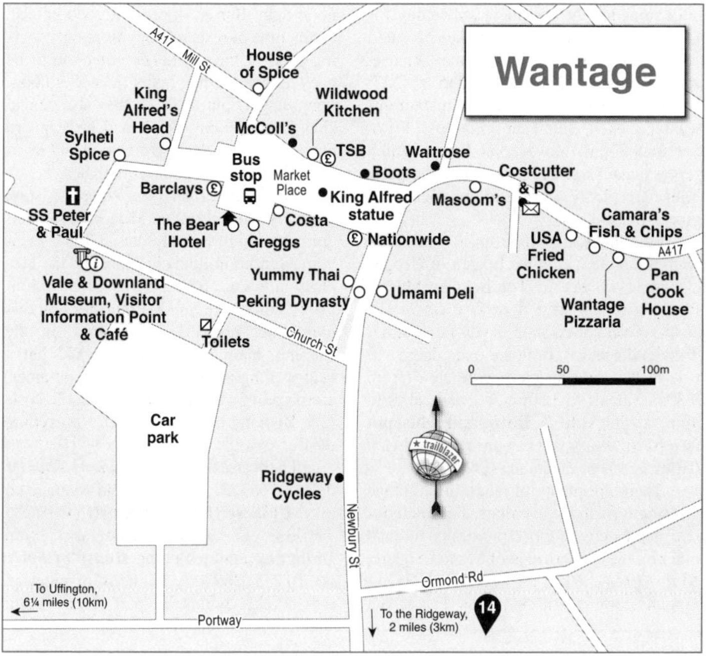

Stagecoach's S8); see pp48-51 for further details.

Go Green Taxis (☎ 01235 811100, 🖳 www.gogreentaxisltd.co.uk) offers a **taxi** service in the Wantage area and will go to villages such as Uffington, Woolstone, Sparsholt and Letcombe Regis but may make an additional charge to cover the petrol for the return journey (or vice versa).

Where to stay

If you are walking from the Ridgeway to Wantage, the chances are you'll be intending to stay overnight here, too.

Right on Market Place is the 500-year-old ***The Bear Hotel*** (☎ 01235 766366, 🖳 thebearwantage.co.uk; 9S/16D/6T/2Tr/1Qd, all en suite; ▾; WI-FI). B&B costs from £42.50pp (sgl/sgl occ £65).

Apart from this you could check the dozen or so options listed on **Airbnb** (see pp20-1).

Where to eat and drink

There are two very good upmarket eateries open during the day. ***Umami Deli*** (☎ 01235 766245, 🖳 umami-deli.co.uk; WI-FI; 🐕; Mon-Sat 9.30am-3pm), on Newbury St,

SYMBOLS USED IN TEXT

▾ Bathtub in, or for, at least one room **WI-FI** means wi-fi is available
Ⓛ packed lunch available if requested in advance
🐕 Dogs allowed but subject to prior arrangement for accommodation (see p197)
fb signifies places that have a Facebook page (for latest opening hours)

does some lovely 'gourmet sandwiches' for £5.50, such as pastrami, chicken, roasted vegetables, cranberry sauce & mayonnaise, and **Wildwood Kitchen** (☎ 01235 424327, 🖳 wildwoodrestaurants.co.uk/restaurant/ wantage; WI-FI; Sun-Thur noon-9pm, Fri & Sat to 9.30pm), on Market Place, which serves salads, pasta, pizzas and burgers. There are plenty of vegetarian, vegan and gluten-free options.

Less fancy lunchtime snacks and sandwiches can be had at the branch of **Greggs** (🖳 greggs.co.uk), by The Bear on Market Place. Virtually next door is a **Costa** (🖳 costa.co.uk) coffee shop if you fancy a hot drink and a snack. Both are open daily.

In the light and airy **café** area (from 9.30am, meals to 3.30pm, tea and cakes to 4pm) at the **Vale & Downland Museum** (see p126; WI-FI) you can enjoy a sandwich (from £4.15) or cream tea (£4.50).

There are plenty of places in Wantage offering food in the evenings. This includes two good pubs in close proximity to each other on the western side of Market Square. **King Alfred's Head** (☎ 01235 771595, 🖳 kingalfs.com; WI-FI; 🐾; food Fri & Sat

noon-8pm, Sun to 4pm) is a good choice. At the time of research they were only serving food at the weekends but hope to be back to their normal hours (Mon-Sat noon-9pm, Sun to 6pm) in 2021; they also plan to change their menu but it will be standard pub food. They also serve a good and regularly changing selection of real ales.

The Bear Hotel (see Where to stay; WI-FI; 🐾 bar only; food Mon-Fri 11.30am-2pm & 6-9pm, Sat 11.30am-2.30pm & 6-9pm, Sun noon-3pm) is probably the best place in town. They serve breakfast (Mon-Fri 7-9am, Sat & Sun 8-10am) for non residents but booking is required. In the evening, main courses start at £13 but a beef wellington with dauphinoise potatoes, carrot purée & tenderstem broccoli costs £25. Booking is recommended for evening meals.

There are also: **Thai** (***Yummy Thai*** (☎ 01235 768222, 🖳 yummythaiwantage.co .uk); **Chinese** (***Peking Dynasty*** (☎ 01235 771338, 🖳 pekingdynasty.org); and **Indian** options including ***House of Spice*** (☎ 01235 760707, 🖳 houseofspicewan tage.co.uk), which is part of a chain;

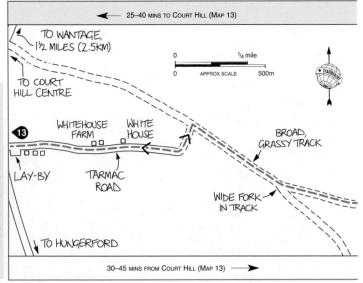

25–40 MINS TO COURT HILL (MAP 13)

TO WANTAGE, 1½ MILES (2.5KM)

TO COURT HILL CENTRE

13 WHITEHOUSE FARM   WHITE HOUSE

LAY-BY   TARMAC ROAD

TO HUNGERFORD

0   ¼ mile
0   APPROX SCALE   500m

★ trailblazer

BROAD, GRASSY TRACK

WIDE FORK IN TRACK

30–45 MINS FROM COURT HILL (MAP 13) →

Sylheti Spice (☎ 01235 764164/762651, 🖥 sylhetispice.webs.com) and *Masoom's* (☎ 01235 799537, 🖥 wantage-masooms.co.uk) options but at the time of research some were only offering takeaway or delivery.

Fast food and **takeaway** outlets abound and include *Camara's Fish & Chips* (☎ 01235 770492; **fb**; Mon-Sat 11am-2pm & 4-10.30pm, Sun noon-2pm &

4-10pm), *Wantage Pizzaria* (☎ 01235 770055, 🖥 wantagepizzaria.co.uk; daily 4pm to late) and *USA Fried Chicken* (☎ 01235 760779; **fb**; daily 3pm to late). *Pan Cook House* (☎ 01235 766287; **fb**; Sun-Thur 5-11.30pm, Fri noon-11.30pm, Sat noon-2.30pm & 5-11.30pm) is a standard Chinese takeaway.

E→(WANTAGE &) COURT HILL TO GORING   [MAPS 13-19]

This is an easy **14-mile/22.5km (4¼-6hrs)** section; add 2 miles/3km if you have stayed in Wantage. From Court Hill the path is level, broad, grassy and exposed, similar to what you've become used to from the previous section.

The first point of interest is the **Baron Wantage Monument** (Map 14) after which you pass a **reservoir** (Map 15) before reaching the cars parks and road crossing at **Bury Down** (Map 16). Less than a mile from there is the **A34 road crossing**, followed closely by a **stone memorial** (Map 17).

There are various options for reaching **East Ilsley** (see pp132-3) from the Ridgeway and around here you'll notice more tree cover and the grassy track changing to a much harder surface for the rest of the stage.

An option to visit **Compton** (see p133) presents itself before you arrive at the **railway bridge** (Map 17) for the now defunct Didcot, Newbury & Southampton Junction Railway.

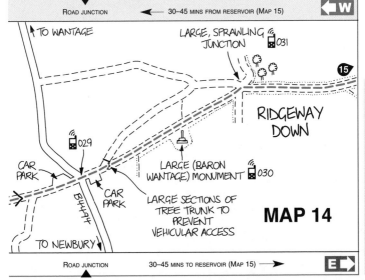

ROAD JUNCTION   ← 30–45 MINS FROM RESERVOIR (MAP 15)   ◄W

↑ TO WANTAGE

LARGE, SPRAWLING JUNCTION   031

15

RIDGEWAY DOWN

029

CAR PARK

B4494

CAR PARK

LARGE (BARON WANTAGE) MONUMENT   030

LARGE SECTIONS OF TREE TRUNK TO PREVENT VEHICULAR ACCESS

MAP 14

TO NEWBURY↓

ROAD JUNCTION   30–45 MINS TO RESERVOIR (MAP 15) →   E►

ROUTE GUIDE AND MAPS

There's an **important junction** (Map 18) that you need to navigate with care and which also offers a route to **Aldworth** (off Map 18). Enjoy the isolation along here as when you reach **Post Box Cottage** (Map 19) the surface becomes tarmac, the houses start and so does the traffic. You gradually descend into the small town of **Streatley**, on the western bank of the river Thames, before crossing into **Goring** on the opposite bank.

At the time of writing there is no source of **drinking water** on the trail between Court Hill and Streatley, so do make sure you set off with plenty.

Baron Wantage monument Not far from the B4494 road crossing is a **large monument** (Map 14), to the south of the track. It consists of a marble column set on a large square base with steps on all sides. At the top of the column is a cross; it is in memory of Baron Wantage (1832-1901) who, amongst other things, expanded the nearby Lockinge estate. The steps provide good seating if you want to rest a while and the column provides some shade – something lacking on this stage on a hot day.

Reservoir Just to the north of the track you will see a reservoir (Map 15). It's a low, square red-brick structure, surrounded by trees and fenced in.

Bury Down There are **car parks** either side of the road crossing here (Map 16). It's a popular place for people to come and stretch their legs, walk their

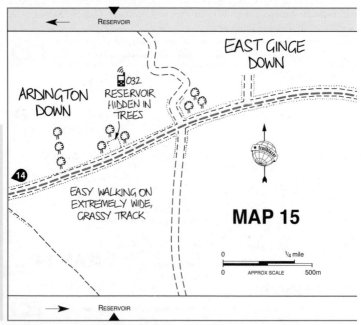

MAP 15

dogs and cycle. Harwell International Business Centre is clearly visible just over a mile to the north from here.

The road goes north to Chilton and south to **West Ilsley**, about one mile (1.5km) away; Newbury & District's Nos 6 & 6a **bus** services call there.

A34 Junction You'll hear the traffic on the A34 for some time before you arrive at the junction (Map 16). You can either use the tunnel under the road, or try to cross it, but it is far safer to use the tunnel. The track down to it drops steeply and once inside, there are some murals depicting traditional historical scenes from the area on one side and graffiti on the other.

Stone memorial Just a few minutes from the tunnel under the A34, on the northern side of the track, almost enclosed by the shrubbery, is a stone memorial inscribed with the name of Hugh Frederick Grosvenor, a 2nd lieutenant in the Lifeguards who, aged just 19, was killed here in an armoured car accident on 9 April 1947.

Visiting East Ilsley There are four possible ways down (Map 17) into East Ilsley from the Ridgeway and they are all less than a mile apart. The direction in which you are headed might have some bearing on your choice, but it doesn't really matter though – leaving by any of the four tracks you'll have to walk about a mile into the village.

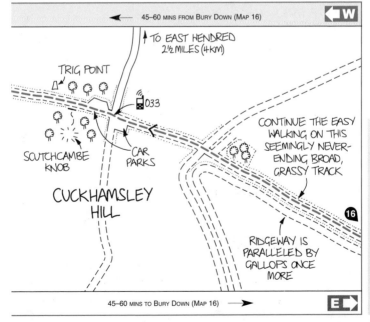

45–60 MINS FROM BURY DOWN (MAP 16)

◀W

TO EAST HENDRED
2½ MILES (4KM)

TRIG POINT

033

CONTINUE THE EASY
WALKING ON THIS
SEEMINGLY NEVER-
ENDING BROAD,
GRASSY TRACK

SCUTCHCAMBE
KNOB

CAR
PARKS

CUCKHAMSLEY
HILL

16

RIDGEWAY IS
PARALLELED BY
GALLOPS ONCE
MORE

45–60 MINS TO BURY DOWN (MAP 16) ⟶

E▶

ROUTE GUIDE AND MAPS

EAST ILSLEY [MAP 17, p134]

From the 17th century to 1934 East Ilsley was known as a venue for huge **sheep markets**. At their peak, drovers would descend on the village filling it with up to 70,000 sheep; it has been a lot quieter here since the market stopped. Today it's an attractive-enough place with a lovely pub that provides food and accommodation and this makes it a convenient place to break your journey.

There is no shop or post office but Newbury & District's **bus** No 6 calls here; see pp48-51.

Where to stay and eat

The *Crown & Horns* (☎ 01635 281545, 🖳 crownandhorns.co.uk; 8D/1T/2Tr, all en suite; 🛏; WI-FI; ⓛ; 🐾) has a cosy interior – in the colder months there is a welcoming

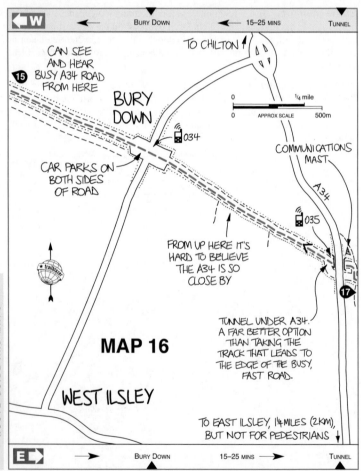

ROUTE GUIDE AND MAPS

open fire to sit beside – and a shady garden. It's always popular with walkers. The **accommodation** is in well-kept rooms and costs from £44.50pp (sgl occ room rate). Breakfast costs £7.95pp. Their menu (**food** Mon-Sat noon-9pm, Sun to 8pm) is varied and includes vegetarian and vegan options. Their Sunday lunches (from £12.95/15.95/18.95 for 1/2/3 courses) are deservedly popular. They serve real ales from local breweries which are well worth sampling.

Visiting Compton If you want to go to Compton, 1½ miles/2.5km, it's best to leave the Ridgeway at 'D' junction (marked on Map 17) and follow the concrete track to Compton.

COMPTON

The Saxon name given to this village means 'Coombe Town', or, 'town in the valley', but there is evidence of Bronze and Iron Age settlement in the area even before the Saxons were here. Plenty of Roman artefacts, coins in particular, have been found near Compton.

The **village shop** (☎ 01635 578682; Mon & Wed-Sat 8am-6.30pm, Tue 9am-6.30pm, Sun 9am-1pm) stocks a surprisingly large range of groceries; it also contains the local **post office** (Mon-Fri 12.30-4pm, Sat 9.30-10.30am).

Foinavon (☎ 01635 579400, 💻 the comptonswan.com; 5D/1D or T, all en suite; 🛁; WI-FI; ①; 🐕 in bar only), formerly the Compton Swan, is a large, white building on the main road through the village. It is often busy with a mixture of locals and visitors and has a large garden. At the time of writing they were serving a limited menu, along with reduced serving times (**food** Thur 5.30-8.30pm, Fri 4.30-8.30pm, Sat noon-3pm & 4.30-8.30pm, Sun 2-6pm) though had a good selection of pizzas from £10. The smartly furnished

accommodation costs from £45pp (sgl occ room rate). Be sure to book ahead if you want to stay here.

From here you can take a **bus** (Newbury & District's No 6) to Newbury as well as West and East Ilsley; see pp48-51 for more details.

Didcot, Newbury and Southampton Junction (DN&SJ) Railway Bridge In what seems like the middle of nowhere, you will cross a **concrete bridge** (Map 17). This takes you over the old, and dismantled, railway that was once the **DN&SJ Railway**. It's been closed since the 1960s and the strip where the track once lay is now covered by bushes and trees. *(cont'd on p136)*

❏ **IMPORTANT NOTE – WALKING TIMES**
All times in this book refer only to the time spent walking. You will need to add 20-30% to allow for rests, photography, checking the map, drinking water etc.

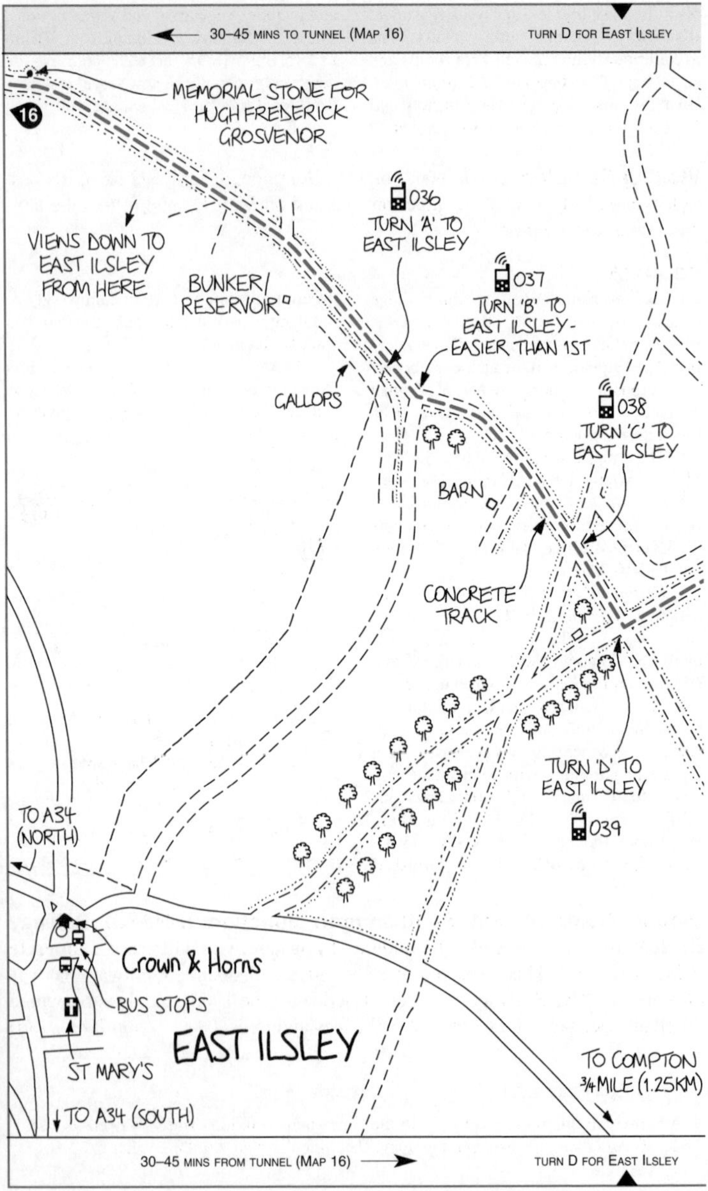

← 30–45 MINS TO TUNNEL (MAP 16)

TURN D FOR EAST ILSLEY

16

MEMORIAL STONE FOR
HUGH FREDERICK
GROSVENOR

VIEWS DOWN TO
EAST ILSLEY
FROM HERE

BUNKER/
RESERVOIR

GALLOPS

036
TURN 'A' TO
EAST ILSLEY

037
TURN 'B' TO
EAST ILSLEY-
EASIER THAN 1ST

038
TURN 'C' TO
EAST ILSLEY

BARN

CONCRETE
TRACK

TURN 'D' TO
EAST ILSLEY
039

TO A34
(NORTH)

Crown & Horns

BUS STOPS

ST MARY'S

↓ TO A34 (SOUTH)

EAST ILSLEY

TO COMPTON
¾ MILE (1.25KM)

30–45 MINS FROM TUNNEL (MAP 16) →

TURN D FOR EAST ILSLEY

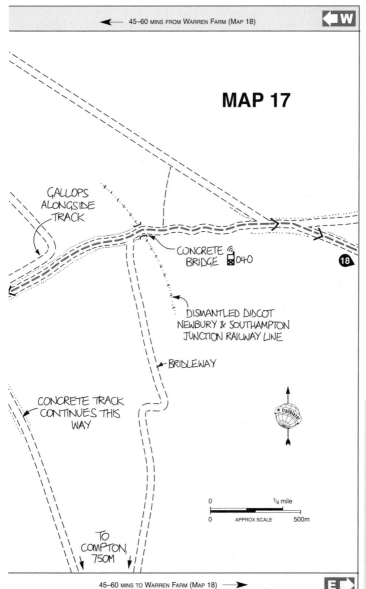

W

MAP 17

GALLOPS
ALONGSIDE
TRACK

CONCRETE
BRIDGE 📱040

18

DISMANTLED DIDCOT
NEWBURY & SOUTHAMPTON
JUNCTION RAILWAY LINE

BRIDLEWAY

CONCRETE TRACK
CONTINUES THIS
WAY

★ trailblazer

0   1/4 mile
0   APPROX SCALE   500m

TO
COMPTON,
750M

E

(cont'd from p133) The section that you cross lies between the old stations of Churn and Compton. This part of the line was opened in 1882 and owing to its course through remote countryside was given the nickname of the 'Desert Line'.

Important junction (if heading east) If heading east, when you arrive at the slightly **staggered crossroads** (Map 18), at which a track turning heads north to the wonderfully named Aston Tirrold while the right turning heads for the less-enticing Greyladies, you should continue straight ahead for a short distance until the track forks. Make sure you are not daydreaming when you reach here as you need to take the less-obvious option, a turn to the left. It's an ascending flinty track, closed in by trees, which bends left after about 200m. It is signposted but if you're not paying attention the natural tendency is to carry straight on.

Visiting Aldworth To reach Aldworth from the Ridgeway, take one of the tracks branching off at either WPT 042 or WPT 043 (Map 18). These routes join

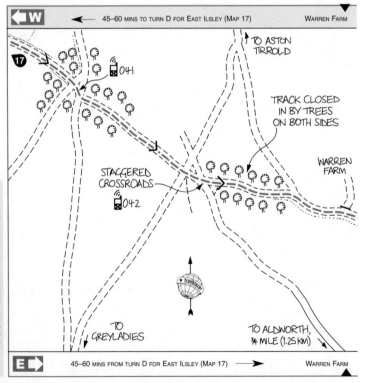

up with each other before entering Aldworth, but the route from WPT 043 involves a little less road-walking.

ALDWORTH [off MAP 18]

The main reason why you might like to detour to this quiet village is to visit *The Bell* (☎ 01635 578272; 🐾 on lead; Tue-Sun noon-7pm). No doubt about it, this is a real country pub. The building dates back to the 15th century and the pub has been in the same family for over 200 years. Take note that the pub is closed on Mondays, except at lunchtime on Bank Holidays. A wide selection of filled rolls is served to go with a choice of varied and interesting real ales and farmhouse cider. By the way, in case you need any more encouragement, it was voted CAMRA (see box on p22) 'National

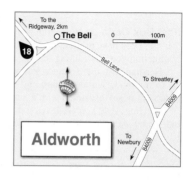

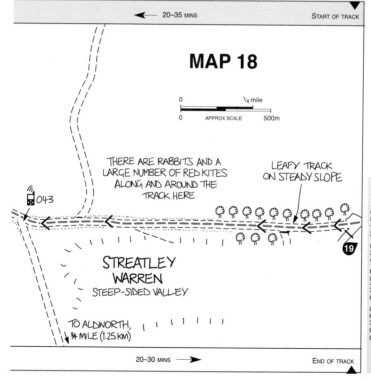

20-35 MINS ← | START OF TRACK

MAP 18

0   ¼ mile
0   APPROX SCALE   500m

THERE ARE RABBITS AND A LARGE NUMBER OF RED KITES ALONG AND AROUND THE TRACK HERE

LEAFY TRACK ON STEADY SLOPE

043

19

STREATLEY WARREN
STEEP-SIDED VALLEY

TO ALDWORTH,
¾ MILE (1.25 KM)

20-30 MINS → | END OF TRACK

Pub of the Year' in 2019, has won the regional award several times and even won an award for being 'the most unspoilt pub in England'. Its high regard amongst real ale drinkers means that it's often very busy despite its quiet location. Morris dancers (see box on p120) can be seen here at certain times of the year.

Post Box Cottage When you arrive at the sealed road by Post Box Cottage (Map 19) you have reached the beginning of a new type of Ridgeway, whichever direction you are walking in.

Heading east, there are no more windswept wanderings up on grassy tracks 20 metres wide without a building in sight. For the next few miles at least, things are positively urban with a long stretch of tarmac walking coming up.

Heading west, you are leaving the towns and villages in exchange for solitude and wide open space, pretty much all the way to the end of the trail. Enjoy it!

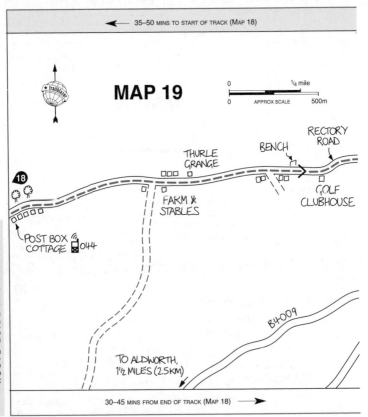

35–50 MINS TO START OF TRACK (MAP 18)

MAP 19

RECTORY ROAD

BENCH

THURLE GRANGE

18

FARM & STABLES

POST BOX COTTAGE 044

GOLF CLUBHOUSE

B4009

TO ALDWORTH, 1½ MILES (2.5KM)

30–45 MINS FROM END OF TRACK (MAP 18)

ROUTE GUIDE AND MAPS

STREATLEY [MAP 19]

This West Berkshire village is now very much smaller than its neighbour, Goring (see pp141-3), across the river in Oxfordshire, but historically it was the larger of the two. Both places were mentioned in the *Domesday Book* with Streatley being valued higher than its neighbour. Even up until the early 19th century it was larger owing to its location on the road to Reading.

For shops, restaurants and other services you should head across the bridge to Goring, just a couple of minutes' walk away.

Thames Travel's No 143 (Goring to Reading) **bus** service stops here, as does Going Forward Buses' No 133 (Goring to Wallingford); see pp48-51 for details.

Where to stay, eat and drink

At the time of writing, YHA Streatley-on-Thames (☎ 0845 371 9044, 🖳 yha.org.uk/hostel/yha-streatley-on-thames) was operating on an 'exclusive hire' basis and sadly that is likely still to be the same in 2021. Hopefully it will re-open as a hostel for independent travellers; for updates check the website or contact the YHA.

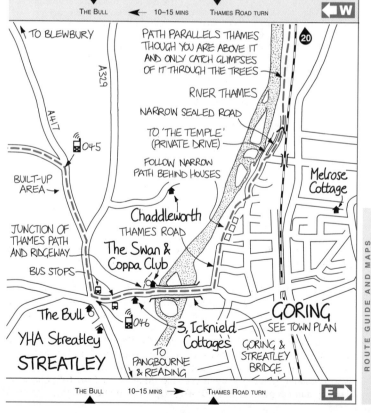

THE BULL   ← 10–15 MINS   THAMES ROAD turn   ◄ W

↑ TO BLEWBURY

PATH PARALLELS THAMES THOUGH YOU ARE ABOVE IT AND ONLY CATCH GLIMPSES OF IT THROUGH THE TREES

A329

RIVER THAMES

NARROW SEALED ROAD

A417

TO 'THE TEMPLE' (PRIVATE DRIVE)

045

FOLLOW NARROW PATH BEHIND HOUSES

BUILT-UP AREA →

Melrose Cottage

Chaddleworth

JUNCTION OF THAMES PATH AND RIDGEWAY

THAMES ROAD

The Swan & Coppa Club

BUS STOPS

The Bull

YHA Streatley

046

STREATLEY

3, Icknield Cottages

TO PANGBOURNE & READING

GORING SEE TOWN PLAN

GORING & STREATLEY BRIDGE

THE BULL   10–15 MINS →   THAMES ROAD turn   E ►

B&B options include *The Bull* (☎ 01491 872392, 💻 bullinnpub.co.uk; 4D/2T, all en suite; 🛏; WI-FI; (🌓); 🐾), a 15th-century former coaching inn, owned by Marstons, where the spacious bar has a relaxed atmosphere. The restaurant (**food** Mon-Sat noon-8.45pm, Sun to 8pm) serves a range of standard pub food; the chicken, leek & cider pie (£9.25) is recommended. The **accommodation** is in a separate building; B&B costs £40-45pp (sgl occ room rate).

Just outside Streatley, and only a few minutes from the Ridgeway, is the beautiful *Chaddleworth* (☎ 07711 420586, 💻 chaddleworthbedandbreakfast.com; 1D/1D or T all en suite, 1D or T separate bathroom; 🛏; WI-FI; (🌓)) which charges from £50pp (sgl occ £85). They have a lovely garden where you can relax after a long day on the trail.

B&B at *3 Icknield Cottages* (☎ 01491 875152; 1S private bathroom; 🛏; WI-FI; (🌓)) is very good value (£35) if you are walking on your own; it has a good location too. However, they may not open after 2021.

Just before crossing the river to Goring is a large upmarket hotel known as *The Swan* (Map 19; ☎ 01491 878800, 💻 the swanatstreatley.com; 2D/39D or T, all en suite; 🛏; WI-FI; 🐾). It is right on the bank of the Thames and boasts a spa, gym, options for eating as well as a spacious riverside terrace – an ideal spot for a break during a long day of walking. Room rates vary depending on demand but expect to pay £50-100pp (sgl occ room rate); breakfast is additional. Snacks are available all day in the hotel's bar and coffee shop (Sun-Thur 8am-8pm, Fri & Sat to 9pm, Sun 10am-7pm) and it is also possible to eat takeaway meals from Coppa Club there. Alternatively you can eat in *Coppa Club* (☎ 01491 529315, 💻 coppaclub.co.uk; WI-FI; Tue-Sat noon-10pm, Sun to 7pm) itself; it is part of the same building, and feels welcoming towards walkers. Mains here cost £13.50-26 and there is a good range for vegetarians/vegans. However, the food (such as burgers and pizzas) served is not what you would expect for somewhere that provides 4-star accommodation.

Goring & Streatley Bridge The double-span bridge linking the village of Streatley and the town of **Goring** offers some lovely views of the Thames to the north and Goring Lock below. This bridge was built in 1923 though there has been a bridge here since the 1830s.

W← GORING TO COURT HILL (& WANTAGE)   [MAPS 19-13]

[Route section begins on Map 19, pp138-9] This is an easy **14-mile/22.5km (4¼-6¼hrs)** section; add 2 miles/3km if you are going to stay in Wantage. The first section, from Goring, through **Streatley**, and out into the countryside is a bit of a dull plod along the gradually ascending road. Once the road finishes at **Post Box Cottage** (Map 19) and the track starts it's fairly isolated walking all the way to the end of the stage.

There's an option to visit **Aldworth** (off Map 18) and further along you'll reach the **railway bridge** (Map 17) for the now defunct Didcot, Newbury & Southampton Junction Railway. Just after the bridge is a turn for **Compton** (map p133) and another one about half a mile further along.

By the time you reach the four turnings for **East Ilsley** (Map 17), you'll notice that the going underfoot has changed to a grassy track and the tree cover is petering out by the time you reach the **stone memorial** (Map 16). The peace is then broken by the **A34 road crossing** (Map 16) and the following road crossing and car parks at **Bury Down** (Map 16), but after this there's a good section of isolated trekking past a **reservoir** (Map 15) and all the way to the **Baron Wantage Monument** (Map 14). From here it's an easy walk to the end of the stage at **Court Hill** (Map 13).

At the time of writing there was no source of drinking water on the trail between Streatley and Court Hill, so do make sure you set off with plenty.

[Next route overview on p125]

GORING [map p142]

After the Great Western Railway came through here in 1840, the town started to grow larger than its neighbour, Streatley. This growth has continued and as a result nearly all the shops, restaurants and services are on this side of the river. The place seems to be at least 90% inhabited by young mums pushing their babies around – we don't know why.

Services

Tourist information (☎ 01491 873565, ⌨ visitgoringandstreatley.co.uk; Mon-Fri 10am-noon, plus Sat 10am-noon in July & Aug) is available through the website, or in the Community Centre on Station Rd but this was closed at the time of writing. The office has a lot of leaflets about the area but staff are not able to do accommodation-booking, nor do they sell maps or books.

The **ATM** on the wall of the estate agents Davis Tate is the only one in town. On the High St you'll also find a **chemist** (☎ 01491 872124; Mon-Fri 9am-6pm, Sat to 5pm) and a **newsagent** (☎ 01491 875369; Sun-Fri 7am-9pm, Sat to 10pm) which sells most groceries and also houses the **post office** (open same hours).

The Goring Grocer (☎ 01491 875609, ⌨ goringgrocer.co.uk; Mon-Sat 9am-3pm), a **delicatessen**, has a great selection of locally produced food including sandwiches and savouries, filos and tartlets. There is a Tesco Express (⌨ tesco.com; daily 7am-11pm) **supermarket** near the station and there are public **toilets** in the car park.

Transport

Going Forward's **bus services** operate from the railway station to Wallingford via Streatley (No 133) and also via South and North Stoke (No 134X/L); Thames Travel's No 143 goes to Reading via Streatley. For further details see pp48-51.

Goring & Streatley station is a stop on GWR's **rail** services (see box on p46).

If you need a **taxi** you could try Pangbourne Taxis (☎ 01491 671979, ⌨ pangbournetaxis.co.uk); they are very helpful, but try to book well in advance.

Where to stay

There are some good accommodation options here: the first is *Melrose Cottage* (Map 19; ☎ 01491 873040, ⌨ howarthr 523@gmail.com; 1D en suite/1T private bathroom; ☛; WI-FI; Ⓛ), a 10-minute walk from the town centre. The rooms (£37.50-42.50pp, sgl/sgl occ from £50) are fairly self contained with their own fridges and microwaves; guests are also welcome to use the large garden. At the time of research they were only using two rooms so the facilities could be private but they hope to use all their rooms (plus 1S/1D or T) in 2021 but then if all booked some of the rooms would share two bathrooms. To get there walk straight up Wallingford Rd, looking out for Milldown Rd on your right, but be careful not to confuse this with Milldown Avenue, also on your right. The B&B is at No 36, pretty much at the far end of the road, again on your right.

An accommodation option right in the centre of the village on Station Rd is *Beams End* (☎ 01491 875949, ☎ 07741 005338 ⌨ jeanturner@btinternet.com; 1S/1D shared bathroom; WI-FI; Ⓛ). At the time of research the room rate for a night in this quiet and friendly place was from £40pp (sgl/sgl occ £40). However, the proprietor may start doing breakfast again in which case the rate will probably go up.

You can also stay at one of the inns in town such as *The Miller of Mansfield* (☎ 01491 872829, ⌨ millerofmansfield.com; 11D/2Tr, all en suite; ☛; WI-FI; 🐾). This lovely 18th-century building, situated right

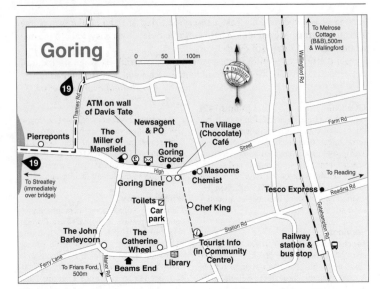

in the town centre, has a collection of striking, individually styled rooms with B&B for £54-94pp (sgl occ room rate). At the time of research they were only open Wednesday to Saturday but it is possible that may change.

At the time of writing new people were about to take over *The John Barleycorn* (🖥 thejohnbarleycornpub.com) and details about accommodation and/or food provision weren't available; hopefully by the time you read this there will be information on the website.

Slightly out of the centre, to the south, but well worth the walk, is *Friars Ford* (☎ 07801 138410, 🖥 friars-ford.co.uk; 1D/2D or T, all en suite; self-contained apartment 1D; 🐾; WI-FI). It would be hard to find a grander place to stay – the walk up the driveway, the house, the garden and the large rooms are all fabulous. The proprietor now requires a minimum stay of two nights and charges from £195 (sgl occ room rate) for a room for two nights; breakfast is no longer served but each room has a kettle, tea/coffee and mini fridge. Friar's Ford is about 500m from the centre of the village.

Walk straight down Manor Road – the entrance is at the end of the road, on your right, through the wrought-iron gates.

Don't forget **Airbnb** (see pp20-1) – there are various options in both Goring and Streatley.

Where to eat and drink

If you're in one of the inns enjoying a drink anyway, you could try eating there. *The Miller of Mansfield* (see Where to stay; WI-FI; 🐾; food Wed-Sat noon-2pm & 6-9pm, Sun 8am-3pm) serves some interesting dishes; their prices certainly aren't the cheapest but may include such treats as sea trout with onion seed, mange tout, baba ganoush & red pepper sauce (£22.50), or char-grilled aged steak with chimichurri, acid onions, mushroom duxelle & beef chips (£32.50).

A minute further along the road is *The Catherine Wheel* (☎ 01491 872379, 🖥 tcw goring.co.uk; WI-FI; 🐾 but not in restaurant; food Mon & Tue 6-9pm, Wed-Sat noon-3pm & 6-9pm, Sun noon-4pm), a Brakspear pub serving a range of pizzas (Wed-Sat £9-13), with vegan and gluten-free options available. A roast is served on Sundays. When you are here *The John Barleycorn* (see Where to stay) may also be open again for food and drink.

For lunch or snacks you could try *The Village Café* (*The Village Chocolate Café*; ☎ 01491 874264, 🖥 chocolatecafegoring .co.uk; Mon-Fri 10am-4pm, Sat & Sun to 5pm; WI-FI; 🐾 on lead), a small, jolly, café in the centre of town serving cakes, panini, sandwiches (£6), jacket potatoes and drinks. At the weekend they also serve cooked breakfasts (from £7.50).

Alternatively, *Pierreponts* (☎ 01491 874464, 🖥 pierreponts.co.uk; WI-FI; 🐾; Wed-Sun 9.30am-4pm) is just before the bridge. In normal circumstances it serves breakfast, lunch and afternoon tea but at the time of research they were only offering takeaway food though they have some

tables outside where people can sit. Their home-made cakes are delicious!

Chef King (☎ 01491 872485; Fri-Sun noon-2pm, Wed-Mon 5.30-10.30pm), in the arcade by The Village Café, is a Chinese takeaway; the menu has all the dishes you'd expect.

Masooms (☎ 01491 875078, 🖥 masooms.co.uk; daily 5.30-10pm), an Indian restaurant on the High St, has a mouth-watering and varied menu; most main courses cost between £8 and £17. The selection of fish curries is worth a look: the red mullet *biraan* is especially good. However, at the time of research they were only offering takeaway.

There is also a fish & chip shop, *Goring Diner* (☎ 01491 871612, 🖥 goring diner.com; Sun-Fri 4.30-9.30pm, Sat noon-9.30pm) on the High St.

E➜ GORING TO WATLINGTON [MAPS 19-26]

This stretch of the Ridgeway totals **14½ miles/23km (6½-9hrs)** and is very enjoyable, especially after the previous sections. From the twin towns of Streatley and **Goring** (Map 19) the path is easy and follows the **River Thames** for around 5½ miles/9km, sometimes right on its bank. From Goring to the charming village of **South Stoke** (Map 20) the Ridgeway shares its route with **Swan's Way** and it passes under the impressive **Moulsford Railway Bridge** before reaching **North Stoke** (Map 21).

Where the path turns east you can either head into either **Wallingford** or **Crowmarsh Gifford** (both off Map 22), or keep on the Ridgeway, heading along **Grim's Ditch** (see box on p154) for several miles before emerging at **Nuffield** (Map 23). One of the most bizarre sections of the Ridgeway is here – a walk across a golf course – after which you head into woodlands and across open fields, passing through **Ewelme Park Estate** and by **St Botolph's** (both on Map 24) and then the turns to **Watlington** (off maps 25 & 26).

Through Goring The route through Goring is straightforward and well-signposted. But it does pay to keep a look out for the official Ridgeway signs, especially when heading south (west), to keep on the path.

River Thames Though the path is parallel and close to the River Thames on this section, you might not always be able to see it. There are some grand houses along here, with gardens stretching all the way to the banks of the river and there's also a restaurant, right on the Thames. *Don Giovanni at The Leatherne Bottel* (Map 20; ☎ 01491 872667, 🖥 leathernebottel.co.uk; WI-FI; 🐾; food daily noon-3pm, Mon-Sat 6-10.30pm) is a riverside restaurant. It's a deservedly popular place serving high-quality food either on the terrace by the river bank or inside the restaurant itself. Their lunch menu (2/3 courses £17.90/20.90) would be worth stopping off for. Main dishes on their à la carte menu are mostly around the £16-22 mark and include *spigola Don Giovanni* (fillet of sea bass cooked in a creamy lobster sauce with prawns & smoked salmon) and spaghetti sautéed with garlic, black olives, parsley & olive oil. Booking is recommended.

SOUTH STOKE   [MAP 20]

This is yet another attractive village on the route. The Ridgeway path follows 'The Street' through the village, lined with a real variety of old, new and renovated houses. You'll pass a primary school and a church, **St Andrew's**.

The Goring to Wallingford **bus** (Going Forward Buses' No 134X/L) service stops outside the Perch & Pike and also on the main B4009 road just outside the village; see pp48-51 for further details.

There is a small shop here, the *South Stoke Community Shop* (☎ 01491 871633, 🖥 southstokeshop.co.uk; Mon-Fri 10am-3pm, Sat & Sun 9.30am-noon but in 2021 they hope to be back to their normal hours Mon-Fri 9am-5pm, Sat to 4pm, Sun to noon) that sells food, beer, takeaway coffee and snacks (but no hot food) and does 'cashback' if you spend £5 or more and if they have cash in the till.

The main place of interest to walkers will be **The Perch & Pike** (☎ 01491 872415, 🖥 perchandpike.co.uk; 3D/1T, all en suite; ✎; WI-FI; 🐾 bar only), which is an excellent example of a rare phenomenon – a pub actually on the Ridgeway! For this reason it's a popular stop for many walkers. The pub itself is a 17th-century coaching inn that has been tastefully refurbished. At the time of writing it had just been taken over by new people and was closed on Mondays though this may change. B&B costs from £47.50pp (sgl occ room rate) and one of the rooms even has a Jacuzzi which would be just the thing after a long day's walk!

Mains (**food** Tue-Fri noon-2pm & 6-9pm, Sat noon-3pm & 6-9pm, Sat noon-3pm) cost £12-18 and they serve Brakspear ales (see box on p22).

Another option is **Airbnb** (see p20-1).

Swan's Way   At the northern end of 'The Street' in South Stoke, you'll see signs for Swan's Way pointing east. Swan's Way is a 65-mile (105km), long-distance bridlepath starting in Salcey Forest, on the border with Northamptonshire and finishing at Goring. The Ridgeway crosses and shares its route at several points.

Moulsford Railway Bridge   The Ridgeway passes directly under this low, wide viaduct (Map 20) that carries the railway over the Thames. From a distance it looks like a standard four-arched viaduct with flattened elliptical arches, as opposed to the semi-circular ones more favoured at the time of its construction. It's only when you get fairly close, and even right under the viaduct, that you see it is really something special. It's not a single viaduct, but **two viaducts**, built alongside each other with a narrow gap between them. The first was built in 1838 and the second in 1892. You'll also see that the viaducts are heavily skewed as they cross the Thames on an angle. The red Berkshire brickwork is another interesting feature as the bricks are laid diagonally as opposed to horizontally. The visual effect of this, combined with the skewing of the viaduct, creates a sort of optical illusion as you stand under the arches following the lines of bricks with your eyes.

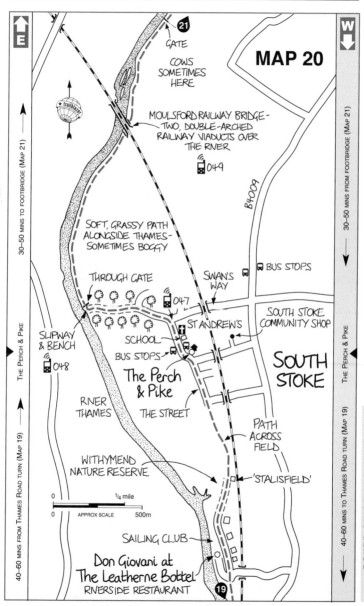

21

GATE

COWS
SOMETIMES
HERE

MAP 20

MOULSFORD RAILWAY BRIDGE—
TWO, DOUBLE-ARCHED
RAILWAY VIADUCTS OVER
THE RIVER

📱049

B4009

SOFT, GRASSY PATH
ALONGSIDE THAMES—
SOMETIMES BOGGY

THROUGH GATE

🚌 BUS STOPS

SWAN'S
WAY

📱047

SOUTH STOKE
COMMUNITY SHOP

ST ANDREW'S

SLIPWAY
& BENCH

📱048

SCHOOL

BUS STOPS

SOUTH
STOKE

**The Perch
& Pike**

RIVER
THAMES

THE STREET

PATH
ACROSS
FIELD

WITHYMEND
NATURE RESERVE

'STALISFIELD'

0   ¼ mile

0   500m
APPROX SCALE

SAILING CLUB

**Don Giovani at
The Leatherne Bottel**
RIVERSIDE RESTAURANT

19

E

W

trailblazer

30–50 MINS TO FOOTBRIDGE (MAP 21)

THE PERCH & PIKE

40–60 MINS FROM THAMES ROAD turn (MAP 19)

30–50 MINS FROM FOOTBRIDGE (MAP 21)

THE PERCH & PIKE

40–60 MINS TO THAMES ROAD turn (MAP 19)

ROUTE GUIDE AND MAPS

NORTH STOKE [MAP 21]

You arrive in this village via the grounds of the 14th-century **church**, the main building of which remains largely unaltered since its construction; even some of the original stained glass remains in the windows. Once you've had a look at it there isn't much else to do here; the village is smaller even than South Stoke and there are no facilities for the walker.

Going Forward Buses' No 134X/L **bus** service stops on the main B4009 road just outside the village; see pp48-51 for further details.

Visiting Wallingford The Ridgeway turns 90 degrees by the pedestrian tunnel under the busy A4130 (Map 22). It is here that you should leave the trail to visit Wallingford or Crowmarsh Gifford. To do so, go through the tunnel under the A4130. If heading **for Wallingford**, take the path on your left to lead you up onto the A4130, soon after you emerge from the tunnel. Then follow the road bridge across the River Thames and descend from the bridge to the riverside path which leads straight to Wallingford (1 mile/1.6km).

If heading directly for **Crowmarsh Gifford** (1¼ miles/2km), stay on the bridleway after going through the tunnel under the A4130. The bridleway turns

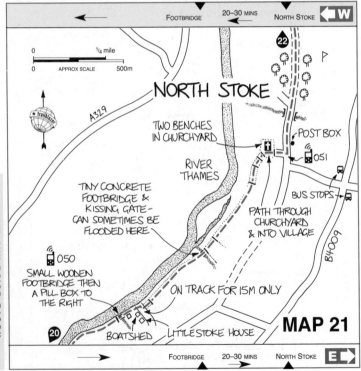

ROUTE GUIDE AND MAPS

into a road and you pass a farm on your left. On a curve in the road there is a footpath turning off to your left. Take this and stay on it to Crowmarsh Gifford. Alternatively, you can reach Crowmarsh Gifford by walking along the A4074 from the roundabout where it joins the A4130, though this is a less pleasant route.

WALLINGFORD [see map p149]

This is the largest town you will have come across 'on' the Ridgeway so far which might merit a visit, especially if you need to stock up, or just take some time out.

This historically important town was established by King Alfred in the 10th century and later a fortified castle was built here by William the Conqueror who arrived after the Battle of Hastings in 1066. The fortifications were added to over the years until it became one of the most important castles in England and remained so for several centuries. It was, however, completely destroyed on the orders of Oliver Cromwell in 1652. You can still visit the **Castle Gardens**, the site of the castle, to the north of town, but there is virtually no evidence of the castle itself.

Although the railway was closed to passengers in 1959, it has since reopened as the **Cholsey & Wallingford Railway**, linking Wallingford, via the old GWR branch line to Cholsey, and the national rail network. At the time of writing, train services were suspended, but they usually run on various weekends and bank holidays during the year and are sometimes pulled by a steam engine. For more information call ☎ 01491 835067, or go to the railway's website: ▪ cholsey-wallingford-railway.com.

Wallingford Museum (☎ 01491 835065, ▪ wallingfordmuseum.org.uk; Mar-Nov Tue-Fri & bank hols 2-5pm, Sat 10.30am-5pm, June-Aug also Sun 2-5pm; £5 adults, children free if with an adult) traces the history of the town from its Saxon roots to the present day. Agatha Christie lived in the Wallingford area for over 40 years and an exhibition includes details about her life and her books as well as some of her original letters. The museum was closed at the time of writing but very much hopes to be open as normal in 2021 – check their website for details.

Services

There is a **tourist information centre** (TIC; ☎ 01491 826972, ▪ wallingford.co .uk – click on Visitors; Mar to end Nov Mon-Fri 9.30am-12.30pm & 1-3.30pm, Sat to 1.30pm, Dec to Feb Mon-Sat 10am-2pm but the hours can depend on the weather) in the Town Hall, built in 1670. The staff here are helpful and there is a huge amount of information for walkers in the form of free leaflets. They also have some information about accommodation (but cannot do bookings) though there is also information on their website – click on Stay; for a full list scroll down to the link to a pdf.

The **post office** (Mon-Fri 9am-5.30pm, Sat to 12.30pm) is in Reynold's, just off Market Place. On St Mary's St the branches of Nationwide, Lloyds and Barclays have **ATMs**.

There is a **Lloyds Pharmacy** (☎ 01491 836206; Mon-Fri 9am-6pm, Sat to 5.30pm) on Market Place and a branch of **Boots** (☎ 01491 839061, ▪ boots.com; Mon-Fri 9am-6pm, Sat to 5.30pm, Sun 10am-4pm), the chemist, on St Mary's St.

A large Waitrose **supermarket** (▪ waitrose.com; Mon-Fri 8am-9pm, Sat to 8pm, Sun 10am-4pm) is on the corner of St Martin's St and the High St; you'll also find **public toilets** here and there are more public toilets in the car park on Wood St.

There are also four **markets** here: a general market every Friday and an independent market every third Tuesday and fifth Saturday, both on Market Place. At the country market in St Mary le More Church every Friday morning homemade produce is sold. Finally, there's a local producer's market in the car park off Kinecroft Lane every Saturday morning.

If you need bicycle repairs try **Rides on Air** (☎ 01491 836289, ▪ ridesonair .com; Mon-Fri 9am-5.30pm, Sat to 5pm) on St Martin's St.

Transport

[See pp48-51] Several Thames Travel **bus** services call here: the frequent X2/X38/X39/X40/NX40 (to Oxford & Reading via Crowmarsh Gifford and Nuffield) and the No 136 (Cholsey to Benson via Crowmarsh Gifford). Going Forward Buses' No 134X/L service goes to Goring via North Stoke & South Stoke. Check you are at the correct bus stop.

There is a **taxi** rank next to the Town Hall. Go Green Taxis (☎ 01491 524343, 💻 gogreentaxisltd.co.uk) offers a service in the area as does Wallingford Taxi Services (☎ 01491 352012, 💻 wallingfordtaxiservices.co.uk).

Where to stay

George Hotel (☎ 01491 836665, 💻 peelhotels.co.uk/george-hotel; 9S/19D/8D or T/1Qd, all en suite, ☕; WI-FI; Ⓛ; 🐕) is a large, upmarket place with a central location. The hotel is in a 16th-century building also incorporating a 'tavern' and a separate restaurant and bar called Bistro George (see Where to eat). It's a very comfortable place: room rates start from £50pp (sgl/sgl occ from £100). Breakfast costs an extra £10pp.

The ***Royal Standard*** (☎ 01491 599105, 💻 royalstandardwallingford.co.uk; 1D en suite, 3D or T share shower facilities; ☕; WI-FI; Ⓛ; 🐕) is where The Partridge used to be, at the southern end of St Mary's St. Rates are fair value, given that only one of the rooms has en suite facilities, with prices starting at £37.50pp, rising to £50pp for the en suite (sgl occ room rate); breakfast is continental.

Opposite, the ***Coachmakers Arms*** (☎ 01491 838229, 💻 coachmakersarms.com; 1D/2Tr, all en suite; ☕; WI-FI; Ⓛ; 🐕) offers B&B from £45pp (sgl occ room rate) and includes a cooked breakfast.

Back at the other end of town, on the High St and near the river, is ***The Town Arms*** (☎ 020 3887 0391, 💻 thetownarmswallingford.com; **fb**; 5D/1Qd all en suite; WI-FI; 🐕). The simple and modern rooms cost from £32.50pp (sgl occ room rate). Breakfast was not available at the time of writing.

Once again, apart from the pubs your best chance of securing accommodation might be **Airbnb** (see pp20-1); there are several places advertised for both Wallingford and Crowmarsh Gifford.

Where to eat and drink

There are plenty of places to eat in Wallingford and lots of variety, too. All the places listed here are in or around the town centre.

Early risers just have a choice of two ubiquitous chains, ***Greggs*** (☎ 01491 836237, 💻 greggs.co.uk; Mon-Sat 7am-5pm, Sun 9am-4pm) and ***Costa*** (☎ 01491 837990, 💻 costa.co.uk; daily 8am-5pm), close to each other on Market Square. At ***Mollie's*** (☎ 01491 836237, 💻 mollieswallingford.co.uk; Mon-Fri 9am-3pm, Sat to 1.30pm; WI-FI) you can get a cooked breakfast (or their vegetarian version) for £6.50. They also do a great range of healthy lunches here with vegan and gluten-free options. They have some excellent cakes too. The proprietor hopes to be able to extend the opening hours in 2021.

For a lunchtime baguette (from £3.20) or evening pizza (from £8) you could try ***The Pizza Café*** (☎ 01491 826222, 💻 thepizzacafewallingford.co.uk; Mon-Sat 10am-2.30pm, Mon-Thur & Sun 5.30-10.30pm, Fri & Sat 5.30-11pm), on St Mary's St. For such a small place they certainly provide a wide choice including plenty of vegetarian options. They even have lactose-free cheese for pizzas, if you require. Also on St Mary's St is a branch of the chain restaurant, ***Pizza Express*** (☎ 01491 833431, 💻 pizzaexpress.com/wallingford; Mon-Fri 11.30am-11pm, Sat 11am-11pm, Sun 11.30am-10.30pm; WI-FI), which dishes up various pizzas and pastas for slightly higher prices and has more room inside. ***Avanti*** (☎ 01491 835500, 💻 avantiitalian.com; Tue-Thur 4.30-10pm, Fri to 10.30pm & Sat noon-10.30pm) serves a good range of pizza and pasta dishes (around £10) and they have a vegan menu too.

Just south of Market Place ***The Old Post Office*** (☎ 01491 836068, 💻 opowallingford.co.uk; WI-FI; 🐕 bar area only;

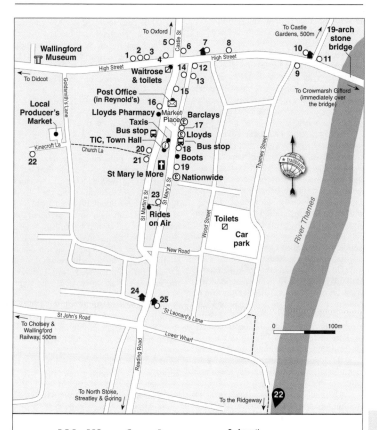

Wallingford

Where to stay
7 George Hotel
10 The Town Arms
24 Coachmakers Arms
25 Royal Standard

Where to eat and drink
1 Smart's Fish & Chips
2 Delhi Brasserie
3 Domino's
4 Chinese Whisper
5 Hong Kong House
6 Thai Corner
7 George's Bistro (in George Hotel)

8 Avanti
9 Wallingford Tandoori
10 The Town Arms
11 The Boathouse
12 Shellfish Cow
13 The Dolphin
14 Bean & Brew
15 Eat @ East Café
16 Mollie's
17 Costa
18 Greggs
19 Pizza Express
20 The Old Post Office
21 USA Chicken & Pizza
22 Coach & Horses
23 The Pizza Café
25 Royal Standard

food Mon-Sat 8am-10pm, Sun 9am-9pm) is described as 'a modern interpretation of an original public house'. Food is served all day, starting with cooked breakfasts (until 11am; £4.50-11) and finishing with evening meals such as roast pork belly, mashed potato, green beans, peas, apple sauce, crackling & gravy (£16.50). They also have a decent choice of vegetarian, vegan and gluten-free meals.

Shellfish Cow (☎ 01491 832807, ☐ shellfishcow.co.uk; wi-fi; ✷; Tue-Thur noon-2.30pm & 6-9pm, Fri same but to 9.30pm, Sat noon-9.30pm) is a restaurant and bar spread over three floors. As you might expect, the focus is on shellfish and there is a fantastic selection – Fowey mussels, Devon scallops and Cornish oysters. Prices are from £8/12 at lunchtime/in the evening. There are only a couple of vegetarian choices, but this is a shellfish restaurant after all.

On the High Street is *Delhi Brasserie* (☎ 01491 826666, ☐ delhibrasserie.co.uk; Mon-Fri noon-2pm & 5.30-11.30pm, Sat & Sun to 11.30pm) which is a pretty standard Indian restaurant though perhaps marginally better than the other choice, *Wallingford Tandoori* (☎ 01491 833133, ☐ wallingfordtandoori .com; Mon-Sat 5.30-11.30pm, Sat also noon-2pm, Sun noon-11pm) which has a similar menu and prices to match.

There's a Thai restaurant in Wallingford too – *Thai Corner* (☎ 01491 825050; Thur-Sat 5.30-9.30pm); it's a small place with an extensive and tasty menu and most main courses cost around £8.

Also worth checking out is *Eat @ East Café* (☎ 01491 598340; normal hours Mon-Sat 11.30am-3pm & 5-10pm but at the time of research due to COVID-19 they were open Tue-Thur 5-8.30pm, Fri & Sat to 9.30pm), a café/restaurant serving a real mixture of food from the Far East with plenty of choice for vegetarians and vegans. From *pho* to *ramen* to *godo gado*, their main courses cost £7.25-8.50.

Both *Hong Kong House* (☎ 01491 835453, ☐ hongkonghouse.org.uk; Sun-Wed 5-9pm, Thur to 9.30pm, Fri & Sat to 10pm) and *Chinese Whisper* (☎ 01491 300300, ☐ chinesewhisper.co.uk; Wed-Mon 5-10pm) are standard Chinese takeaways.

Fast-food options in Wallingford include *Smart's Fish & Chips* (☎ 01491 824411; Mon-Thur noon-2pm & 4.30-10pm, Sat 4-10pm, Sun 4-9pm), on the High St; a branch of *Domino's* (☎ 01491 833000, ☐ dominos.co.uk/wallingford; daily 10am-11pm), the pizza chain, nearby: and *USA Chicken & Pizza* (☎ 01491 83273; Tue-Thur & Sun 5-10pm, Fri & Sat to 11pm), on St Martin's St.

Plenty of **pubs** here serve food. If the weather is good you should visit the *Coach & Horses* (☎ 07488 914003, ☐ coachand horseswallingford.co.uk; wi-fi; ✷; food Wed & Thur 5-8.30pm, Fri & Sat noon-3pm & 5-8.30pm, Sun noon-4pm), just out of the town centre and owned by Fullers, whose garden opens onto a large grassy park. The menu has half a dozen pub standards and a similar number of more interesting Greek choices including *chicken tava* (chicken thighs slow cooked in tomatoes with chips & Greek salad) for £11.95.

The Dolphin (☎ 01491 837377, ☐ thedolphinwallingford.co.uk; ✷; food Sun-Wed 9am-2pm, Fri & Sat to 7pm), nearer the centre of town, has a standard bar menu, and they serve a 'full English' breakfast (small/large £5.50/6.50) all day; eat this before setting out and you'll definitely be up for a day of walking!

The Boathouse (☎ 01491 834100, ☐ greeneking-pubs.co.uk/pubs/oxfordshire/boat-house; wi-fi; ✷; food daily noon-9pm) has a large patio area for dining, right on the bank of the Thames. It's a Greene King pub and serves their usual menu. It can get quite noisy at weekends but you can always sit outside if the weather is warm enough. Just opposite is *The Town Arms* (see Where to stay; food Wed to Sat noon-3pm & 5-9pm, Sun noon-5pm) which specialises in tasty burgers and hot dogs (£5.50-8.50) with both vegetarians and vegans catered for. They also serve beer from West Berkshire Brewery (see box on p22).

Bistro George (food Fri-Sun noon-3pm, daily 6-9pm), in **George Hotel** (see Where to stay), has a lovely outdoor eating area in the hotel courtyard; main courses here are £10-22 and include a couple of vegetarian options such as butternut risotto topped with sage & cashew nut crumb (£12.95). Their *Tavern Bar* (food daily noon-3pm & 6-9pm) serves substantial sandwiches, burgers and some 'classics' such as sausage & mash and steak & chips.

Our favourite place for lunch, however, is just round the corner. *Bean & Brew* (☎ 01491 520685; **fb**; wi-fi; 🐾; Mon-Sat 8.15am-5.15pm, Sun 9am-4pm) does some delicious ciabattas (from £6.25)

including a chicken, chorizo & sundried tomato one for eat in or takeaway. They also make picnic boxes for two people with meat and vegetarian options available. They're not cheap at £32.50, but are very generously packed with sandwiches, savoury tarts, cheese, biscuits, cake and more.

The *Royal Standard* (see Where to stay; Wed-Fri 5-9pm, Sat noon-9pm, Sun to 8pm) has pub food for around a tenner (steak & ale pie, sausage & mash), but little for vegetarians.

To reach **Crowmarsh Gifford** (see below) from Wallingford you'll have to walk across the **19-arch stone bridge** crossing the Thames. Believe it or not this was the main road crossing of the Thames in this area until the A4130 bypass and new bridge were opened in 1993.

CROWMARSH GIFFORD
This town has now become an extension of Wallingford. It's separated from its larger neighbour only by the bridge and, to be honest, most shops and services are located in Wallingford, on the other side of the bridge. There are, however, two campsites here (though one closed at the time of writing) and it's easy to walk into Wallingford should you need to.

The main claim to fame for this place is that **Jethro Tull** lived here. No, not them, but him, the inventor of the seed drill. You can still see his house on The Street where he lived from 1700 to 1710. It's only a couple of minutes' walk from the bridge, but is not open to the public. It's the middle one of the three terraced Tudor houses.

The seed drill was essentially a device that enabled you to plant three rows of seeds at the same time. He also invented other machines in an effort to improve crop yields. At the time his ideas weren't implemented fully but, looking back, he is

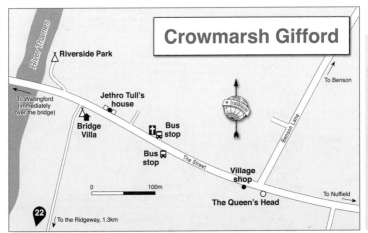

now recognised as one of the most important figures in the modernisation of farming methods.

Services

There is a well-stocked **village shop** (☎ 01491 837176; Mon-Fri 7am-6pm, Sat 8am-5pm, Sun 8am-noon) on The Street.

Thames Travel's **bus** Nos 136, X38, X39, X40 and NX40 stop here; see pp48-51 for further details.

Where to stay

On the right as you walk in from the Ridgeway is *Bridge Villa* (☎ 01491 836860, 🖥 bridgevilla.co.uk; Feb-Dec; WI-FI; 🐕 on lead). They offer **camping** (£10-14 for a tent and one person, £16-24 for two people); the rate includes use of the shower and toilet facilities. They also offer a **room** (1T en suite) from £25pp (sgl occ £45), but do not serve breakfast. Booking ahead is now essential for both forms of accommodation.

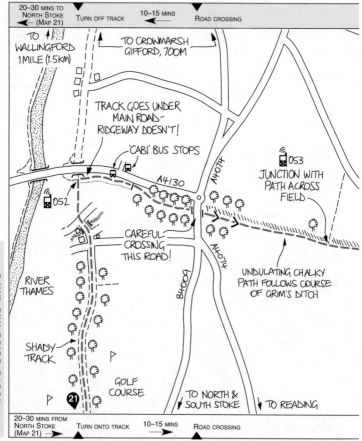

ROUTE GUIDE AND MAPS

On the banks of the Thames, **Riverside Park** (☎ 01491 835232, 🖳 better.org.uk/leisure-centre/south-oxfordshire/riverside-park-and-pools; late May to early Sep) was closed at the time of writing but it was a busy and very well-run **campsite**, with 18 pitches and shower/toilet facilities and also a heated open-air swimming pool so hopefully it will be open again in 2021.

Where to eat and drink

Since The Bell closed, there is now only one pub in the village. The 13th-century Fuller's pub, **The Queen's Head** (☎ 01491 839857, 🖳 queensheadcrowmarsh.co.uk; WI-FI; 🐾; food Mon-Fri noon-2.30pm & 5-8.30pm, Sat noon-8.30pm, Sun noon-4pm) serves some hearty meals such as treacle-roasted gammon steak (£11.50). They also have various vegetarian options – risotto verde with spinach, pea & hazelnut pesto (£11.50).

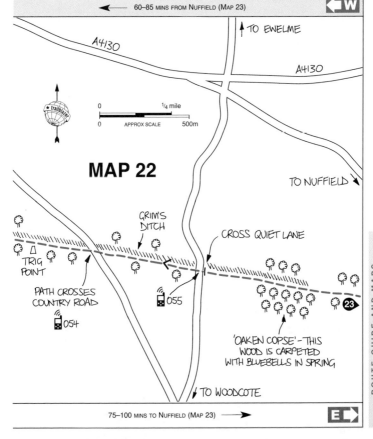

Grim's Ditch Between the A4130/A4074 roundabout near Wallingford and **Nuffield** the Ridgeway is almost entirely comprised of narrow, undulating paths following Grim's ditch.

Sometimes the path is on top of the ditch and sometimes to one side. Most of the way is shaded by trees and you also pass through some attractive

---

❏ **GRIM'S DITCHES**

There are many Grim's ditches in England. The reason is that Grim is the Anglo-Saxon word for the devil and his name was often attributed to unnatural features in the landscape. This particular Grim's ditch (see Map 22, pp152-3, but also Map 23, below) was probably built during the Iron Age and probably to mark a boundary as it's not big enough to be a defensive earthwork. 'Probably' being the operative word as, even now, little is known about this stretch.

60–85 MINS TO ROAD CROSSING (MAP 22)

TO CROWMARSH GIFFORD & WALLINGFORD

A4130

MAP 23

★ trailblazer

TO CROWMARSH GIFFORD

KISSING GATE

GRIM'S DITCH

22

BACHELOR'S HILL

'WOODLANDS' - PRIVATE HOUSE. WATER TAP TO SIDE OF WHITE ENTRANCE GATE

75–100 MINS FROM ROAD CROSSING (MAP 22) ⟶

ROUTE GUIDE AND MAPS

woodland. There are plenty of tree roots sticking through the surface of the path in places so be careful you don't trip. This is a popular stretch for day walkers and dog walkers.

Several areas of woodland along this section (for example '**Oaken Copse**', Map 22) are carpeted with bluebells in the late spring and make for a much-visited and very colourful sight. There's a **water tap** by 'Woodlands' (Map 23).

Golf course crossing Rather than skirting discreetly around it, you will be directed across several fairways (watch out for the bunkers!) of **Huntercombe Golf Course** (Map 23) at Nuffield.

You'll need to follow the strategically placed wooden posts to make your way from one side of the course to the other while always taking into account what the golfers are up to.

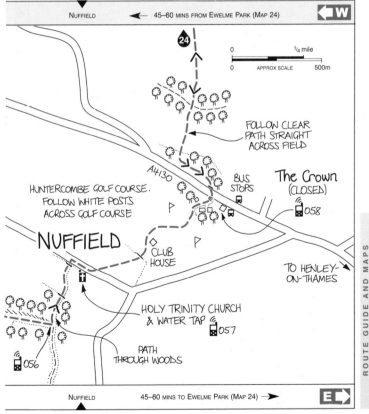

NUFFIELD   ← 45–60 MINS FROM EWELME PARK (MAP 24)   ◄W

0   ¼ mile
0   APPROX SCALE   500m

FOLLOW CLEAR PATH STRAIGHT ACROSS FIELD

A4130

HUNTERCOMBE GOLF COURSE. FOLLOW WHITE POSTS ACROSS GOLF COURSE

BUS STOPS

The Crown (CLOSED) 058

NUFFIELD

CLUB HOUSE

TO HENLEY-ON-THAMES

HOLY TRINITY CHURCH & WATER TAP 057

056

PATH THROUGH WOODS

NUFFIELD   45–60 MINS TO EWELME PARK (MAP 24) →   E►

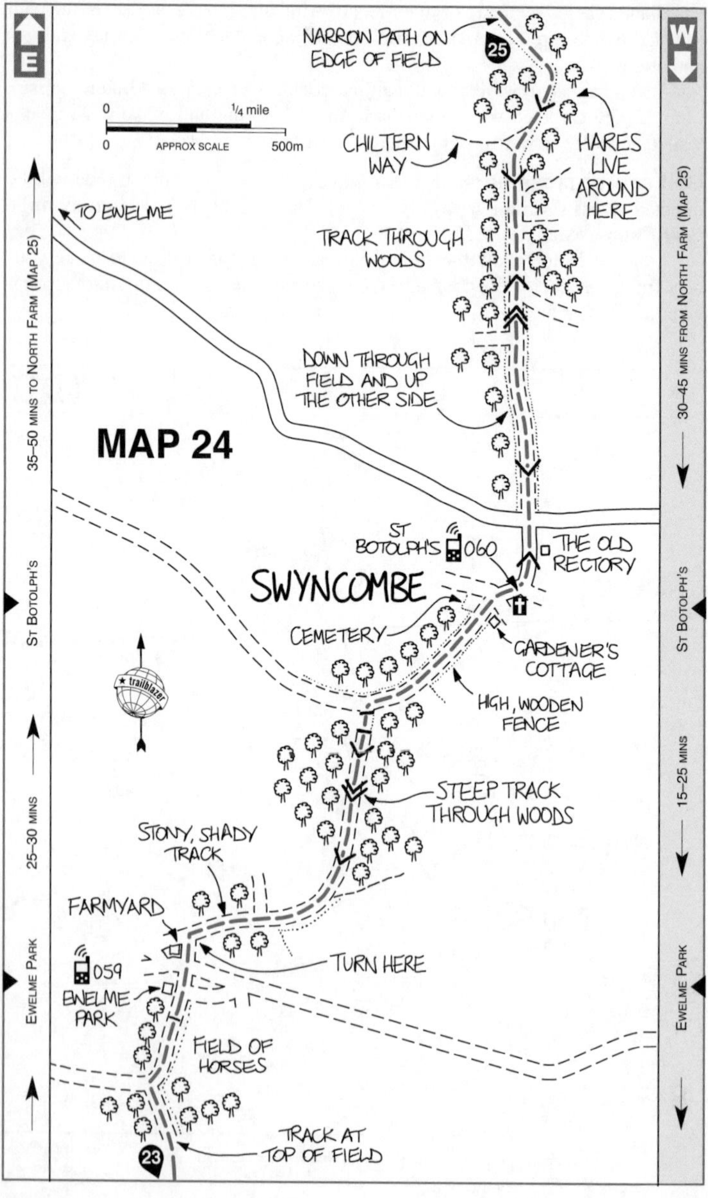
MAP 24
E
W
0 ¼ mile
0 APPROX SCALE 500m
35–50 MINS TO NORTH FARM (MAP 25)
30–45 MINS FROM NORTH FARM (MAP 25)
ST BOTOLPH'S
25–30 MINS
15–25 MINS
EWELME PARK
NARROW PATH ON EDGE OF FIELD
25
CHILTERN WAY
HARES LIVE AROUND HERE
TO EWELME
TRACK THROUGH WOODS
DOWN THROUGH FIELD AND UP THE OTHER SIDE
ST BOTOLPH'S 060
THE OLD RECTORY
SWYNCOMBE
CEMETERY
GARDENER'S COTTAGE
HIGH, WOODEN FENCE
trailblazer
STEEP TRACK THROUGH WOODS
STONY, SHADY TRACK
FARMYARD
TURN HERE
059
EWELME PARK
FIELD OF HORSES
TRACK AT TOP OF FIELD
23

NUFFIELD   [MAP 23, p155]

Nuffield is basically a small, quiet village with a church and a golf course: there is no post office, shop, pub, accommodation or food. **Holy Trinity** church, built in 1189, is the final resting place of Viscount William Morris (1877-1963), founder of Morris Motors. He was the Henry Ford of England, starting a mass-production car factory to build the Morris Oxford car. You can use the **water tap** by the bench next to William Morris's grave.

Thames Travel's X38 **bus** service (Reading to Oxford via Wallingford) stops at Nuffield Common, near The Crown (now closed); see pp48-51 for further details.

Ewelme Park Estate The picturesque Ewelme Park Estate (Map 24) was formed around 450 years ago from several smaller estates and was an important **royal deer park** under Henry VIII, Elizabeth I, James I, and Charles I, before being broken up and sold. Nowadays the estate is better known for its pheasants rather than deer, though the finale for both animals is the same. A large cache

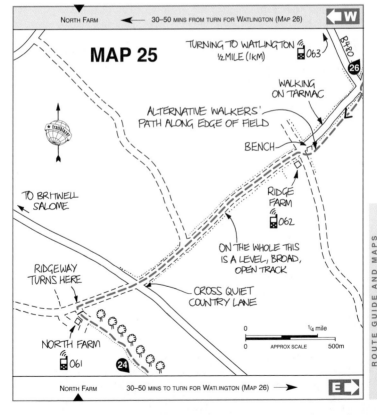

of Roman coins was also found on the estate, among several other finds in the area. Local schools make trips to the estate to learn about its history and see the archery corridor used by Henry VIII. When you walk through you'll see the **beautiful gatehouse** and views of the main house itself which, despite its appearance, is not very old. You may also see some peacocks and will definitely hear several dogs barking, announcing your arrival in the area.

St Botolph's church   Considering the location of the 11th-century **St** Botolph's church at **Swyncombe**, you might be surprised at how large it is. The cemetery around the church is full and there is another diagonally across the crossroads. You may recognise the name of the church as it's famous for the drifts of snowdrops that surround it in early February; so famous, in fact, that there have even been cases of snowdrop-bulb rustling in the churchyard.

Visiting Watlington   There are two turnings (Maps 25 & 26) but if you're heading for the centre of town it matters little which you take; if aiming for either White Mark Farm campsite or Spire & Spoke the easternmost (Map 26) is best; see p160 for details. Either way it's about half a mile into the town.

W ← WATLINGTON TO GORING   [MAPS 26-19]

[Route section begins on Map 26, opposite]   This stretch of the Ridgeway totals **14½ miles/23km (5-7½hrs)** and is actually something of a red-letter day on the trail. Once completed, you'll be virtually halfway on your Ridgeway odyssey. You'll notice that the path changes character after today, too, as you cross to the southern side of the Thames, leave the wooded upland scenery of the Chilterns behind and enter the Wessex Downs. To appropriate that old footballing cliché, the Ridgeway is a trek of two halves – and after the end of this stage you'll have reached half-time.

There is some pretty straightforward walking along decent tracks as you leave the road turnings for Watlington behind. It's when you turn off the track at **North Farm** (Map 25) that things get more interesting. You climb and descend through woodland to reach **St Botolph's church** (Map 24) before enduring a really steep climb through more woods. But that's the hardest part of the day done.

Once across the golf course at **Nuffield** (Map 23) you can enjoy the company of **Grim's Ditch** (see box on p154) and the shady, undulating path that follows it all the way to the turn for **Wallingford** and for **Crowmarsh Gifford** (both off Map 22). From here there's an easy and picturesque walk along the Thames to enjoy, passing through **North Stoke** (Map 21) and **South Stoke** (Map 20), before finishing for the day in **Goring** (Map 19) – a town with all the facilities that a weary walker might need. *[Next route overview on p140]*

❏ IMPORTANT NOTE – WALKING TIMES

All times in this book refer only to the time spent walking. You will need to add 20-30% to allow for rests, photography, checking the map, drinking water etc.

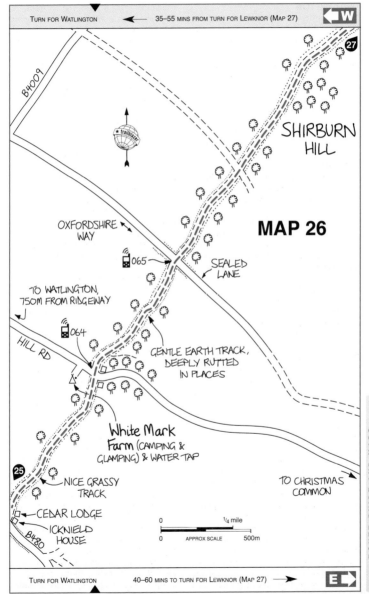

B4009

SHIRBURN HILL

MAP 26

OXFORDSHIRE WAY →

065

SEALED LANE

TO WATLINGTON, 750M FROM RIDGEWAY

064

HILL RD

GENTLE EARTH TRACK, DEEPLY RUTTED IN PLACES

White Mark Farm (CAMPING & GLAMPING) & WATER TAP

25

NICE GRASSY TRACK

CEDAR LODGE

ICKNIELD HOUSE

B480

TO CHRISTMAS COMMON

0 ¼ mile

0 APPROX SCALE 500m

ROUTE GUIDE AND MAPS

WATLINGTON

This is officially the smallest town in England. However, some people, the residents of Manningtree in Essex for instance, might like to take issue with this. For the record the royal charter giving town status to Watlington was issued in 1154.

If you are stopping here for the day most services and shops that you'll need are on one of two streets. The town is pleasant enough and has a few interesting old buildings to look at so it might be nice to relax here for an hour or two over lunch.

Services

For the **post office** (Mon-Fri 9am-5.30pm, Sat to 1pm) or an **ATM**, you'll have to go to the Co-op **supermarket** (☎ 01491 612472; daily 6am-10pm), on Couching St; the ATM is just inside the door.

Near the Co-op there is a **chemist,** Watlington Pharmacy (☎ 01491 612248; Mon-Fri 9am-1pm & 2-6pm, Sat to 1pm) and if you need a bike repair go to **Sprocket Science** (☎ 07712 775218, 🖳 sprocket science.co.uk; Tue-Sat 10am-4pm).

There are **public toilets** on the High St.

Thames Travel's No 11 **bus** goes to Oxford from the stops near The Fat Fox Inn; see pp48-51 for further details.

Where to stay

Campers should head for *White Mark Farm* (Map 26; ☎ 01491 612295, 🖳 white markfarm.co.uk; 🐾 on lead; Mar-late Oct), just a few minutes' walk from the Ridgeway. There are around 40 pitches for tents on this friendly, well-run campsite and they charge from £10 per adult (£4 if aged 15 or below). The rate includes use of the toilet and shower facilities as well as a microwave oven, kettle and fridge and they can charge your phones/laptops etc for 50p-£1 per item. At the time of writing, their well-stocked shop was closed but they hope to be able to open it in 2021 and for their normal hours (daily 9am-6pm). However, it's no more than 10 minutes to walk to the centre of town from here. Officially they are closed from the end of October to the beginning of March but if you are walking between November and February and

would like to camp here, contact them. On the same site is *White Mark Glamping* (Map 26; ☎ 07543 375464, 🖳 whitemark glamping.com; 🐾 on lead) for those who might like more creature comforts during their stay. There are three tents sleeping two adults, or one that can sleep two adults and two children; they charge from £100 per tent. The tents have real beds, outdoor seating, BBQ, fire pit, a kettle, crockery and cutlery. Toilets and showers are shared with the campsite.

The Fat Fox Inn (☎ 01491 613040, 🖳 thewatlingtonfox.co.uk; 5D/4T, all en suite; ▼; WI-FI; Ⓛ; 🐾) is a delightful old pub near the centre of town. The accommodation here is in a tastefully converted coach barn next to the pub and each room is different. B&B costs from £45pp (sgl occ room rate).

Airbnb (see pp20-1) boasts several options in and around the town so that may be your best bet for accommodation.

Where to eat and drink

A good option for lunch (eat in or takeaway) is *Granary Deli* (☎ 01491 613585, 🖳 granarydeli.co.uk/cafe; WI-FI; 🐾; Mon-Sat 9am-5pm) with a fine array of wholesome sandwiches, cakes and lunches.

If you get here early enough you could also check out *Orange Bakery* (☎ 07585 454241, 🖳 theorangcbakery.org; Wed-Fri from 9.15am, Sat from 10.30am, they close when they sell out, usually around 1pm) where there are some delicious cinnamon buns and cheese & marmite swirls on offer.

On the way into Watlington, from the easternmost turning off the Ridgeway, is *Spire & Spoke* (☎ 01491 614956; **fb**; WI-FI; 🐾; food Mon-Sat noon-3pm & 6-9pm, Sun noon-8pm). This freehouse has five handpumps serving an excellent selection of local beers to go with pizzas (around £8.50; evenings and Sun only) from their wood-fired oven; they serve wraps and paninis at lunch time. It is convenient if you're staying at White Mark Farm Campsite and it's a popular place with cyclists.

The Fat Fox Inn (see Where to stay; food Wed-Sat noon-2.30pm, Tue-Sat 6-9.30pm, Sun noon-5pm) offers a varied

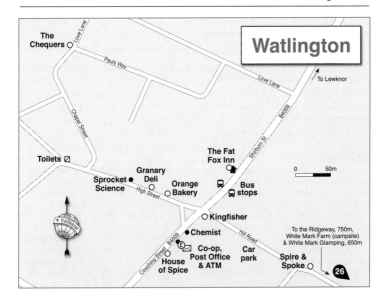

menu with choices such as fish & chips, steak and lasagne but only one vegetarian option. Main courses cost £10-13.50.

The Chequers ☎ 01491 612874, 🖥 the chequerswatlington .co.uk; WI-FI; 🐾 garden only; food Tue-Sun noon-3pm), a pub on Love Lane, is well known as one of the best places in town for food and it has friendly staff. However, at the time of writing the inside part of the pub was closed but they had set a bar (Tue-Sat noon-9pm, Sun to 4pm) up in the garden and they were offering food at lunch only – choice of

ploughman's (£8.50), butternut squash and chickpea burger with chips (£10.95) – but hope to return to normal service in 2021.

At *House of Spice* (☎ 01491 613865, 🖥 houseofspicewatlington.co.uk; daily 5-10pm), the menu contains all the usual Indian dishes; lamb dopiaza costs £9.

Alternatively *Kingfisher* (Mon noon-2pm & 4-10pm, Tue-Thur 11.30am-2pm & 4.30-10pm, Fri & Sat 11am-2pm & 4-10pm) serves takeaway fish & chips, burgers and fried chicken.

E➔ WATLINGTON TO PRINCES RISBOROUGH [MAPS 26-31]

Although this **11.2 mile/18km (4-5¼hrs)** section of the Ridgeway is pleasant enough, it's fairly uneventful. The walking is easy with few steep sections so you can really slow down, relax and enjoy the scenery.

Perhaps take a diversion into **Lewknor** before crossing under the **M40 motorway** (both on Map 27). After this there are several small villages off the Ridgeway which might be useful: **Aston Rowant** for the Mercure Lambert Thame Hotel (off Map 28) and **Kingston Blount** (Map 28) for bus services.

The final mile of the path before the turn for **Chinnor** is paralleled by the **Chinnor chalk pits** (both on Map 29) and after the village there is a great stretch of walking on **Chinnor Hill** (Map 30). You'll walk through a **golf course** before two crossing two **railways** in quick succession (both on Map 30). The stage finishes on the outskirts of **Princes Risborough** (Map 31).

Visiting Lewknor About 250m from the M40 is the signposted turning off the Ridgeway for Lewknor (see below). Follow the single lane road to the B4009. When you get there you might wonder why so many cars are parked along the road – they are Oxford Tube/Bus customers (see p47). Cross the road into the layby opposite and take the path from here leading into the trees. This turns into a road, leading you into Lewknor.

LEWKNOR   [MAP 27]

Lewknor is a small, picturesque village, much like many others around here. Easy access to the M40, and therefore London, has added to its value on the property market. It's a very quiet place as nearly all the traffic coming through is for the village itself.

The Oxford Tube and Oxford Bus 'airline' **coach** services (see box on p47) stop on the B4009, just off junction 6 of the M40 near Lewknor. Carousel's link40 **bus** (High Wycombe to Thame) also stops there. See pp48-51 for details.

At the crossroads in the village, and a good reason to come here, is *Ye Olde Leathern Bottel* (aka *The Leathern Bottle*; ☎ 01844 351482, 🖥 theleathernbottle.co.uk; food Tue-Sat noon-2pm & 6-9pm, Sun noon-3pm). Note that they close in the afternoon during the week (Tue-Sat 2.30-5.30pm) and also at 5pm on Sundays. At the time of writing they were only open outside – they had a marquee in their garden – and were serving a limited menu but it was still varied and included vegetarian options. They also were closed all day on Mondays and weren't certain what would happen in 2021.

Another good reason to visit is for the excellent **B&B** at *Moorcourt Cottage* (☎ 01844 351419, 🖥 moorcourt2002@yahoo .co.uk; 1T en suite, 1S with private bathroom; 🛁; WI-FI; Ⓛ; Apr-end Oct). Accommodation in this picture-perfect house is from £42.50pp, or £55 if you're on your own. The friendly owners will even pick you up from where the Ridgeway joins the road to Lewknor, saving you a fairly tedious stretch of road walking at the end of the day. This is another popular place for walkers to stay so be sure to book well in advance. If arranged in advance they will transport your luggage to your next destination on the Way; a charge is made. Credit cards are not accepted.

M40 motorway You'll probably hear the M40 motorway up ahead long before you see it. There are no two ways about it: this motorway completely dominates the countryside it passes through, especially as it runs along an embankment at this point. Luckily for walkers there is a large **tunnel** underneath which is without murals, unlike the tunnel under the A34 near East Ilsley. About 250m east of the tunnel is a path into the **Aston Rowant Discovery Trail** (see box on p36 for details).

Kingston Blount About half a mile from the Ridgeway you can find **bus stops** at Kingston Blount (Map 28). Services from here are: Carousel's Link40 (Thame to High Wycombe) and Red Rose's No 275 (High Wycombe to Oxford); see pp48-51 for further details.

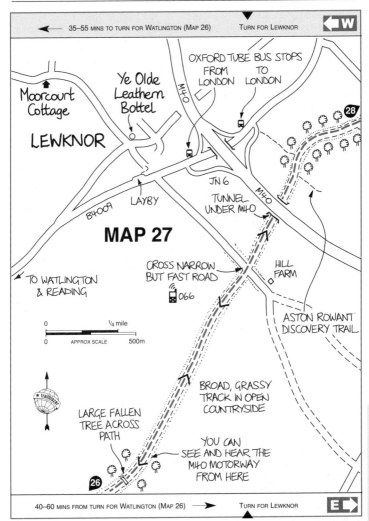

ASTON ROWANT [off MAP 28, p164]
Mercure Lambert Thame Hotel (☎ 01844 351496, 🖳 lambertarms.co.uk; 49D or T, all en suite; ☕; WI-FI; (Ⓛ); 🐾) is part of the Mercure Hotel chain and is situated just under half a mile from the Ridgeway. Rooms cost from £37pp (sgl occ £69)

including breakfast, which is very good value around these parts. What's more, they have a good restaurant and bar, *The Red Kite*, so no more walking is required once you've checked in. They serve dinner every day (6-9pm) – there is a varied menu including such options as fillet of hake with crushed new potatoes, green beans, spinach & parsley cream (£10), or grilled artichoke, Paris mushroom, sunblushed tomato, goat's cheese & tagliatelle (£11.50) as well as more traditional dishes such as local beer-battered cod & chunky chips with butter minted peas (£12). They always have vegetarian, vegan and gluten-free options.

The hotel is about 650m from the Ridgeway. To get there leave the Ridgeway where it crosses the A40 at Beacon Cottage (Map 28). Follow the A40 in the signposted direction of **Postcombe** and cross over the staggered junction with the B4009, keeping on the A40. You'll be able to see the hotel just up ahead, on your left – it's the Tudor-style building.

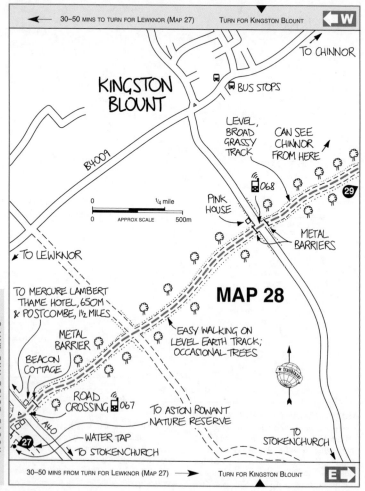

MAP 28

Chinnor chalk pits To the south of Chinnor are several huge pits that were quarried out to provide chalk for the local cement works (Map 29). The works closed in 1999 and the site is now a housing estate. However, the Ridgeway passes between the pits and although it's not easy to get a proper view of them, most have water at the bottom. On a sunny day, this can be bright turquoise which contrasts with the brilliant white chalk-pit sides – a bizarre sight in the middle of this countryside. In the summer you'll probably come across security guards patrolling the perimeter of the pits to prevent people from swimming in them.

Oakley Hill nature reserve (⌨ bbowt.org.uk/nature-reserves/oakley-hill), run by Berks, Bucks & Oxon Wildlife Trust (see p63) is just to the south of the pits and there is a path leading to the reserve from the Ridgeway.

Visiting Chinnor When you reach the main road that crosses the Ridgeway (Map 29), you'll see a signpost pointing down the road to Chinnor. Follow the road for about a third of a mile/500m into the village. Although Chinnor is a large village there isn't a great deal here, so if you don't want to go on the railway (see below) you might want to keep walking.

CHINNOR [MAP 29, p167]

In the 19th century this place was well known for producing lace and chair legs. The Chiltern beech forests were the source of wood for the legs. In the early 20th century a cement factory was opened and this steadily expanded as new technology allowed for ever-increasing production levels. The population in the village grew as the works expanded but they were eventually closed in 1999.

One thing that has survived is the railway line between Chinnor and Princes Risborough along which **Chinnor & Princes Risborough Railway** now run steam trains. By 1961 the line from Watlington to Chinnor had closed completely, though the section from Chinnor to Princes Risborough was used by the cement factory. In the early 1970s Chinnor station and platform were demolished and by the late '80s all freight traffic had ceased. However, within five years the wholly volunteer-run Chinnor & Princes Risborough Railway Association had rebuilt the platform and station and started running their heritage steam services. Since then the volunteers have extended the line and trains can now reach Princes Risborough station providing an 8-mile (12.9km) return trip. Services were suspended during COVID-19 but at the time of writing were just restarting on a trial basis; normally steam and vintage diesel services run most Sundays and the *tea room* is open for walkers. For updates, check their website (⌨ chinnorrailway.co .uk), before making your way down there.

Services

The village is centred on Church Rd where there is a line of shops. This comprises a **supermarket**, Manor Stores (☎ 01844 354925, ⌨ nisalocally.co.uk; Mon-Sat 6.30am-9pm, Sun 7.30am-9pm), **Lloyds Pharmacy** (Mon-Fri 9am-6pm, Sat to 1pm), and Godwins **Bakery** (☎ 01844 690589; **fb**; Mon-Fri 6am-5pm, Sat 6am-3pm) where you can find some good lunch items such as vegan spicy chickpea rolls, sausage breakfast pasties and peppered steak slices (£1.60-2.20).

The **post office** (Mon-Fri 9am-5.30pm, Sat to 2pm) is just around the corner on the High St. There is an **ATM** outside the Co-op petrol station on Oakley Rd and also a Co-op **supermarket** (daily 6am-11pm) and a **public toilet** here.

Both Carousel's Link40 (Thame to High Wycombe) **bus** service and Redline's No 320 to Princes Risborough stop at the

Village Centre and Red Lion. Red Rose's No 275 (High Wycombe to Oxford) stops at the Village Hall (next to the Crown pub) and the Village Centre; see pp48-51 for further details.

If you want a **taxi** call Chinnor Cabs (☎ 01844 353637, 💻 chinnorcabs.co.uk).

Where to stay near Chinnor

There is nowhere to stay in the village itself, but a very good B&B close to the Ridgeway (about 300m from it) is *The Courtyard* (Map 30; ☎ 07815 562921, 💻 wainhill.co.uk; 1D en suite; WI-FI; ⓛ; 🐾) at **Wainhill**. The large, stylish and comfortable room is in a detached wooden lodge, separate from the main cottage, and costs from £62.50pp (sgl occ room rate) for a single-night stay but the rate is discounted for stays of two nights or more. You'll need to book well in advance for this place.

It would also be worth checking **Airbnb** (see pp20-1) which was showing a couple of options when we checked.

Where to eat and drink

A good place for a break is *Village Centre* (☎ 01844 353733, 💻 chinnorvillagecentre .org); the staff are friendly and the menu includes tea, coffee, breakfasts and toasted sandwiches but at the time of writing they were open limited days/hours (Tue-Thur

9.30am-2.30pm) and booking was required. When they have more volunteers they hope to return to their normal hours (Mon-Fri 9am-4pm, Sat 9.30am-2.30pm).

There are two Indian restaurants in the village: *Duo Chefs* (☎ 01844 353752, 💻 duochinnor.com; daily noon-2.30pm & 6-11pm) in the 'centre' and *Chinnor Indian Cuisine* (☎ 01844 354843, 💻 chinnor indiancuisine.co.uk; Tue-Sat 5.30-11pm, Sun noon-3pm & 5.30-10pm) a couple of minutes' walk from the 'centre'.

If a Chinese takeaway is more your thing head to *Golden Chopsticks* (☎ 01844 354284; Mon & Wed-Sun 5.30-9.30pm).

Alternatively, there is the rather grandly named *Kingston Fisheries* (☎ 01844 353874; Mon-Thur 5-9pm, Fri noon-1.30pm & 5-9.30pm, Sat noon-1.30pm & 5-9pm). It's the only fish & chip shop in the village.

Our favourite pub, though food is not served, is the *Red Lion* (☎ 01844 353468, 💻 theredlionchinnor.co.uk; WI-FI; 🐾; bar Mon-Thur 4-11pm, Fri 2-11pm, Sat noon-11pm, Sun noon-10pm), a freehouse which has four handpumps serving interesting real ales from all over the country.

The Crown (☎ 01844 351244; **fb**; WI-FI; 🐾 but not in restaurant; food Mon-Sat 10am-3pm, Sun 10am-4pm) on Station Rd; it does breakfasts as well as lunches.

Chinnor Hill For about a mile the Ridgeway follows a track contouring the shady, wooded slopes of Chinnor Hill (Map 30). This really is a lovely section of the walk in all seasons. The hill rises on one side of the track and, on the other side, you get occasional views through the trees across the countryside below. This area is a **nature reserve** and there are several paths branching off, leading up the hillside further into the woods. Near the top of the hill there are **three ancient barrows**.

Golf course The path cuts through **Princes Risborough Golf Course**. No navigation across the fairways is necessary as the route is fenced in with hedges and trees.

Railway crossings The Ridgeway crosses two sets of railway tracks – one via a **level crossing** and the other over the top of a tunnel. It hardly needs to be mentioned to take great care at the level crossing – it's on a bend so visibility is limited in both directions. You can take a more leisurely approach when crossing the other set of tracks, walking on the roof of **Saunderton Tunnel**. The station north of here is Princes Risborough and to the south it's Saunderton.

Kingston Fisheries

Chinnor Indian Cuisine

B4009

TO PRINCES RISBOROUGH

TO THAME

Red Lion

Golden Chopsticks

BUS STOPS

SHADY TRACK, CLIMBING GENTLY

Village Centre

LLOYDS PHARMACY

30

CHINNOR

Godwins Bakery

MANOR STORES

The Crown

Duo Chefs

CO-OP PETROL STATION, SHOP, ATM & TOILET

POST OFFICE

B4009

BUS STOP

BENCH

CHINNOR & PRINCES RISBOROUGH RAILWAY STATION

TO LEWKNOR & WATLINGTON

0.70

'STEPPING HILL' & 'GREENWAY' PRIVATE HOUSES

CHALK PIT

SPACE FOR CARS TO PARK

PREVIOUSLY CHINNOR CEMENT & LIME WORKS, NOW A HOUSING ESTATE

trailblazer

CHALK PIT

CHALK PIT

TO BLEDLOW RIDGE

069

MAP 29

PATH TO OAKLEY HILL NATURE RESERVE - GOOD VIEWS OVER CHINNOR AND FURTHER NORTH FROM UP HERE

0   ¼ mile

CHALKY TRACK

0   APPROX SCALE   500m

28

Between these two stations the double track divides for about two miles before rejoining, hence the need for two crossings at this point.

Visiting Princes Risborough The Ridgeway follows the outskirts of this town. Unless you're heading east and need the railway station, the best way into Princes Risborough is along New Rd (Map 31) which conveniently leads to a roundabout near the top of the High St.

W← PRINCES RISBOROUGH TO WATLINGTON   [MAPS 31-26]

[Route section begins on Map 31, p170] Although this **11.2 mile/18km (3½-5¼hrs)** section of the Ridgeway is pleasant enough, it's fairly uneventful. The

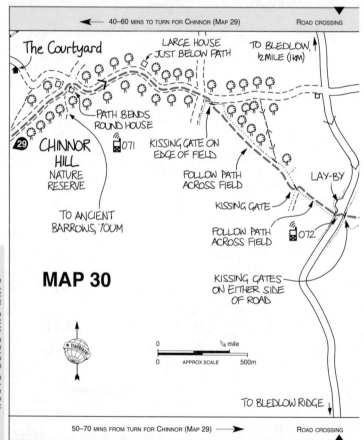

← 40–60 MINS TO TURN FOR CHINNOR (MAP 29)   ROAD CROSSING

The Courtyard

LARGE HOUSE JUST BELOW PATH

TO BLEDLOW, ½ MILE (1KM)

PATH BENDS ROUND HOUSE

29 CHINNOR HILL NATURE RESERVE

📱 071 KISSING GATE ON EDGE OF FIELD

FOLLOW PATH ACROSS FIELD

LAY-BY

KISSING GATE

TO ANCIENT BARROWS, 700M

FOLLOW PATH ACROSS FIELD 📱 072

MAP 30

KISSING GATES ON EITHER SIDE OF ROAD

★ trailblazer

0   ¼ mile
0   APPROX SCALE   500m

TO BLEDLOW RIDGE

50–70 MINS FROM TURN FOR CHINNOR (MAP 29) →   ROAD CROSSING

walking is easy with few steep sections so you can really slow down, relax and enjoy the scenery.

Leaving **Princes Risborough**, there is a section of dull road walking to get you back out into the countryside. You'll need to cross two railways in quick succession before walking through a **golf course** (both on Map 30). It's after here that the countryside walking starts again in earnest and eventually you'll reach the track through the woods on **Chinnor Hill** (Map 30) – this is a lovely stretch of walking. Once past the turn for **Chinnor**, the path is paralleled by the **Chinnor chalk pits** (both on Map 29) for around a mile.

You'll pass turnings for **Kingston Blount** (Map 28) where there are bus stops and **Aston Rowant** for Mercure Lambert Thame Hotel (off Map 28).

← 35–50 MINS   LONGWOOD FARM ◄W

31

TO SAUNDERTON

PATH HEADS STRAIGHT ACROSS FIELD

CROSS RAILWAY ON TOP OF SAUNDERTON TUNNEL 074

LEVEL CROSSING

PATH CUTS THROUGH PRINCES RISBOROUGH GOLF COURSE

KISSING GATE

CROSS FIELD

PATH ACROSS FIELD

WALK BETWEEN MEADOWS

COWS

FOLLOW PATH ROUND THE SIDE OF THE HOUSE

GATE ON EDGE OF WOODS

FOLLOW EDGE OF FIELD AS IT BENDS ROUND

BENCH

STEEP PATH ON LODGE HILL

NOTE SIGNPOST SAYS YOU GO OVER THE STILE; YOU DON'T!!

STEEP PATH ON HILLSIDE

WALK DOWN DRIVE FOR LONGWOOD FARM 073

TO BRADENHAM, 2½ MILES (4KM)

SAUNDERTON LEE

35–50 MINS →   LONGWOOD FARM ►E

ROUTE GUIDE AND MAPS

Shortly after crossing under the **M40 motorway** you can take a diversion into **Lewknor** (both on Map 27), or continue on the good, mainly level track to the turn for **Watlington** (Map 26).   *[Next route overview on p158]*

PRINCES RISBOROUGH

This is one of the biggest towns on the Ridgeway. Despite this, the centre is still compact with most of the shops and services occupying the old High St and large supermarkets at either end. As the Ridgeway passes about 400m from the town centre it makes a convenient overnight or lunch stop.

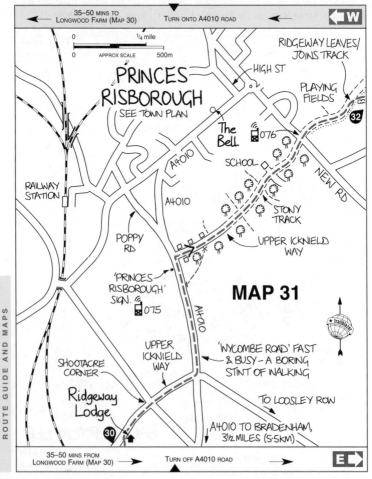

Like many of the towns around here, this one dates back a very long way, possibly to Roman times. The Saxons were certainly here and a couple of hundred years after they arrived there is a mention of this town in the Domesday Book as 'Riseburg'.

Edward, 'The Black Prince', had his palace here in the 14th century, hence the town's name, though the site of the palace is now unfortunately a car park, so not really worth investigating.

The arrival of the railway in 1862 caused the town to grow considerably and by the 1930s the previously separate towns of Princes Risborough and Monks Risborough had merged.

Services

There is a **post office** (☎ 01844 275366; Mon-Fri 9am-5.30pm, Sat to 1pm) by the roundabout at the southern end of town. The library also plays host to the **Information Centre** (✉ lib-prr@bucking hamshire.gov.uk; Tue, Thur & Fri 10am-2pm, Sat to 1pm); they have local information as well as an accommodation list and can make bookings.

On the High St itself you'll also find branches of Barclays, Nationwide and TSB banks, all with **ATMs**.

There is a **supermarket** at either end of the High St: Tesco Superstore (Mon-Sat 6am-11pm, Sun 10am-4pm) at the top – which has **toilets** – and M&S Simply Food (Mon-Fri 8am-8.30pm, Sat to 8pm, Sun 10am-4pm) at the bottom; there are also free public **toilets** in the car park nearby. Next to M&S Simply Food there is a **newsagent** (Mon-Sat 6am-8pm, Sun 7am-8pm).

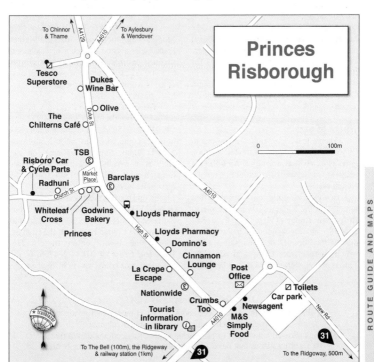

You'll also find two branches of Lloyds Pharmacy, a **chemist**; one at 62-68 High St (☎ 01844 347095; Mon-Fri 8am-6pm, Sat 9am-5.30pm), the other (☎ 01844 343321; Mon-Fri 9am-6pm, Sat to 1pm) is at 52 High St. There's also a shop for **cyclists**, Risboro' Car and Cycle Parts (☎ 01844 273092, 🖳 risborocarcycleparts.co .uk; Mon-Sat 9am-5pm, Sun 10.30am-12.30pm), on Church St, where the staff will repair your bike.

There is a **market** in the High St every Thursday (9am-3pm) and a bi-monthly farmers' market (🖳 princesrisborough towncouncil.gov.uk).

Transport

Unlike in many of the surrounding towns the railway line is still open; Chiltern Railways operates **train** services between London Marylebone & Aylesbury/Banbury; see box on p46.

Arriva's No 300 and Redline's No 321 **bus** services (High Wycombe to Aylesbury) pass through; Redline's No 320 also operates from here to Chinnor. See pp48-51 for further details.

If you need a **taxi** contact Risborough Cars (☎ 01844 274111, 🖳 risboroughcars .co.uk).

Where to stay

It's a shame that accommodation options in Princes Risborough are so limited as it's a good place to stop overnight. **Airbnb** (see pp20-1) was advertising two options when we checked.

However, slightly out of town, but directly on the Ridgeway, is a great place: *Ridgeway Lodge* (Map 31; ☎ 01844 345438, 🖳 ridgewaylodge.co.uk; 1D/1T private facilities/1D or T en suite; WI-FI) which charges from £50pp (sgl occ £78). This is a very well-run B&B in a beautiful

location; however, at the time of research it was closed but the proprietor expects to open in 2021 though may not accept advance bookings for a single night on a Saturday. The double and twin are only let to a group and in that case the facilities are shared.

Where to eat and drink

Crumbs Too (☎ 01844 344462, 🖳 crumbs too.co.uk; WI-FI; 🐾; Mon-Sat 8am-5pm, Sun 9am-5pm), at the southern end of the High St, continues to be a popular stop for coffee, cakes and lunchtime bites. At the time of research they are open on Sundays but this may not be the case in 2021.

Also on the High St, *La Crepe Escape* (☎ 01844 275600; **fb**; WI-FI; Mon-Sat 10am-4pm, Sun to 3pm) is very popular, serving both sweet and savoury crêpes from around £4-7; vegetarian, vegan, gluten- and dairy-free options are available.

Godwins Bakery (☎ 01844 347187; Mon-Fri 6am-4pm, Sat to 3pm), on Market Place, sells a good selection of cakes and savoury pastries. *The Chilterns Café* (☎ 01844 273223; **fb**; WI-FI; Mon-Sat 7.30am-4pm) is worth a look too for all-day breakfasts, baguettes and salads.

There's a good choice of curry houses for such a small town. *Cinnamon Lounge* (☎ 01844 345654, 🖳 cinnamonloungeris borough.com; Mon-Sat noon-2.30pm & 5.30-11.30pm, Sun noon-10pm), on the High St, is usually busy, but for a quieter Indian meal try *Olive* (☎ 01844 274443, 🖳 oliveindianrestaurantpr.co.uk; daily 5-11pm), on Duke St; there is also *Radhuni* (☎ 01844 273741, 🖳 radhunihp27.co.uk; Mon-Sat noon-2pm & 6-11pm, Sun noon-2pm to 6-10pm), on Church St, just off the High St.

In the town centre, there's *The Whiteleaf Cross* (☎ 01844 274706, 🖳 the whiteleafcross.co.uk; WI-FI; 🐾 on lead; bar

---

SYMBOLS USED IN TEXT

🛁 Bathtub in, or for, at least one room   WI-FI means wi-fi is available

Ⓛ packed lunch available if requested in advance

🐾 Dogs allowed but subject to prior arrangement for accommodation (see p197)

fb signifies places that have a Facebook page (for latest opening hours)

Sun-Wed noon-11pm, Thur & Sat to midnight, Fri to 12.30am). At the time of research their kitchen is closed because of COVID so they are allowing customers to bring food in but that will change once their kitchen can reopen and then they are likely to serve food daily (Mon-Sat noon-9pm, Sun to 4pm). Just down from the library, there is *The Bell* (Map 31; ☎ 01844 274702; **fb**; WI-FI; 🐾; bar Sun-Thur noon-11pm, Fri & Sat noon-midnight).

For a more interesting selection of drinks, and a stylish location head to *Dukes*

Wine Bar (☎ 01844 274060, 🖳 dukeswine bar.co.uk; WI-FI; 🐾; food Tue-Sat noon-2pm & 6-9pm, bar Tue-Sat noon-3pm & 5.30-10pm, Sun 4-8pm).

There is also a very busy fish & chip shop on Market Place called *Princes* (☎ 01844 343751; **fb**; Mon-Thur & Sat 11.30am-9.30pm, Fri to 10pm).

Finally, for late-night fodder there's a branch of the pizza joint *Domino's* (☎ 01844 344244, 🖳 dominos.co.uk/princesrisborough; daily 11am-11pm), for take away or delivery.

E➔ PRINCES RISBOROUGH TO WIGGINTON (& TRING)
[MAPS 31-37]

This section is **12½ miles/20km (5½-8¼hrs)**, but be aware that there are many steep ups and downs to tire you out before the end is in sight. A great deal of the walking is through mature woodlands on good paths and there is plenty of variety.

The first task of the day is to climb to the top of **Whiteleaf Hill** before descending the other side to **Cadsden** (both on Map 32). You'll pass by **Chequers**, the Prime Minister's country house, shortly after which is a **farm shop** (both on Map 33). This is followed by some very enjoyable woodland walking, marked with **acorn guideposts**, to take you to the top of **Coombe Hill** (both on Map 33) where there's a **Boer War monument** and stunning views. Descend to the attractive and useful town of **Wendover** following the route past **St Mary the Virgin church** and into more woodland walking through **Barn Wood** and **Hale Wood** (all on Map 34). Decide whether to avoid a stretch of the path in a **ditch** (Map 35) before reaching the turn for **Hill Farm Campsite** (off Map 35). More woodland walking follows, before you reach **Hastoe** then **Tring Park** (both on Map 36), after which you'll find the turn for **Wigginton** (Map 37).

If you decide you want to walk right through **to Ivinghoe Beacon** in one day, be prepared for a tough time. On paper the **17½ miles/28km** doesn't sound unreasonable but the steep up and down sections will leave you weary well before you get your first sight of the Beacon. From there it's a strenuous last few miles to the end. Then there is the matter of walking from the Beacon to accommodation or to transport – a walk into Ivinghoe village is entirely possible but that would add another couple of miles. For this reason, starting the last day from somewhere closer, such as Wendover or Wigginton, can make a lot of sense. It'll also mean you'll have some energy left at the end of the day to celebrate finishing the Ridgeway.

Whiteleaf Hill In whichever direction you are walking, you'll have to endure a steep climb up to the top of **Whiteleaf Hill Nature Reserve** (Map 32; 🖳 chilternsociety.org.uk/our-sites/whiteleaf-hill); this nature reserve is known for

ROUTE GUIDE AND MAPS

its variety of butterflies and wild flowers. Even if you're not looking specifically, you're bound to notice a chalkhill blue butterfly (see opp p65) or two and you'll probably also see the common blue. Flowers that grow well on this chalky soil have wonderful names, such as squinancy wort and viper's bugloss.

On the west side of the hill, facing Monks Risborough, there is a chalk cross on a triangular base cut into the hill – the **Whiteleaf Cross**. The history of this monument is hazy to say the least, but it was recorded as far back as the mid 1750s. It's probably been enlarged since then and now a concerted effort has been made to restore and maintain it. There are fantastic views from up here across Princes Risborough and to Chinnor Hill.

Cadsden The Ridgeway passes through a part of this hamlet (Map 32), but the only thing of interest to the walker will be the pub, *The Plough* (☎ 01844 343302, 🖥 ploughatcadsden.co.uk; 4D or T/1Tr, all en suite; 🛢; WI-FI; ⓛ; 🐾 bar area only). It's a popular place and they charge from £42.50pp (sgl occ room rate) for B&B.

The menu (**food** Mon noon-2pm, Tue-Fri noon-2pm & 6-9pm, Sat noon-3pm & 6-9pm, Sun lunch sittings at noon & 2.30pm) includes fish & chips (£14.95), burgers/veggie burgers (from £12.95). The lunch menu includes a choice of baguettes and jacket potatoes for £5-6.50; on Sundays they serve a roast (from £12.95). At the time of research (because of COVID) booking is required for meals but this may have changed by the time you read this. The pub itself is open Monday-Friday 11am-3pm & 5-10pm, Saturday 11am-9pm, Sunday noon-6pm. For dogs and walkers (!) there is a **water tap** in the pub's garden on the other side of the road.

Chequers There are sections of steep woodland walking either side of the **Chequers Estate** (Map 33) but its isolated position in the middle of the valley floor makes it impossible to miss. The dwelling you might be able to see today dates from the 16th century though there has been a house on this site since the 12th century. Over time, Chequers has been modified by its various inhabitants, but a Mr Arthur Lee and his wife Ruth restored the house to its original Tudor glory in the early part of the 20th century. During World War I Chequers was used as a hospital and convalescent home after which it was donated to the then prime minister, David Lloyd George, by the Lees. Since then it has been at the disposal of the current serving Prime Minister, though now it isn't used as much as it previously was. Although the route cuts straight across the driveway to Chequers, no other part of the grounds or the house is open to the public. Naturally, security around here is tight: you'll certainly see surveillance cameras and perhaps police on patrol.

Farm shop Just 100m off the Ridgeway, south of the Chequers Estate is **Buckmoorend Farm Shop & Kitchen** (Map 33; ☎ 01296 624425, 🖥 buckmoorendfarm.co.uk; 🐾; **shop** Tue 10am-4pm, Wed-Fri 10am-6pm, Sat & Sun to 4pm; **food** Fri-Sun 10am-4pm). They serve hot food, snacks, drinks and icecreams from their kitchen and have a shop packed with interesting local produce. They also have an outdoor seating area.

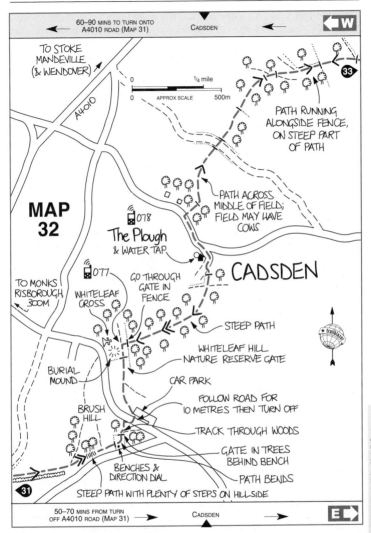

CADSDEN

W

TO STOKE MANDEVILLE (& WENDOVER)

A4010

MAP 32

078

The Plough & WATER TAP

077

TO MONKS RISBOROUGH 300M

WHITELEAF CROSS

BURIAL MOUND

BRUSH HILL

31

GO THROUGH GATE IN FENCE

PATH RUNNING ALONGSIDE FENCE, ON STEEP PART OF PATH

PATH ACROSS MIDDLE OF FIELD; FIELD MAY HAVE COWS

33

CADSDEN

STEEP PATH

WHITELEAF HILL NATURE RESERVE GATE

CAR PARK

FOLLOW ROAD FOR 10 METRES THEN TURN OFF

TRACK THROUGH WOODS

GATE IN TREES BEHIND BENCH

PATH BENDS

BENCHES & DIRECTION DIAL

STEEP PATH WITH PLENTY OF STEPS ON HILL-SIDE

Acorn guideposts Between Chequers and Coombe Hill there is some great walking through **mature woodland** and thankfully it stays fairly level for some time. However, there are many other paths through the woods here and you'll need to look out for the black 'acorn' guideposts and the occasional Ridgeway signpost, to keep on the right path.

ROUTE GUIDE AND MAPS

Coombe Hill There is a monument and **trig point** (Map 33) on the north-west corner of Coombe Hill and the Ridgeway visits both. This is a very popular place for day-trippers and it's quite surprising to see so many people up here. The **monument** commemorates those men from Buckinghamshire who were killed in the Boer War. It was completed in 1904 but had to be partially rebuilt in 1939 after being damaged when struck by lightning. If heading east, do not take the obvious gravel path as you leave the monument as this goes to a car park, not **Wendover**. Take the path to the left of it.

WENDOVER   [see map p180]

Even if the Ridgeway didn't go straight through the centre of Wendover it would still be a good idea to stop off here. It's an attractive town with a compact centre where all the shops and services you are likely to need are located.

This town was mentioned in the **Domesday Book** but probably dates from a good deal earlier than that. Its position on the road from London to Aylesbury has always ensured it plenty of passing trade and in days gone by it had a large number of inns to cater for weary travellers. There are still some very old pubs to stop off at for a few drinks. Wendover's proximity to London by train also means this is a popular place for city workers to commute from; as a result the town has an air of affluence.

Services

The **post office** (☎ 01296 623378; Mon-Fri 9am-5.30pm, Sat to 4pm) is on the High St along with a branch of Lloyds Pharmacy (☎ 01296 622166; Mon-Fri 9am-6.30pm, Sat to 5.30pm).

Nearby there's a Budgens **supermarket** (☎ 01296 625864, 🖳 budgens.co.uk/our-stores/wendover; Mon-Sat 6.30am-10pm, Sun 9am-6pm) with an **ATM**.

There is a **market** here every Thursday (9am-3pm) and a local produce market on the third Thursday of every month (9am-1pm), both on the pedestrian area outside Budgens.

There is no tourist information centre as such but there are lots of leaflets in **Wendover Community Library** (🖳 www .buckscommunitylibraries.org/wendover; Tue, Thur, Fri & alternate Sat 10am-2pm) and the librarians do their best to help. In the adjacent car park is a noticeboard with contact details for local accommodation and there are free **public toilets** (daily 7am-7.30pm) here too.

Transport

Red Rose's No 50 **bus** service (Aylesbury to Ivinghoe) stops here; Redline's No 50 provides a weekend service but on a slightly different route. Red Rose's No 55 calls here en route between Aylesbury and Amersham; see pp48-51.

Wendover **railway** station is on the Chiltern Line which runs from Aylesbury to London Marylebone; see box on p46.

There is a **taxi** firm called Alexander's (☎ 01296 620888, 🖳 alexandersofwen dover.co.uk) at the railway station.

Where to stay

Just 150m from the Ridgeway, south of the centre of Wendover, is the excellent and stylish, four-star B&B at *Hale House* (Map 34; ☎ 01296 625742, 🖳 halehousebnb.co .uk; 1D private bathroom, 2Tr, all en suite; ☻; WI-FI; ⓛ). As well as offering large and well-appointed guest rooms for £50-62.50pp (sgl occ £90-110) in a modern, eco-friendly house, they also serve award-winning breakfasts. The owner can pick you up or drop you off somewhere further along the Ridgeway and offers a discount for stays of two nights or more which means Hale House could be a base for starting or finishing the walk. They can also put a camp bed in one room for a fourth person.

An atmospheric place in which to stay is ***Red Lion Hotel*** (☎ 01296 622266, 🖳 red lionhotelwendover.co.uk; 2S/17D/3T, all en suite; ☻; WI-FI; ⓛ; 🐾). This is a 16th-century coaching inn that used to be the start/end point for coaches to/from London.

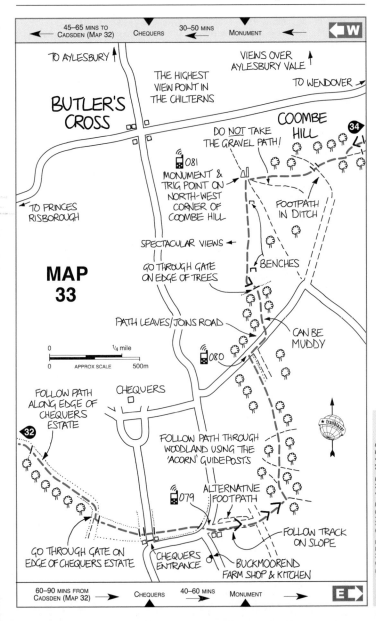

TO AYLESBURY ↑

THE HIGHEST VIEW POINT IN THE CHILTERNS

VIEWS OVER AYLESBURY VALE ↑

TO WENDOVER →

BUTLER'S CROSS

COOMBE HILL

34

DO NOT TAKE THE GRAVEL PATH!

📱 081

MONUMENT & TRIG POINT ON NORTH-WEST CORNER OF COOMBE HILL

TO PRINCES RISBOROUGH

FOOTPATH IN DITCH

SPECTACULAR VIEWS ←

GO THROUGH GATE ON EDGE OF TREES

MAP 33

BENCHES

PATH LEAVES/JOINS ROAD

CAN BE MUDDY

0 ¼ mile

0 APPROX SCALE 500m

📱 080

FOLLOW PATH ALONG EDGE OF CHEQUERS ESTATE

CHEQUERS

32

★ trailblazer

FOLLOW PATH THROUGH WOODLAND USING THE 'ACORN' GUIDEPOSTS

📱 079

ALTERNATIVE FOOTPATH

FOLLOW TRACK ON SLOPE

GO THROUGH GATE ON EDGE OF CHEQUERS ESTATE

CHEQUERS ENTRANCE

BUCKMOOREND FARM SHOP & KITCHEN

ROUTE GUIDE AND MAPS

The front of the hotel looks as if it has changed little since those days and it really is a place worth stopping off at even if you are not staying here – but if you are you can have a very comfortable room from £39.50pp (sgl £69). They also have two rooms which sleep a couple and up to two children but these are not suitable for a group of adults. This is another popular place so book well in advance.

The **Airbnb** website (see pp20-1) advertises a handful of options in Wendover so is worth checking out.

Where to eat and drink

If you want something quick you have several good choices. A popular place is *Whitewaters Deli Café* (☎ 01296 623331; WI-FI; Mon-Sat 9am-5pm, Sun 9.30am-4pm); it serves delicious cakes, sandwiches and salads and has at least one vegan options.

Close by, *Rumsey's Chocolaterie* (☎ 01296 625060, 💻 rumseys.co.uk/pages/rumseys-wendover; WI-FI; 🐈; daily 9.30am-5.30pm) specialises in handmade chocolates, but also serves breakfasts, tea,

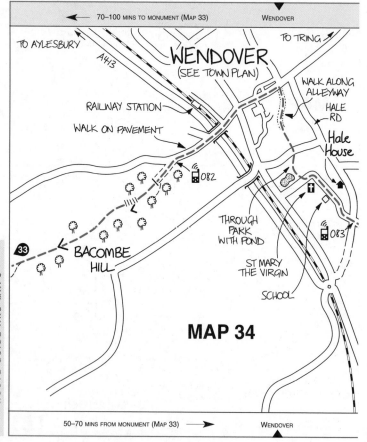

ROUTE GUIDE AND MAPS

coffee and light lunches. There's also ***Crumbs Café*** (☎ 01296 820238; WI-FI; Mon-Sat 8am-5.30pm, Sun 9am-5pm) which serves all-day breakfasts, paninis and burgers with generous portion sizes; ***The Bakers Shop*** (☎ 01296 624642; daily 6am-6pm) for rolls, cakes and milkshakes; and finally, for something more traditional, there's ***Lady Grey Tearoom*** (☎ 07519 834251, 💻 ladygreytearoom.co.uk; 🐕; Wed-Sun 10am-4pm) in a lovely little spot in Barn Courtyard – and thus away from the noise of the traffic on the main drag – with some tasty fare including sandwiches from £5.50 and some tempting afternoon tea (£5-17.50) options.

For more substantial fare, on Pound St, ***Shoulder of Mutton*** (☎ 01296 623223, 💻 chefandbrewer.com; WI-FI; 🐕 bar only; food daily 11.30am-9pm) is a large, old, Chef & Brewer establishment serving a decent range of pub grub such as chicken & woodland mushroom pie (£12.49). There are few vegetarian or vegan options though.

Also on Pound St, ***Tres Corazones*** (☎ 01296 622092, 💻 trescorazones.co.uk;

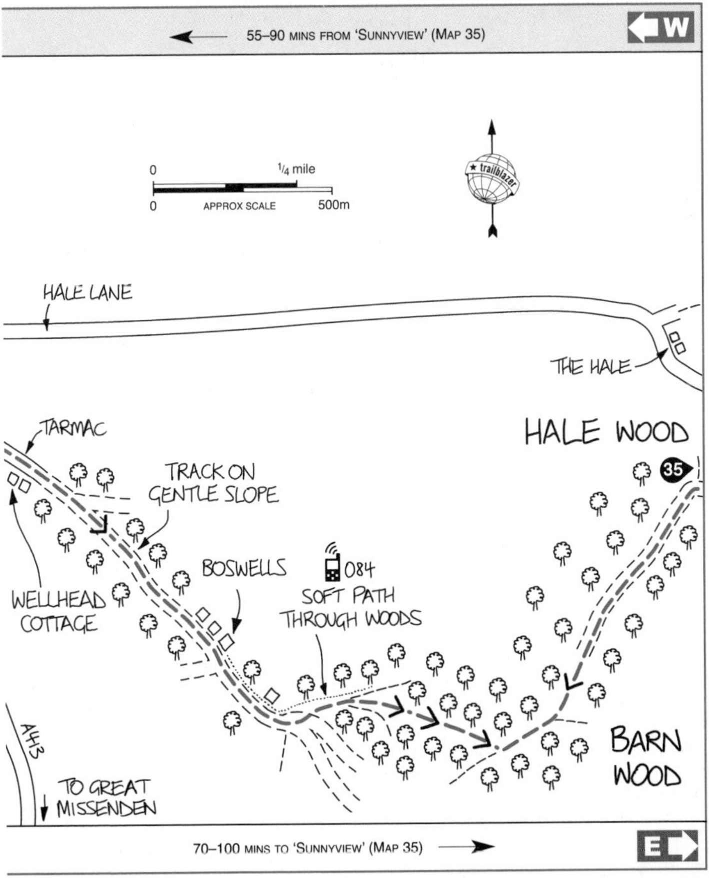

55–90 MINS FROM 'SUNNYVIEW' (MAP 35)
W
0
1/4 mile
0
APPROX SCALE
500m
trailblazer
HALE LANE
THE HALE
TARMAC
HALE WOOD
35
TRACK ON
GENTLE SLOPE
BOSWELLS
084
SOFT PATH
THROUGH WOODS
WELLHEAD
COTTAGE
A413
TO GREAT
MISSENDEN
BARN
WOOD
70–100 MINS TO 'SUNNYVIEW' (MAP 35)
E

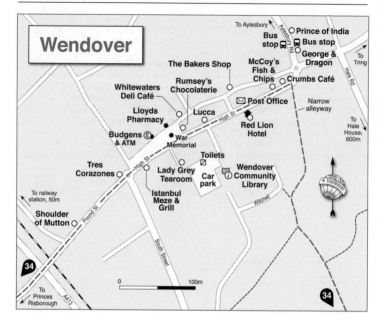

Wendover

To Aylesbury
Prince of India
Bus stop
Bus stop
McCoy's Fish & Chips
George & Dragon
To Tring
The Bakers Shop
Crumbs Café
Rumsey's Chocolaterie
Whitewaters Deli Café
Post Office
Narrow alleyway
Lloyds Pharmacy
Lucca
High St.
Red Lion Hotel
To Hale House, 600m
Budgens & ATM
War Memorial
Toilets
Tres Corazones
High St.
Lady Grey Tearoom
Car park
Wendover Community Library
To railway station, 50m
Pound St.
Istanbul Meze & Grill
Witchell
Shoulder of Mutton
South Street
0   100m
34
To Princes Risborough
A413
34

Wed noon-3pm & 5-9pm, Thur noon-2.30pm & 5.30-9pm, Fri & Sat noon-10pm, Sun noon-6pm) is a spacious tapas restaurant with most dishes around the £6-7 mark and plenty of vegetarian and vegan choices.

On High St, the bar at *Red Lion Hotel* (see Where to stay; food Mon-Fri 7-10am & noon-9pm, Sat 8-10.30am & noon-9pm, Sun 8-10.30am & noon-8pm) serves a full English breakfast for £10.50 (vegan option £9.50) and has four real ales that change on a regular basis but they always have London Pride. The restaurant menu varies but usually includes burgers (£12.75) and fish & chips (£13.25).

On the other side of the road, you'll find *Lucca* (☎ 01296 696380, 🖥 luccarestaurant.co.uk; Tue-Thur noon-3pm & 5-9pm, Fri-Sun noon-9pm, Sun noon-3pm); it's a friendly place with a large array of tasty Italian dishes on offer, including pizzas (£9.95-13), pasta (£10-12.95) and salads (£11.95-12.95).

There's also *Istanbul Meze & Grill* (☎ 01296 709276, 🖥 istanbulwendover.com; Tue-Sun 9.30am-11pm) a Mediterranean restaurant with a wide selection of kebabs, moussakas, and seafood, with vegetarian options.

Just down from the post office is a chippy, *McCoy's Fish & Chips* (☎ 01296 708243; daily noon-2pm & 5-9pm).

Inside the *George & Dragon* (☎ 01296 586152, 🖥 georgeanddragonwendover .com; food Mon-Thur 5-9pm, Fri-Sun noon-2pm & 5-9pm) is a Thai restaurant and takeaway; mains cost from £7.95 (takeaway), or £8.95 if you're eating in.

The *Prince of India* (☎ 01296 623233, 🖥 prince-of-india.co.uk; daily noon-2.30pm & 6-11.30pm), almost next door to the George & Dragon, serves tasty Indian food.

St Mary the Virgin church This church (Map 34), not far from the centre of Wendover, was built in the 14th century and was used briefly as a camp by some of Oliver Cromwell's New Model Army troops during the English Civil War. In the churchyard there are several benches in the shade – a pleasant rest-stop on a hot day.

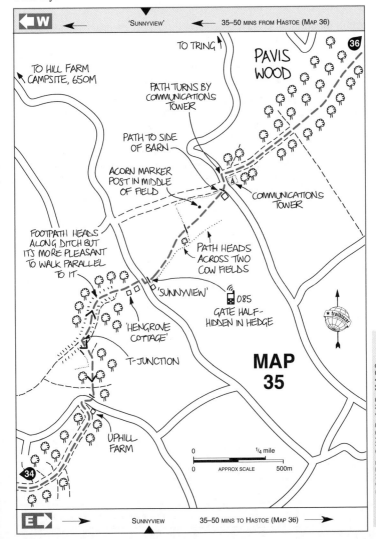

Woodland walking The Ridgeway passes through two woods – **Barn Wood** and the Forestry Commission's **Hale Wood** (both on Map 34) – on decent trails and mainly level, except for the western side of Barn Wood. This is a lovely walk surrounded by mature woodlands including many conifer trees and plenty of bluebells in the spring. Although there are good views to Wendover from here, the wood blocks them for most of the time.

Ditch avoidance There is a section of ditch (Map 35) that the Ridgeway follows for several hundred metres. The official signposts send you to the bottom of the steep ditch and along it, but there is also a path running through the woodland parallel to it which is far preferable. Having walked in the ditch I wouldn't recommend it unless you like muddy boots and swarms of flies for company.

Route to campsite *Hill Farm Campsite* (☎ 01296 630819, 🖳 hillfarmcamp site.co.uk; 🐕 on lead) is about 1½ miles from the Ridgeway. Simply follow the road north at Sunnyview House until you see the campsite on your left. There is no pavement on the road, but most of the way there is a verge to hop onto when cars are passing. This small, well-run campsite has 10 pitches (from £10pp for Ridgeway walkers). The rate includes toilet, shower and washing up facilities as well as use of a kettle, an electric socket and free tea/coffee. On the same site but managed differently are six pre-pitched tents (☎ 07703 020329,

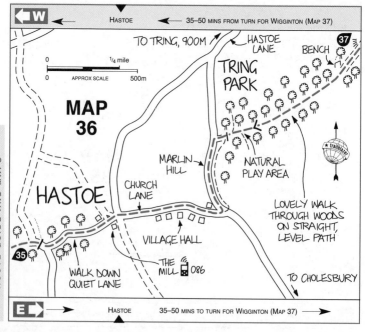

⌨ prepitchedtents@gmail.com). Options include a three-man tent sleeping up to two people on camp beds (from £35 per night), and a six-man tent sleeping up to four for £45 as well as larger tents. A luxury bell tent (£230-260 min two nights; 1D but can add camp beds for children) is also available. The facilities mentioned above are available to people staying in a pre-pitched tent but they can also hire a fire pit and BBQ and buy wood, firelighters and matches; a solar-powered charger is also available.

Hastoe The Ridgeway follows the road through this tiny **hamlet** (Map 36) and there's little to stop for, but at the eastern end of the hamlet, where the Ridgeway goes up Marlin Hill, there is a **convenient route into Tring**. Simply follow Marlin Hill north for about ¾ mile, all downhill, and you'll enter Tring near the Natural History Museum after having gone under the A41.

Tring Park Leased to the **Woodland Trust** (see p64), this park used to be much bigger but in 1974 the A41 was cut straight through the centre of it in an east–west direction. The manor house is now located in the top half, while the Ridgeway passes through the bottom half. It's a really enjoyable section of the walk along decent paths with plenty of wildlife to look out for, including fallow deer.

Visiting Wigginton or Tring The Ridgeway passes about 750m from the 'centre' of **Wigginton** (Map 37) and it's a good place to stay the night if you are heading east and want a relaxed last day of walking up to Ivinghoe Beacon. From either of the two places where the Ridgeway crosses the road north of the village, it's about 800m along the road to the pub.

You can also reach **Tring** from either of these road crossings. Follow either road north, cross under the A41, go past the Tesco Superstore and follow the road to Tring's High St, about 1½ miles from the Ridgeway.

The advantage staying in Tring has over Wigginton is that there are far more facilities, but Wigginton is closer to the Ridgeway so you'll have to take into account the time and effort of walking there and back.

W ← WIGGINTON (& TRING) TO PRINCES RISBOROUGH
[MAPS 37-31]

[Route section begins on Map 37, p185] This section is **12½ miles/20km (5½-8¼hrs)**, but be aware that there are many steep ups and downs to tire you out before the end is in sight. A great deal of the walking is through mature woodlands on good paths and there is plenty of variety.

Shortly after leaving **Wigginton**, walk through the wooded **Tring Park** before emerging near **Hastoe** (both on Map 36). Just after the turn to **Hill Farm Campsite** (off Map 35) you enter more woods and decide whether to avoid a stretch of path in a **ditch** (Map 35). Woodland walking through **Hale Wood** and **Barn Wood** is followed by **St Mary the Virgin church** on the way into **Wendover** (all on Map 34). From here there's a long climb to the top of **Coombe Hill** with its **Boer War monument** and stunning views, before descending through woodland, marked with **acorn guideposts** (all on Map 33). There's a **farm shop** just before you pass by **Chequers** (both on map 33), the Prime Minister's country house. After this you'll reach **Cadsden** at the foot of the steep ascent to the top of **Whiteleaf Hill** (both on Map 32). From the summit you descend to **Princes Risborough** (Map 31).

[Next route overview on p168]

WIGGINTON   [MAP 37]

This small village has been here for centuries. It's probably now best known for the exclusive Champneys Health Spa just out of the village on the Chesham Rd. It's a sleepy place with little to do, but there is good accommodation in the village pub – a perfect place to wind down after a long day on the Ridgeway.

There is no post office, but there is a **village shop** stocked with local produce (☎ 01442 891061, 🖳 wiggintonshop.org.uk; **fb**; Mon, Tue, Thur & Fri 8.30am-4.30pm, Wed & Sat 9.30am-4.30pm, Sun 8.30am-1pm) that also has a *café* which serves tea, coffee, homemade cakes, bacon baps and snacks. Note that hot drinks/food are only served up to 30 minutes before closing and up to an hour before on Sunday.

A **taxi** can be ordered through Diamond Cars (☎ 01442 890303; Diamond also offer luggage transfer between Watlington and Ivinghoe Beacon) which is just as well because Red Rose's No 397 **bus**

to Tring is the only service calling here; see pp48-51.

The Greyhound (☎ 01442 824631, 🖳 greyhoundtring.co.uk; 1D/1T/1Tr; all en suite; WI-FI bar only; ⓛ; 🐾) is the only pub in the village, hence its popularity with the locals – and also deservedly so with walkers, so book well ahead if you want to stay here. The rate (from £37.50pp, sgl occ £60) does not include breakfast and none is available. They are happy to do packed lunches if requested in advance but these are not available till 10am unless you are happy to keep it in your room – but note that the rooms don't have fridges. This friendly place has a changing selection of real ales and their menu (**food** Mon-Sat noon-8.30pm, Sun to 5pm) mainly consists of pub standards (£13-17), though there are a few vegetarian options. They also serve jacket potatoes (£7.95) and a range of ciabattas (£8.95) at lunch times during the week.

TRING   [see map p187]

This is the largest town close to Ivinghoe Beacon. It has all the shops and services you might need and there are good public transport links too. There aren't, however, many places to stay in the town, so you might prefer to make your visit brief.

Like many of the towns in this chain of settlements along the edge of the Chilterns, there is evidence of Saxon settlement in Tring and it's also mentioned in the **Domesday Book**.

The town has always been on a natural pathway and when the **Grand Junction Canal** (now called the **Grand Union Canal**, see box on p189) was cut through here in the late 18th century commerce in the town really started to expand. In the

early 19th century a large **silk mill** was established in Tring and this gave employment to many of the town's women and children. In 1835 a railway was built along the course of the canal which runs to the east of Tring. Although this meant that the railway station (see Map 38) was not built in the town it still further improved Tring's accessibility, especially to London.

You might well expect a museum in this town to include some of this history, but in fact its subject is something altogether different. The **Natural History Museum at Tring** (🖳 nhm.ac.uk/tring; Mon-Sat 10.30am-4.30pm, Sun 1.30-5pm; entry is free, but at the time of writing, you needed to book online in advance) is at the corner of Akeman St and Park St, just a few minutes' walk from the High St. It comprises about 4000 stuffed animals from Walter Rothschild's personal collection. You'll be able to see anything from a coelacanth to a great auk to a platypus. It really is worth a visit!

Services
The **post office** (Mon-Fri 9am-3pm, Sat 9am-noon) can be found on the High St. There are no banks in Tring, but there is an **ATM** outside McColls (see p186).

Tring Information Centre (☎ 01442 823347, 🖥 tring.gov.uk/information-cen tre) was closed at the time of writing and

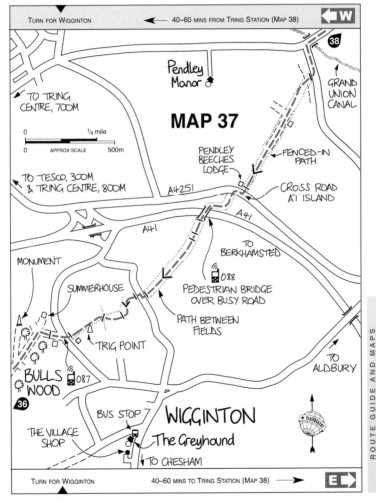

TURN FOR WIGGINTON

◄— 40–60 MINS FROM TRING STATION (MAP 38)

◄W

38

Pendley Manor

GRAND UNION CANAL

TO TRING CENTRE, 700M

MAP 37

0   ¼ mile

0   APPROX SCALE   500m

PENDLEY BEECHES LODGE

FENCED-IN PATH

TO TESCO, 300M & TRING CENTRE, 800M

A4251

CROSS ROAD AT ISLAND

A41

A41

MONUMENT

A41

TO BERKHAMSTED

🕿088

SUMMERHOUSE

PEDESTRIAN BRIDGE OVER BUSY ROAD

PATH BETWEEN FIELDS

TRIG POINT

TO ALDBURY

BULLS 🕿087 WOOD

36

BUS STOP

WIGGINTON

★ trailblazer

THE VILLAGE SHOP

The Greyhound

TO CHESHAM

TURN FOR WIGGINTON

40–60 MINS TO TRING STATION (MAP 38) —►

E►

ROUTE GUIDE AND MAPS

staff were working from home, but you can leave a message or email them. It is conveniently located just off the High St on Akeman St and, when open (generally Mon-Fri 9.30am-3pm, Sat 10am-1pm), has plenty of literature and advice about Tring and the surrounding area and also some information on accommodation

There is an M&S Simply Food **supermarket** (Mon-Sat 8am-9pm, Sun 10am-4pm) in a precinct just off the High St and a Tesco Superstore (Mon-Sat 6am-midnight, Sun 10am-4pm), to the east of town, on London Rd. On the High St there is a McColls supermarket (☎ 01442 890957, 🖳 mccolls.co.uk/storelocator/tring-high-street; Mon-Sat 7am-8pm, Sun 8am-8pm) and also a branch of **Lloyds Pharmacy** (Mon-Fri 9am-6pm, Sat to 5.30pm) can be found on the High St. There's also a **cycle shop** here, Mountain Mania Cycles (☎ 01442 822458, 🖳 mountainmaniacycles.co.uk; Mon, Tue, Thur-Sat 9am-5.30pm, Wed to 7.30pm) at 10 Miswell Lane.

The **farmers' market** (🖳 tringfarmersmarket.co.uk) is held on Church Square on every 2nd and 4th Saturday of the month.

There are free **public toilets** (Mon-Sat 7am-5pm) in the car park.

Transport
Tring is a stop on both London Northwestern's frequent **rail** services from London Euston to Cheddington & Northampton and Southern's (Clapham Junction to Milton Keynes) services; see box on p46.

There is a reasonable number of **bus services** from Tring: Red Rose's No 387 stops both at Church Square in Tring and at the railway station, their 397 at Church Square only, and their 501 at Church Square and also opposite Tesco (London Rd); Red Eagle's No 61 and Arriva's No 500 only stop at Church Square as do Redline's No 50 and 164; see pp48-51 for further details.

If you need a **taxi** you should phone John's Taxis (☎ 01442 828848, 🖳 johns taxisoftring.co.uk), based at Tring Station (Map 38). They frequently taxi Ridgeway walkers around.

Where to stay
In a good location, just off the eastern end of the High St, is *Wellbrook House* (☎ 01442 824912, 🖳 wellbrookhome.com; 2D or T, both shared bathroom; 🛏; WI-FI; 🐾) which charges from £32.50pp (sgl occ £65), but they do not provide breakfast or a packed lunch. It's the first house on the right, behind the Robin Hood pub and is owned by the same people.

About 1¼ miles/2km west of the town centre there is a *Premier Inn* (☎ 0333 321 9101, 🖳 premierinn.com; Tring Hill; 30D, en suite, 🛏; free WI-FI) which has **rooms** from about £41 if you book online and pay at the time of booking; flexible rates are likely to be higher; there is also a Beefeater restaurant (daily Mon-Fri 6.30-10.30am & noon-11pm, Sat 7-10.30am & noon-11pm, Sun 7-10.30am & noon-10.30pm) on site; continental/full English breakfast costs £6.99/8.99.

Much nearer the path and also near Tring Railway Station is *Pendley Manor* (Map 37; ☎ 01442 891891, 🖳 pendleymanor.co.uk; 72 rooms, all en suite; 🛏; WI-FI). The rooms at this hotel include doubles (a few with four-poster beds), twins and 15 rooms which can sleep up to four people. The rates are complex and change according to the day and demand, but you're looking at upwards of about £80pp (sgl occ room rate). The rate includes use of their indoor heated pool and other leisure facilities. **Food** is available throughout the day in either their bar or the restaurant.

If none of the above is suitable or available there is no shortage of options advertised on **Airbnb** (see pp20-1).

Where to eat and drink
If you fancy a lunchtime sandwich head for *P.A.M.S Sandwich Bar* (☎ 01442 824262, 🖳 pamssandwichbar.co.uk; 🐾; Mon-Fri 9am-3pm, Sat 9am-2pm), on the High St. Design your own sandwich, panini, tortilla wrap or breakfast roll.

In the precinct near the M&S, *Sandwich Plus* (☎ 01442 826489, 🖳 sandwich-plus.com; Mon-Fri 8.30am-3pm), a bakery and deli serves sandwiches and some delicious cakes.

Tring

To Ivinghoe, 3¾ miles

Brook St

Station Rd

London Rd

To Pendley Manor, 700m,
Tring Railway Station, 1½ miles
& Aldbury, 2¼ miles

37

37

Bus stops

Tesco
Superstore

To Wigginton, 1¼ miles
& Berkhamsted, 4½ miles

Tring Park

The
Robin
Hood

Wellbrook House

Car park

Olive Limes

High St

The
Espresso
Lounge

Toilets

0   50   100m

Bus stops

Tring Town Council
Information Centre

Post Office

Lussmans

Church Square

Sandwich Plus

M&S Simply Food

McColls

China Town

The Akeman

Natural History
Museum at Tring

Park St

Hastoe Lane

Frogmore St

Ocean Fish & Chips

P.A.M.S Sandwich Bar

Lloyds Pharmacy

High St

Prezzo

Tamarind

Mighty Bite Pizzeria

Akeman St

36

To the
Ridgeway, ¾ mile

Park Rd

Langdon St

High St

Car park

Crockers

Black Goo

To Mountain Mania
Cycles, 300m;
Premier Inn, 1¼ miles
& Aylesbury

Western Rd

The King's
Arms

Coffee shops include the rather swish **Black Goo** (☎ 01442 825937, 💻 blackgoo coffee.co.uk; WI-FI; daily 9am-4pm), at the western end of the High St, and at the other end of the High St is **The Espresso Lounge** (☎ 01442 828228, 💻 theespressolounge.co .uk; WI-FI; Mon-Thur 8.30am-3.30pm, Fri to 4pm, Sat to 5pm, Sun 9am-2.30pm); they serve breakfasts, light lunches and home-made cakes alongside their coffees.

For something special you could try **Crockers** (☎ 01442 828971, 💻 tring.crock ersuk.com; Tue 6-11pm, Wed & Thur noon-2.30pm & 6-11pm, Fri & Sat noon-2.30pm & 6pm-midnight) whose 'dining room' menu includes mains such as Bavette steak with miso mash & bearnaise sauce (£15), or their 'chef's table' where you can watch the chef prepare your food (set menu £100).

Another fine choice is **Lussmanns** (☎ 01442 502250, 💻 lussmanns.com/restau rants/tring; Sun, Mon & Tue noon-9pm, Wed & Thur noon-9.30pm, Fri & Sat noon-10.30pm); it was closed at the time of writing and there's a possibility that it may not reopen in 2021 but it is worth checking as it is highly regarded. Spread over two floors of an old bank, they have a 3-course set menu for £18.50 or interesting mains on their classics menu such as North African spiced organic lamb salad (£14.95), though offer only one vegetarian option.

There are several **Indian restaurants** in Tring. **Tumurind** (☎ 01442 822333; Sun-Thur 6-11.30pm, Fri & Sat 6pm to mid-night) and **Olive Limes** (☎ 01442 828444, 💻 olivelimes.com; Tue-Sun 6-11pm) which has a more contemporary feel. On the High St is a branch of **Prezzo** (☎ 01442 822610, 💻 www.prezzorestaurants.co.uk /restaurant/tring; Mon-Sat noon-11pm, Sun to 10.30pm), another Italian restaurant.

Several **takeaways** are dotted around Tring. They include: **China Town** (☎ 01442 824831; Tue-Thur & Sun 5-10pm, Fri & Sat to 11pm) which serves exactly what you'd expect; **Mighty Bite Pizzeria** (☎ 01442 828556; Sun-Thur 5-11pm, Fri & Sat 1pm-midnight) serving pizzas, burgers and the like; and **Ocean Fish & Chips** (☎ 01442 822524; Mon-Sat 3-9pm).

There are several **pubs** around town that serve food. The most upmarket is **The Akeman** (☎ 01442 826027, 💻 theakeman .co.uk; WI-FI; 🐾 bar area only; food Mon-Sat 8am-10pm, Sun 9am-9pm), a café/pub/restaurant serving Mediterranean-style food. They also serve a pretty good range of breakfasts, with various vegetarian options (£4.50-11). Later on there are brunches, lunches, wood-fired pizzas, grills and salads.

The 16th-century Fuller's pub, **The Robin Hood** (see Wellbrook House, 💻 robinhoodtring.co.uk; WI-FI; 🐾; food Mon-Fri noon-2.15pm & 6-9.15pm, Sat noon-9.15pm, Sun noon-4pm & 6-9.15pm) is a cosy retreat serving large, tasty pub meals such as fish & chips, or ham, egg & chips for £10-12.50. They also have baguettes and sandwiches. On Sunday and Monday evenings they serve a Thai menu.

The most interesting choice is just a short walk away from the western end of the High St; **The King's Arms** (☎ 01442 823318, 💻 kingsarmstring.co.uk; WI-FI; 🐾 on lead; food Mon-Sat noon-2.30pm & 5.30-9pm, Sun noon-4pm) on King St. This is a friendly freehouse on a suburban street serving five real ales in a relaxed atmos-phere. It has won various CAMRA (see box on p22) awards over the years and the food is good too. The menu varies but may include roasted vegetable salad (£10) and beer-battered fish & chips (£12.50).

Outside of the town, both **Pendley Manor** and **Premier Inn** serve food: see Where to stay.

E➔ (TRING &) WIGGINTON TO IVINGHOE BEACON [MAPS 37-39]

This final **5-mile/8km (2¼-4hrs)** section of the Ridgeway may not seem much of a challenge but as most of this stage is uphill, with a steep climb to the fin-ish itself, it'll probably be enough.

The first thing of note on this stage is the long **pedestrian bridge** over the A41 which you must cross. You'll also cross over the **Grand Union Canal** (both on Map 37) and the railway lines outside **Tring Railway Station** (Map 38). Shortly after this there is a turn for **Folly Farm B&B** (off Map 38), and an option to walk to **Aldbury** (Map 38) before you turn off the road for the final three miles to the Beacon. Ascending the tree-lined path you'll reach **Aldbury Nowers** (Map 38) after which the trees thin out. On **Pitstone Hill** you'll arrive at the car park and road crossing followed by some exposed walking before the final steep climb up **Beacon Hill** to finish at **Ivinghoe Beacon** (all on Map 39).

Once at Ivinghoe Beacon what are your options? If you are continuing on foot you could take the steep path down the hillside to the cattle grid on Beacon Rd (Map 39), then walk into **Ivinghoe** (see p195). Be careful as the path is very steep and there are plenty of hidden holes in the ground, plus the B489 road to the village is not particularly wide yet people drive fast. If you get on with it the 1¼-mile/2km walk from the top of Ivinghoe Beacon to Ivinghoe village shouldn't take more than 20-30 minutes. Alternatively you could retrace your steps from Ivinghoe Beacon back down the trail to Tring Railway Station for a train, bus or taxi.

You could arrange for someone with a car to wait for you in one of the car parks near Ivinghoe Beacon – the National Trust car park is closer to the Beacon than the Pitstone Hill car park (both on Map 39). You could also arrange for a taxi (see p186) to pick you up from the National Trust car park and take you to Tring Railway Station or further afield. The closest place to the Beacon from which you could be picked up would be near the cattle grid on Beacon Rd, mentioned above. There is a layby there where someone could wait.

Pedestrian bridge Crossing the crowded A41 dual-carriageway that runs from Bicester down to the M25 is made considerably easier thanks to the pedestrian bridge (Map 37). Opened in 1993 and measuring over a hundred metres long it's quite something, maybe more so when viewed from the road below. You'll also notice that it's not level – the northern end is somewhat lower than the southern.

Grand Union Canal The Ridgeway crosses the Grand Union Canal (Map 37; see box below) on a road bridge on Station Rd. You don't get to see much of the canal from the bridge, but if you feel that you've had enough of the Ridgeway at this point, you could always strike out on the 138-mile Grand Union Canal Walk here. To the north the towpath goes to Gas Street Basin in Birmingham and to the south Thames Lock in Brentford.

❑ **THE GRAND UNION CANAL**

This runs from the River Thames in Brentford, up through the Chilterns via many locks, then on to Birmingham where it finishes 137 miles/220km later. Initially this was the **Grand Junction Canal**, which opened in 1805 and ran only from Brentford, Middlesex, to Braunston, Northamptonshire, to link with the Oxford Canal. In 1929 it was linked to various other branches running up to Birmingham via Warwick and was renamed the Grand Union Canal. Nowadays the main traffic on the canal is boats rented by tourists. The towpath, from the Thames at Brentford to Birmingham, is now also recognised as an official walking path.

ROUTE GUIDE AND MAPS

Tring Railway Station The Ridgeway passes over the rail line on a bridge right outside Tring Railway Station (Map 38). It's now a stop for local services for trains to and from London Euston and there is a taxi company (see p186) in the station car park. There is nothing of interest to the walker here, except perhaps for a place to sit and shelter if it's raining, so if you're not catching a train here there is little reason to stop.

Folly Farm B&B This excellent bed and breakfast is best reached along Northfield Rd (Map 38), the turning for which is about 200m east of Tring Station. The B&B is about 1¼ miles along this road, just off the roundabout. *Folly Farm* (☎ 01442 851645, 🖥 follyfarmbedandbreakfast.co.uk; 1D en suite, 1D & 1S private bathroom; ☛; WI-FI; Ⓛ; 🐾) charges from £50pp (sgl/sgl occ £70/90). If the single and double are booked by friends or a family the bathroom is shared. Book well in advance as it's very popular. In all it's 1½ miles from Ivinghoe, 2 miles from Aldbury and 2½ miles from the centre of Tring.

Visiting Aldbury You can reach Aldbury simply by following Station Rd east into the village from where a gate leads to a concrete track (Map 38).

ALDBURY [MAP 38]

Aldbury is a picture-perfect English village, complete with **duck pond**, church and pub. It would be a good alternative to Wigginton if the accommodation there is full. This idyllic village has been captured on film many times: *The Avengers*, *The Dirty Dozen*, *Inspector Morse*, *Midsomer Murders* (inevitably) and, more recently, *Bridget Jones's Diary: The Edge of Reason*.

You'll be surprised when you look inside the **village shop** (☎ 01442 851233; Mon-Sat 6am-5.30pm, Sun 7.30am-4pm). Not only is it very well stocked and much larger than it looks from the outside, but there is a **post office** (Mon, Tue, Thur & Fri 9am-1pm & 2-5.30pm, Wed 9am-1pm, Sat 9am-12.30pm) in here as well as an **ATM** (the charge per withdrawal is £1.50). However, at the time of research the shop was for sale so the opening hours and ATM availability could well change.

Red Rose Travel's No 387 **bus** service operates to Tring; see pp48-51 for further details.

Where to stay and eat

In a prime location near the duck pond is *The Greyhound Inn* (☎ 01442 851228, 🖥 greyhoundaldbury.co.uk; 5D/2D or T/1Qd in a separate cottage, all en suite; ☛; WI-FI; Ⓛ; 🐾), a much filmed and photographed

place. **B&B** costs from £47.50pp, £80 if you're on your own. The **food** (Mon-Thur noon-8pm, Fri & Sat to 9pm, Sun to 5pm) is of a high standard and there is a varied all-day menu: they have some good sandwiches (around £7) and their traditional mains include home-cooked honey-roasted ham, eggs, chips & peas (£13.50). There is one vegetarian option, mixed bean casserole bound in a tomato & basil sauce with brown basmati rice (£13.50). It's a Hall & Woodhouse pub so serves Badger beers. At the time of research they were open all day but the pub may close between 3pm and 6pm on weekdays.

Another good option for **food**, but especially for beer, is *The Valiant Trooper* (☎ 01442 851203, 🖥 valianttrooper.co.uk; WI-FI; 🐾; food Mon-Wed & Fri noon-3pm, Sat 10am-6pm, Sun 10am-3pm). This free-house pub is open all day, has five hand-pumps, and is less than five minutes' walk from the centre of the village. The menu changes weekly but includes daily specials with options such as smoked haddock fish cakes with leek gratin topped with a poached egg (£13.95) and free-range pork sausages with bubble & squeak and home-made baked beans (£12.50). At the time of research the food hours were more limited than usual but this may change.

Aldbury Nowers With either the end of the trail nearly in sight, or having only recently embarked on it, 99.99% of trekkers on the Ridgeway undoubtedly march through these woods (Map 38) with little thought as to what they're actually walking through. It's forgivable, of course, but it's also a bit of a shame, for this scrumptious little corner of Hertfordshire countryside is actually one of the main butterfly habitats in the UK (see box on p192).

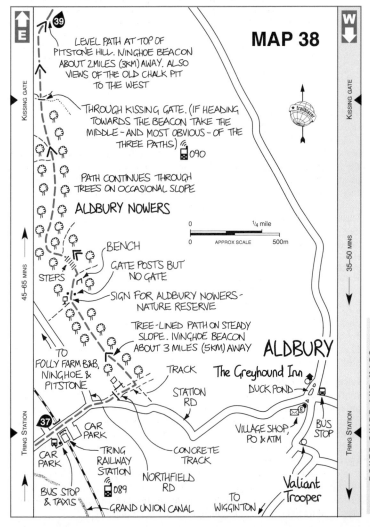

MAP 38

39

LEVEL PATH AT TOP OF PITSTONE HILL. IVINGHOE BEACON ABOUT 2 MILES (3KM) AWAY. ALSO VIEWS OF THE OLD CHALK PIT TO THE WEST

KISSING GATE

KISSING GATE

★ trailblazer

THROUGH KISSING GATE. (IF HEADING TOWARDS THE BEACON TAKE THE MIDDLE - AND MOST OBVIOUS - OF THE THREE PATHS) 📱090

PATH CONTINUES THROUGH TREES ON OCCASIONAL SLOPE

ALDBURY NOWERS

0   ¼ mile
0   APPROX SCALE   500m

BENCH

GATE POSTS BUT NO GATE

STEPS

35-50 MINS

45-65 MINS

SIGN FOR ALDBURY NOWERS - NATURE RESERVE

TREE-LINED PATH ON STEADY SLOPE. IVINGHOE BEACON ABOUT 3 MILES (5KM) AWAY

ALDBURY

TO FOLLY FARM B&B, IVINGHOE & PITSTONE

TRACK

The Greyhound Inn

DUCK POND

STATION RD

VILLAGE SHOP, PO & ATM

BUS STOP

37

CAR PARK

TRING STATION

TRING STATION

CAR PARK

TRING RAILWAY STATION 📱089

CONCRETE TRACK

NORTHFIELD RD

Valiant Trooper

BUS STOP & TAXIS

GRAND UNION CANAL

TO WIGGINTON

❏ **THE BUTTERFLIES OF ALDBURY NOWERS**

Nobody is quite sure why **Aldbury Nowers Nature Reserve** (🖳 hertswildlifetrust
.org.uk/reserves/aldbury-nowers; open all day all year but best Apr-Aug) is so popular with our colourfully winged friends but the truth is that the reserve plays host to
over 30 species – out of the 59 species commonly accepted to live in the UK. Some
of the Albury Nowers' residents, such as the meadow brown and the peacock, are
commonplace enough. But several rarities are also here – Essex skippers, marbled
whites, green hairstreak, brown argus, and the scarce grizzled and dingy skippers.

Some butterflies (such as the orange tip) appear early in the season and are rarely
seen after June; others appear late in the summer. But if you have the time there are
few more enjoyable ways to spend a warm afternoon than to take a decent butterfly
guide, a little magnifying glass or similar (to spot the sometimes subtle differences
between the species) and to sit on the slopes of Albury Nowers, ticking off the species.

Top of Pitstone Hill There's a good view of the Beacon at this point, north
of Aldbury Nowers. For those walking towards it, this will be the first proper
look at the final objective, though you will already have seen it from afar. You'll
always have it in sight now, so however tired you feel you can at least admire
the increasingly stunning views from up here and plod on. For those walking
away from the Beacon, it'd be a good idea to stop, turn around and take a good
look as these will be your last good views of it before entering the woods. Down
to the west you can see a large, **old chalk pit** (off Map 38), now filled with
water; this is a popular place for relaxing and swimming during the summer.
The water takes on a turquoise colour, adding something almost tropical to the
atmosphere of the place. If you are plodding along here under the hot sun, just
the sight of it can make you want to run down there and dive right in.

Pitstone Hill car park The Ridgeway crosses a road and car park (Map 39)
near the top of Pitstone Hill. This isn't the closest car park to Ivinghoe Beacon
– the NT car park is closer, but the Ridgeway doesn't go within 500m of it.

Beacon Hill There is a short, steep section of Ridgeway path by the Beacon.
If you started the day at Princes Risborough, this might just about finish you off.
However, if you are starting your walk from the Beacon and feeling fresh, it will
still provide a decent test and warm-up for your knees and ankles.

Ivinghoe Beacon At the high point on the Beacon there is a **Ridgeway information board** and **trig point** to go with the fantastic panoramic views. There
are often other people up here, but few who have either just finished walking all
87 miles of the Ridgeway, or who are preparing to set out on the trail, so take
plenty of time to relax and enjoy the views before moving on.

If you've just finished walking the Ridgeway and are ready to leave the
Beacon, you have several choices. If you are lucky, someone might be waiting
to pick you up from the car park you passed on your way up here. If not, you'll
need to walk down to Ivinghoe village. The best way to do this is to follow one
of the many paths down the hillside to the main road. Be careful as it's very
steep and there are plenty of hidden holes in the ground.

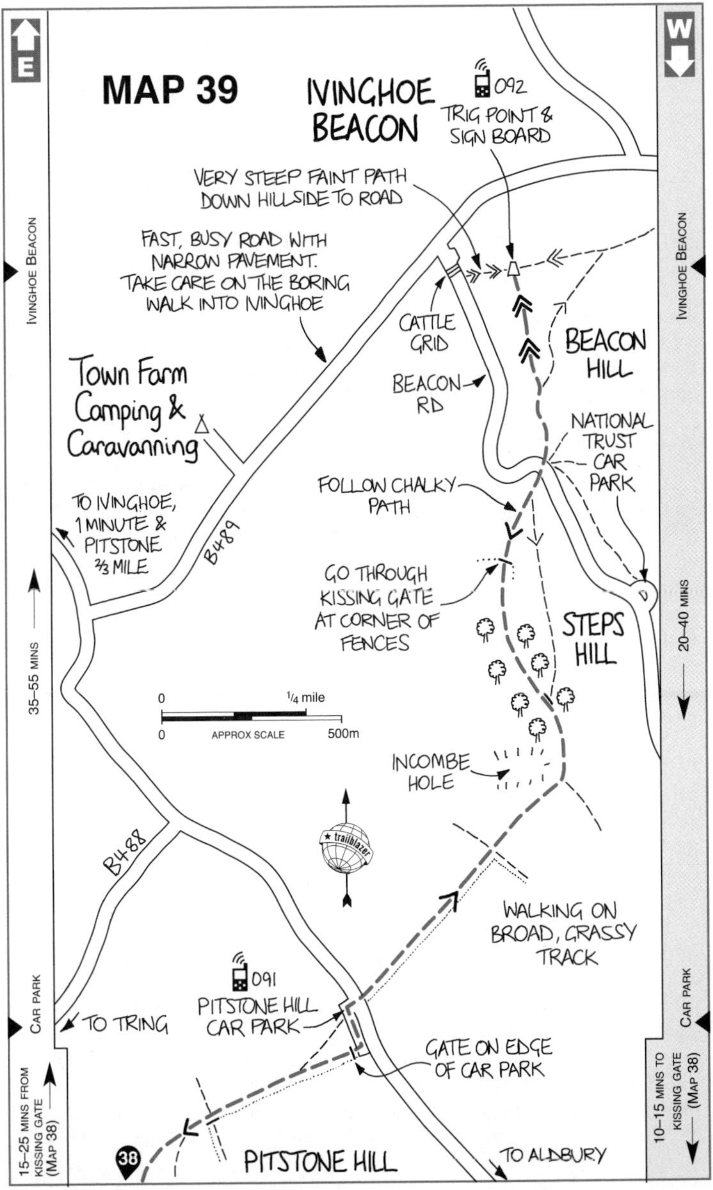

MAP 39

IVINGHOE BEACON

📱092
TRIG POINT &
SIGN BOARD

VERY STEEP FAINT PATH
DOWN HILLSIDE TO ROAD

FAST, BUSY ROAD WITH
NARROW PAVEMENT.
TAKE CARE ON THE BORING
WALK INTO IVINGHOE

CATTLE
GRID

BEACON
HILL

BEACON
RD

NATIONAL
TRUST
CAR PARK

Town Farm
Camping &
Caravanning

FOLLOW CHALKY
PATH

TO IVINGHOE,
1 MINUTE &
PITSTONE
⅔ MILE

GO THROUGH
KISSING GATE
AT CORNER OF
FENCES

STEPS
HILL

0   ¼ mile
0   500m
APPROX SCALE

INCOMBE
HOLE

★ trailblazer

WALKING ON
BROAD, GRASSY
TRACK

📱091
PITSTONE HILL
CAR PARK

GATE ON EDGE
OF CAR PARK

TO TRING

38

PITSTONE HILL

TO ALDBURY

IVINGHOE BEACON

IVINGHOE BEACON

35-55 MINS

15-25 MINS FROM
KISSING GATE
(MAP 38)

CAR PARK

20-40 MINS

CAR PARK

10-15 MINS TO
KISSING GATE
(MAP 38)

ROUTE GUIDE AND MAPS

Most paths finish near the B489 from where it's a boring walk into Ivinghoe (see opposite). This road is not particularly wide yet people drive very fast along it so be careful. If you get on with it the 1¼-mile/2km walk from the top of Ivinghoe Beacon to **Ivinghoe village** shouldn't take more than 20-30 minutes.

Starting from Ivinghoe Beacon

Start here if you're walking in a **westerly direction** (Ivinghoe Beacon to Overton Hill and Avebury) and follow the maps in a descending order (from 39 to 1) and the text with a **red background**, looking for the **←W symbol** on overview text and on map borders, working back through the book.

For **map profiles** see the colour pages and **overview maps** at the end of the book. For an overview of this information see the **Itineraries** on p32 & p34 and the **town and village facilities tables** on p33 & p35.

W ← IVINGHOE BEACON TO WIGGINTON (& TRING) [MAPS 39-37]

[Route section begins on Map 39, p193] This first **5-mile/8km (1¾-2¾hrs)** section of the Ridgeway is easy to walk and straightforward to navigate. It's pretty much all downhill on a good path. But before you can enjoy all that, how are you going to get to Ivinghoe Beacon in the first place?

Someone with a car, or a taxi (see p186), could drop you off near the Beacon. This could be at either of the car parks, but the National Trust car park is closer to the Beacon than the Pitstone Hill car park (both on Map 39). Closer still, you could be dropped off by the cattle grid on Beacon Rd (Map 39), shortly after you've turned off the B489. From there you'll see a very steep signposted path off left up to the Beacon.

You could also walk **from Ivinghoe village** (see opposite) to the Beacon. Walk out of the village and turn left onto the B489. Follow this fast, but not particularly wide road and turn off onto Beacon Rd (Map 39). About 80m along the road is a cattle grid, after which is a very steep signposted path up to the Beacon. Of course, you could get public transport to Tring Railway Station then walk up to the Beacon and back down again, before continuing westwards on the Ridgeway, but that's a tough start to your Ridgeway walk.

Starting your walk at **Ivinghoe Beacon** you first need to descend the steep slope of **Beacon Hill** before enjoying some excellent open walking to the road crossing and car park at **Pitstone Hill** (all on Map 39). Once over the hill you descend for the next couple of miles, passing through **Aldbury Nowers** before reaching Station Rd where you can turn left for **Aldbury** (both on Map 38), or continue on the Ridgeway past a right turn for **Folly Farm B&B** (off Map 38) and then past **Tring Railway Station** (Map 38). Shortly afterwards you cross the **Grand Union Canal** and then the A41 via a long **pedestrian bridge** (both on Map 37). Not long after this you will reach the turn for **Wigginton** (Map 37).

[Next route overview on 183]

IVINGHOE

Given its name you'd be right in presuming that this village is the closest to the end of the Ridgeway at Ivinghoe Beacon. This means that most Ridgeway walkers will pass through, or stay here, at some point.

Services

The village **post office** and **shop** (☎ 01296 660325; opening times for both: Mon-Sat 8am-8pm, Sun 9am-2pm) are in the Old Town Hall. If this doesn't have what you want there is a larger shop (and with longer opening hours) in Pitstone (see below).

If you're in urgent need of plasters, there's a **chemist**, Windmill Pharmacy (☎ 01296 706280; Mon-Fri 8.30am-1pm & 2-6pm), 50m down from the post office.

Red Eagle's No 61 **bus** and Redline's Nos 50 & 164 stop here; see pp48-51 for further details.

Where to stay

If you want to **camp**, head for *Town Farm Camping & Caravanning* (Map 39; book online only at ⌨ townfarmcamping.co.uk; 50 pitches; WI-FI; 🐾; Apr-end Sep) which charges from £10pp (£12pp in high season, generally half price for children under 16) including use of toilet and shower facilities. They also have six 4-person tents, set up with single sleeping mats and a lantern; from £30 per night (£40 high season) plus their usual tariff per person.

There may also be a couple of options on **Airbnb** (see pp20-1).

Where to eat and drink

There's a great eatery, *CuriosiTEA Rooms* (☎ 07775 831153; fb; WI-FI; 🐾; Mon, Tue, Thur, Fri & Sun 10am-3pm, Wed to 2pm, Sat to 4pm), just below The Green in the centre of the village. Lots of outdoor seating, biscuits for dogs, friendly staff and a decent array of cakes, sandwiches, toasties, jacket potatoes and other lunchtime options. It's a pleasant place to relax those

aching muscles while waiting for the bus. For dinner, the 17th-century *King's Head Restaurant* (☎ 01296 668388, ⌨ kings headivinghoe.co.uk; Tue-Sun noon-2.15pm, Tue-Sat 7-9.15pm), right in the centre of the village, is known for its high-quality cuisine. It's not really the place for muddy walkers – the dress code is smart, particularly in the evening – and with their à la carte menu costing £48.95 (though this includes an appetiser, entrée, dessert and coffee), you'll probably not find many walkers in there anyway. However, they do offer a Bon Appetit luncheon menu Tuesday to Saturday (three courses for £26.95, or à la carte) which might be worth considering for a celebratory meal.

The alternative, is the cosy *Rose & Crown* (☎ 01296 668472, ⌨ roseandcrown ivinghoe.co.uk; bar Mon-Sat noon-11pm, Sun to 10.30pm; **food** Tue-Sat noon-2pm & 6-9pm, Sun noon-3pm), down Vicarage Lane. Lunchtime food includes sandwiches with soup or chips (£7.50) while mains are from £12 and choices may include ham, egg & chips, or gnocchi with butternut squash, walnuts & goat's cheese. They sometimes serve beer from Tring Brewery (see box on p22).

PITSTONE [off map above]

Mason's Stores (☎ 01296 660052; Mon-Fri 6.30am-8pm, Sat 7am-8pm, Sun 8am-5.30pm) is on Marsworth Rd about 10 minutes' walk from Ivinghoe. It's also an **off-licence** and **newsagent**.

APPENDIX A: WALKING WITH A DOG

WALKING THE RIDGEWAY WITH A DOG

Many are the rewards that await those prepared to make the extra effort required to bring their best friend along the trail. You shouldn't underestimate the amount of work involved, though. Indeed, just about every decision you make will be influenced by the fact that you've got a dog: how you plan to travel to the start of the trail, where you're going to stay, how far you're going to walk each day, where you're going to rest and where you're going to eat in the evening etc.

If you're also sure your dog can cope with (and will enjoy) walking 10 miles or so a day for several days in a row, you need to start preparing accordingly. Extra thought also needs to go into your itinerary. The best starting point is to study the town and village facilities table on p34 and p35 (and the advice below), and plan where to stop and where to buy food.

Looking after your dog

To begin with, you need to make sure that your dog is fully **inoculated** against the usual doggy illnesses, and also up to date with regard to **worm pills** (eg Drontal) and **flea preventatives** such as Frontline – they are, after all, following in the pawprints of many a dog before them, some of whom may well have left fleas or other parasites on the trail that now lie in wait for their next meal to arrive.

Pet insurance is also a very good idea; if you've already got insurance, do check that it will cover a trip such as this.

On the subject of looking after your dog's health, perhaps the most important implement you can take is the **plastic tick remover**, available from vets for a couple of quid. These removers, while fiddly, help you to remove the tick safely (ie without leaving its head behind buried under a dog's skin).

Being in unfamiliar territory also makes it more likely that you and your dog could become separated. For this reason, make sure your dog has a **tag with your contact details on it** (a mobile phone number would be best if you are carrying one with you); the fact that all dogs now have to be **microchipped** provides further security.

When to keep your dog on a lead

● **When crossing farmland**, particularly in the **lambing season** (around May) as your dog can scare the sheep, causing them to lose their young. Farmers are allowed by law to shoot at and kill any dogs that they consider are worrying their sheep. During lambing, most farmers would prefer it if you didn't bring your dog at all.

The exception to the 'dogs on leads' rule is if your dog is being attacked by cows. Some years ago there were three deaths in the UK caused by walkers being trampled as they tried to rescue their dogs from the attentions of cattle. The advice in this instance is to let go of the lead, head speedily to a position of safety (usually the other side of the field gate or stile) and call your dog to you.

● **Around ground-nesting birds** It's important to keep your dog under control when crossing an area where certain species of birds nest on the ground. Most dogs love foraging around in the woods but make sure you have permission to do so; some woods are used as 'nurseries' for game birds and dogs are only allowed through them if they are on a lead.

What to pack

You've probably already got a good idea of what to bring to keep your dog alive and happy, but the following is a checklist:

● **Food/water bowl** Foldable cloth bowls are popular with walkers, being light and taking up little room in the rucksack. You can also get a water-bottle-and-bowl combination, where the bottle folds into a 'trough' from which the dog can drink. Where there are water taps along the Ridgeway, there is often a trough for your dog to drink from but this is not always the case.

● **Lead and collar** An extendable lead is probably preferable for this sort of trip. Make sure both lead and collar are in good condition – you don't want either to snap on the trail, or you may end up carrying your dog through sheep fields until a replacement can be found.

● **Medication** You'll know if you need to bring any lotions or potions.

● **Bedding** A simple blanket may suffice, or you can opt for something more elaborate if you aren't carrying your own luggage.

● **Poo bags** Essential.

● **Hygiene wipes** For cleaning your dog after it's rolled in stuff.

● **A favourite toy** Helps prevent your dog from pining for the entire walk.

● **Food/water** Remember to bring treats as well as regular food to keep up your mutt's morale. That said, if your dog is anything like mine the chances are they'll spend most of the walk dining on rabbit droppings and sheep poo anyway.

● **Corkscrew stake** Available from camping or pet shops, this will help you to keep your dog secure in one place while you set up camp/doze.

● **Tick remover** See opposite.

● **Raingear** It can rain!

● **Old towels** For drying your dog.

When it comes to packing, I always leave an exterior pocket of my rucksack empty so I can put used poo bags in there (for deposit at the first bin). I always like to keep all my dog's kit together and separate from the other luggage (usually inside a plastic bag inside my rucksack). I have also seen several dogs sporting their own 'doggy rucksack', so they can carry their own food, water, poo etc – which certainly reduces the burden on their owner!

Cleaning up after your dog

It is extremely important that dog owners behave in a responsible way when walking the path. Dog excrement should be cleaned up. In towns, villages and fields where animals graze or which will be cut for silage, hay etc, you need to pick up and bag the excrement.

Staying (and eating) with your dog

In this guide the symbol 🐾 denotes where a **hotel, pub, or B&B** welcomes dogs. However, this always needs to be arranged in advance – many places have only one or two rooms suitable for people with dogs. In some cases dogs need to sleep in a separate building. Some places make an additional charge (usually per night but occasionally per stay) while others may require a deposit which is refundable if the dog doesn't make a mess.

Smaller **campsites** tend to accept dogs, but some of the larger holiday parks do not; again look for the 🐾 symbol in the text.

When it comes to **eating**, most landlords allow dogs in at least a section of their pub and some cafés do, though restaurants generally don't. Make sure you always ask first and ensure your dog doesn't run around but is secured to your table or a radiator.

APPENDIX B: THE GREATER RIDGEWAY

LYME REGIS TO HUNSTANTON

After you've completed the Ridgeway you might like to consider a stroll along parts of the Greater Ridgeway that link Lyme Regis, in Dorset, with Hunstanton, in Norfolk. The Ridgeway covered in this book comprises just the middle section.

Starting from the popular seaside town of Lyme Regis, you can follow the **Wessex Ridgeway** 136 miles (219km) up to its finishing point at Marlborough in Wiltshire, crossing the Ridgeway near Avebury. From Lyme Regis the path goes through Beaminster before meandering through open country and numerous small villages and passing within a few miles of Shaftesbury. You then skirt round the edge of Salisbury Plain taking in the towns of Heytesbury and Warminster. From here you head towards Westbury White Horse and on to Devizes before arriving in Avebury and finally Marlborough.

From there the **Ridgeway** in this book takes you up to Ivinghoe Beacon from where you can follow the **Icknield Way** on to Knettishall Heath in Suffolk, 103 miles (166km) away. The long history of this trail equals that of the Ridgeway and is made evident by the wealth of archaeological remains found along here. The route continues on the high chalky ground visiting numerous towns along the way including Baldock, Royston and Linton. From here the Icknield Way continues to Cheveley and Icklingham before finishing at Knettishall Heath Country Park.

Picking up where the Icknield Way finishes, the **Peddars Way**, from Knettishall Heath to Hunstanton, clocks in at 46 miles (75km) and provides easy walking to the end of the Greater Ridgeway. This largely straight inland route follows a Roman road in open countryside with few villages en route.

You will pass through Little Cressingham, Castle Acre and Ringstead before reaching the coast at Holme-next-the-Sea. From here you walk along the coast to reach Hunstanton, and the end of the Greater Ridgeway.

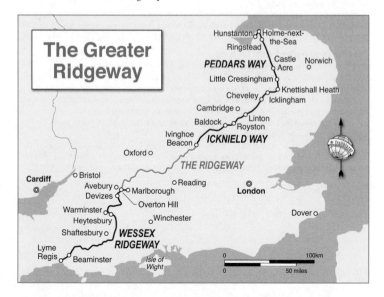

❏ **RIDGEWAY NATIONAL TRAIL CERTIFICATES**

Now you have walked – cycled or ridden – along the Ridgeway what else can you do?

Firstly the Ridgeway National Trail team are very keen to encourage people to **give feedback** (🖳 nationaltrail.co.uk/en_GB/contact) on their experiences because, not surprisingly, it's very useful for them. In return they will send you a free **certificate**!

Another way you can help is to upload **photos** of your walk so the NT team can build an online photo gallery (🖳 nationaltrail.co.uk/en_GB/trails/the-ridgeway/add-your-information).

Some of the work keeping the trail well maintained is done by volunteers but there are also lots of other costs in terms of making improvements to the trail and also providing free online information for everyone to benefit from so the Friends of the Ridgeway are grateful for any **donations** (🖳 nationaltrail.co.uk/ridgeway/donate).

Further information
- *The Wessex Ridgeway*, Anthony Burton, Aurum
- *Ancient Trackways of Wessex*, HW Timperley & Edith Brill, Nonsuch
- *The Icknield Way Path: A Walkers' Guide*, by Sue Prigg and Nigel Balchi, Icknield Way Association
- *Norfolk Coast Path and Peddars Way*, Alexander Stewart, Trailblazer Publications

APPENDIX C: MAP KEY

Map key

♠ Where to stay	ⓘ Tourist Information	☑ Public toilet
○ Where to eat and drink	📖 Library/bookstore	● Other
Λ Campsite	@ Internet	🚏 Bus stop/station
✉ Post Office	🏛 Museum/gallery	▪◻▪ Rail line & station
ⓔ Bank/ATM	🏠 Church/cathedral	▨ Park

╱ Ridgeway	⬀ Slope	⋰ Fence
╱ Other Path	⬀ Steep slope	⟿ Stream/river
╱ 4 x 4 track	⟍ Stile	🌳 Trees/woodland
╱ Tarmac road	⟍ Gate	🔲024 GPS waypoint
╱ Steps	⟍ Bridge	⑭ Map continuation

APPENDIX D: GPS WAYPOINTS

Each GPS waypoint below was taken on the route at the reference number marked on the map as below. This list of GPS waypoints is also available to download from the Trailblazer website – 🖳 trailblazer-guides.com.

MAP	REF	GPS WAYPOINT		DESCRIPTION
Marlborough to Avebury walk				
Map A	AA	N51° 25.113'	W01° 44.031'	Southern end of Marlborough High St
Map A	BB	N51° 25.565'	W01° 44.213'	Gate into cemetery
Map A	CC	N51° 25.957'	W01° 44.954'	Road crossing
Map A	DD	N51° 26.384'	W01° 46.326'	Track to Manton House
Map B	EE	N51° 26.597'	W01° 47.109'	Junction in path
Map B	FF	N51° 26.517'	W01° 47.638'	Underground reservoir
Map B	GG	N51° 26.234'	W01° 48.851'	Cross track
Map C	HH	N51° 26.191'	W01° 51.236'	Junction with Green Street
Map C	II	N51° 25.712'	W01° 51.236'	Red Lion, Avebury
A walk around Avebury				
Map C	II	N51° 25.712'	W01° 51.236'	Red Lion, Avebury
Map C	JJ	N51° 25.246'	W01° 50.749'	Gates to Waden Hill
Silbury Hill option				
Map C	KK	N51° 25.041'	W01° 51.188'	Through gate and follow river
Map C	LL	N51° 25.130'	W01° 51.336'	Left turn after gate
Map C	MM	N51° 24.967'	W01° 51.705'	Silbury Hill car park
Map C	NN	N51° 24.851'	W01° 51.110'	Gate from A4 road up to the Long Barrow
Long Barrow option				
Map C	OO	N51° 24.732'	W01° 51.045'	Turn right for the Long Barrow
Map C	PP	N51° 24.516'	W01° 51.017'	West Kennet Long Barrow
Map C	QQ	N51° 24.496'	W01° 50.096'	Join road into East Kennett
Map C	RR	N51° 24.711'	W01° 49.834'	Start/end of the Ridgeway
Map C	SS	N51° 25.065'	W01° 49.816'	Turn left for quickest route to Avebury
The Ridgeway				
Map 1	001	N51° 24.711'	W01° 49.834'	Car park; start of the Ridgeway
Map 1	002	N51° 25.065'	W01° 49.816'	Turn to Avebury
Map 1	003	N51° 26.191'	W01° 51.236'	Junction with Green Street
Map 2	004	N51° 27.312'	W01° 49.245'	Kink in path
Map 3	005	N51° 28.294'	W01° 48.913'	Hackpen Hill car park
Map 4	006	N51° 29.115'	W01° 47.178'	Barbury Castle
Map 4	007	N51° 29.004'	W01° 46.469'	Upper Herdswick Farm
Map 4	008	N51° 28.325'	W01° 44.461'	Gate
Map 5	009	N51° 27.752'	W01° 43.303'	Turn to Hallam
Map 5	010	N51° 27.746'	W01° 41.822'	Track crossroads
Map 6	011	N51° 28.618'	W01° 41.520'	Cross quiet B4192 road
Map 6	012	N51° 29.224'	W01° 41.694'	Track crossroads by reservoir
Map 6	013	N51° 29.688'	W01° 41.640'	Lower/Upper Upham junction at dog's leg in path

MAP	REF	GPS WAYPOINT	DESCRIPTION
Map 7	014	N51° 30.036' W01° 41.521'	Fork in path
Map 7	015	N51° 30.994' W01° 41.695'	Gate near Liddington Castle
Map 7	016	N51° 31.429' W01° 41.267'	Turn off B4192 to Foxhill
Map 8	017	N51° 31.803' W01° 40.100'	The Burj, Foxhill
Map 9	018	N51° 32.559' W01° 38.213'	Road junction to Bishopstone
Map 10	019	N51° 33.010' W01° 37.270'	Cross track
Map 10	020	N51° 33.432' W01° 36.427'	B4000 road crossing
Map 10	021	N51° 33.969' W01° 35.700'	Entrance to Wayland's Smithy
Map 11	022	N51° 34.459' W01° 34.013'	Eastern gate, Uffington Castle
Map 12	023	N51° 34.452' W01° 32.134'	Cross road Kingston Lisle to Seven Barrows
Map 12	024	N51° 34.217' W01° 31.436'	Tracks for Sparsholt/Down Barn Farm
Map 12	025	N51° 33.826' W01° 30.343'	Sparsholt Firs car park
Map 13	026	N51° 33.241' W01° 28.012'	Cross road to Letcombe Bassett
Map 13	027	N51° 33.317' W01° 26.871'	Segsbury Farm
Map 13	028	N51° 33.437' W01° 25.960'	A338 road crossing
Map 14	029	N51° 33.266' W01° 23.906'	B4494 road crossing
Map 14	030	N51° 33.411' W01° 23.408'	Baron Wantage monument
Map 14	031	N51° 33.513' W01° 23.086'	Large, sprawling junction
Map 15	032	N51° 33.648' W01° 22.047'	Reservoir hidden in trees
Map 15	033	N51° 33.737' W01° 20.428'	Cross road for East Hendred
Map 16	034	N51° 33.194' W01° 18.598'	Bury Down car park
Map 16	035	N51° 32.880' W01° 17.679'	Tunnel under A34
Map 17	036	N51° 32.373' W01° 16.590'	Turn 'A' to East Ilsley
Map 17	037	N51° 32.362' W01° 16.544'	Turn 'B' to East Ilsley
Map 17	038	N51° 32.125' W01° 16.175'	Turn 'C' to East Ilsley
Map 17	039	N51° 32.016' W01° 16.059'	Turn 'D' to East Ilsley
Map 17	040	N51° 32.250' W01° 15.177'	DN&SJ Railway bridge
Map 18	041	N51° 32.021' W01° 13.844'	Cross tracks
Map 18	042	N51° 31.786' W01° 13.331'	Staggered crossroads
Map 18	043	N51° 31.647' W01° 12.551'	Junction with tracks to Aldworth
Map 19	044	N51° 31.639' W01° 11.068'	Post Box Cottage
Map 19	045	N51° 31.726' W01° 09.064'	Path joins A417 road
Map 19	046	N51° 31.363' W01° 08.923'	Streatley crossroads
Map 20	047	N51° 32.929' W01° 08.335'	Turn towards River Thames
Map 20	048	N51° 32.951' W01° 08.701'	Slipway on bank of Thames
Map 20	049	N51° 33.454' W01° 08.544'	Railway viaducts
Map 21	050	N51° 33.862' W01° 08.072'	Small wooden footbridge
Map 21	051	N51° 34.306' W01° 07.271'	Turn in North Stoke
Map 22	052	N51° 35.304' W01° 07.232'	Turn before A4130 road
Map 22	053	N51° 35.121' W01° 05.983'	Junction with path across field
Map 22	054	N51° 35.069' W01° 05.487'	Path crosses country road
Map 22	055	N51° 35.012' W01° 05.012'	Cross road to Ewelme & Woodcote
Map 23	056	N51° 34.716' W01° 02.419'	Path turns 90°
Map 23	057	N51° 34.862' W01° 02.281'	Holy Trinity Church, Nuffield
Map 23	058	N51° 35.048' W01° 01.607'	The Crown (closed), Nuffield
Map 24	059	N51° 35.833' W01° 01.732'	Ewelme Park
Map 24	060	N51° 36.393' W01° 00.979'	St Botolph's
Map 25	061	N51° 37.392' W01° 01.316'	North Farm
Map 25	062	N51° 37.831' W01° 00.254'	Ridge Farm
Map 25	063	N51° 38.022' W00° 59.954'	Westernmost turning to Watlington

MAP	REF	GPS WAYPOINT	DESCRIPTION
Map 26	064	N51° 38.413' W00° 59.528'	Turn to White Mark Farm
Map 26	065	N51° 38.714' W00° 59.110'	Cross sealed lane
Map 27	066	N51° 39.968' W00° 57.546'	Cross narrow but fast road to Lewknor
Map 28	067	N51° 40.404' W00° 56.903'	A40 road crossing
Map 28	068	N51° 40.908' W00° 55.741'	Cross road that goes to Kingston Blount
Map 29	069	N51° 41.309' W00° 54.704'	Path to Oakley Hill Nature Reserve
Map 29	070	N51° 41.749' W00° 54.073'	Cross road to Chinnor
Map 30	071	N51° 42.264' W00° 53.218'	Path bends round house
Map 30	072	N51° 41.864' W00° 51.978'	Cross road that goes to Bledlow
Map 30	073	N51° 41.741' W00° 50.531'	Longwood Farm drive
Map 30	074	N51° 42.205' W00° 50.498'	Saunderton railway tunnel
Map 31	075	N51° 42.930' W00° 50.118'	Princes Risborough sign
Map 31	076	N51° 43.251' W00° 49.502'	Cross road to Princes Risborough
Map 32	077	N51° 43.737' W00° 48.641'	Turn in route direction
Map 32	078	N51° 43.982' W00° 48.287'	The Plough, Cadsden
Map 33	079	N51° 44.221' W00° 46.578'	Cross road to Butler's Cross
Map 33	080	N51° 44.707' W00° 46.326'	Ridgeway briefly follows road
Map 33	081	N51° 45.184' W00° 46.291'	Monument on Coombe Hill
Map 34	082	N51° 45.545' W00° 44.999'	Join/leave road
Map 34	083	N51° 45.366' W00° 44.098'	Cross road to Wendover
Map 34	084	N51° 44.949' W00° 43.456'	Soft path through woods
Map 35	085	N51° 45.825' W00° 41.816'	Gate half-hidden in hedge
Map 36	086	N51° 46.532' W00° 40.269'	The Mill, Hastoe
Map 37	087	N51° 47.138' W00° 38.777'	Road crossing
Map 37	088	N51° 47.460' W00° 38.133'	Pedestrian bridge over A41 road
Map 38	089	N51° 48.042' W00° 37.400'	Tring railway station
Map 38	090	N51° 48.956' W00° 37.379'	Kissing gate
Map 39	091	N51° 49.496' W00° 36.931'	Pitstone Hill car park
Map 39	092	N51° 50.531' W00° 36.502'	Ivinghoe Beacon trig point

INDEX

Page references in **bold** type refer to maps

access 56-8
  disabled 27-8
accidents 58
accommodation 18-21, 96-7
  see also place name
Airbnb 20-1
Aldbourne Circular Route
  36
Aldbury 190, **191**
Aldbury Nowers Nature
  Reserve 64, 191, **191**, 192
Aldworth 137, **137**, 138
Alexander Keiller Museum,
  Avebury 85, **87**
apps:
  birds 44;
  location 58;
  weather 59
Ardington Down **130**
Areas of Outstanding
  Natural Beauty (AONBs)
  61-2
Ashbury 114-15, **114**
Ashbury Circular Walk 36
Ashridge Drovers' Walk 37
Aston Rowant 163-4
Aston Rowant Discovery
  Trail 36, 162, **163**
Aston Rowant National
  Nature Reserve 62
ATMs 24, 25, 33, 35, 41
  see also place name
Aubrey, John 88-9, 91
Avebury **82**, 85-7, **87**, **93**
Avebury Stone Circle 88-9,
  89, **93**
Avebury to Marlborough
  walk 81-2
Avebury walk **82-3**, 90-2

B&Bs see bed and breakfasts
Bachelor's Hill **154**
backpacks see rucksacks
Backpackers' Club 43
Bacombe Hill **178**
baggage transfer 26
bank holidays 24
banks 24, 25, 33, 35, 41
  see also place name

Barber Surgeon Stone 88,
  89
Barbury Castle 102-4, **102**
Barn Wood **179**, 182
Baron Wantage monument
  129, 130
Beacon Hill 192, **193**
Beacon View Walk 37
Beckhampton Avenue 90
bed and breakfasts (B&Bs)
  19-20, 30
beers 22
birds 69-72
Bishopstone 113, **113**
blisters 59
books 43-4, 199
boots 38-9
British Summer Time (BST)
  25
budgeting 29-30
Bulls Wood **185**
bunkhouses 18-19
burial mounds 8, 91, 97,
  98, 122, 166, **168**, **175**
Bury Down 130-1, **132**
bus services **48-9**, 50-1, 52
  see also place name
business hours 24
Butlers Cross **177**
butterflies 65-6, 174, 192
Butterfly Conservation 64

Cadsden 174, **175**
camp fires 55, 57
Campaign for Real Ale
  (CAMRA) 22
campaigning organisations
  63-4
camping & campsites 18, 55
  budgeting 29
  gear 41
  itinerary 32, 34
  supplies 23
cashback 25-6
cash machines see ATMs
cell phones 25, 41, 58
Charlbury Hill **110**, 112
Chequers Estate 174, **177**
Cherhill Hill 98

Cherhill White Horse 118
Chiltern Link, The 37
Chiltern Way **156**
Chilterns AONB 62
Chinnor 165-6, **167**
Chinnor & Princes
  Risborough Railway 165
Chinnor chalk pits 165, **167**
Chinnor Hill Nature
  Reserve 166, **168**
Chiseldon & Marlborough
  Railway Path 106
Cholsey and Wallingford
  Railway 147
climate 14-16
clothing 39-40, 58
coach services
  to Britain 44
  in Britain 46-7
compasses 40
Compton 133, **133**
conservation of the
  Ridgeway 61-4
conservation organisations
  63-4
Coombe Hill 176, **177**
Countryside Code 56-7
Countryside & Rights of
  Way Act 2000 (CRoW) 58
Court Hill 124-5, **125**
COVID-19 impact 20-1
credit cards 25, 41
crop circles 84
Crowmarsh Gifford 151-3,
  151
Cuckhamsley Hill **131**
Cunnington, Maud 90
currency 24
cycling see mountain-biking

day walks 31-2, 34, 36-7
daylight hours 15
debit cards 25, 41
Devil's Punchbowl **121**,
  122-3
Didcot, Newbury and
  Southampton Junction
  Railway 133, **135**, 136
difficulty, of walk 12-13

digital maps 42
direction of walk 30-1
disabled access 27-8
dogs, walking with 29, 57,
    196-7
Dragon Hill **116**, 117
drinking water *see* water
drinks 22
driving: in Britain 47, 52;
    on the Ridgeway 28;
    to Britain 44
duration of walk 13-14

East Ginge Down **130**
East Ilsley 132-3, **134**
East Ilsley/West Ilsley
    Circular Route 36
East Kennett **83**, 90, 92, **93**
economic impact of walking
    53
emergency services 25
emergency signals 58
English Heritage 24, 63, 92
    properties 85
environmental impact of
    walking 53-8
equipment 38-41
erosion 54
European Health Insurance
    Cards (EHICs) 25
events 16
Ewelme Park Estate **156**,
    157-8
exchange rates 24

facilities table 33, 35
farmers' markets 23
    see also place name
ferry services to Britain 44
festivals 16
field guides 43-4
fires 55, 57
first-aid kit 40
flights to Britain 44
flora and fauna 64-72
    see also field guides
flowers 64-5
food 21, 23, 40, 58
footwear 38-9
Forestry Commission 62,
    182
Foxhill **110**, 111

Friends of the Ridgeway 63,
    199
Fyfield Down NNR 62, **80**,
    80-1, **93**, 98

gaiters 39-40
gallops *see* horse gallops
gloves 40
Goring **139**, 141-3, **142**
Goring & Streatley Bridge
    139, 140
GPS 17-18, 42
    waypoints 18, 200-2
Grand Union (Junction)
    Canal **185**, 189
Greater Ridgeway 10,
    198-9, **198**
Green Street 81, **82**, 92, 98,
    99
Greenwich Meantime
    (GMT) 25
Grim's ditches **152-3**, 154,
    154-5
guesthouses 20

Hackpen Hill (nr Avebury)
    101, **101**
Hackpen Hill (nr Sparsholt)
    121, 122
Hackpen White Horse
    101-2, **101**, 118
Hale Wood **179**, 182
Hallam **104**, 106
Hastoe **182**, 183
hats 40
health 59-60
heat exhaustion/heatstroke
    60
Herepath *see* Green Street
Historic England 62
historical background 10-12
Holy Trinity Church,
    Nuffield **155**, 157
horse gallops 80, **81**, **101**,
    103, 108, **121**, **131**, **135**
horse-racing *see* racehorses
horse-riding on the
    Ridgeway 28
hostels 18-19
hotels 20
hyperthermia 60
hypothermia 59-60

Icknield Way 37, 198
Idstone 113
Idstone Hill 113, **114**
Incombe Hole **193**
inns 20, 23
insurance, travel 25
Iron Age hill forts 10, 98,
    102, 117, 123
itinerary planning 30-9
Ivinghoe 195, **195**
Ivinghoe Beacon 192, **193**,
    194

Keiller, Alexander 88-9, 90,
    98
Kendall, Rev HGO 98
Kingston Blount 162, **164**
Kingston Hill **120**, 121

Lambourn Valley Way 36
Letcombe Bassett **124**
Letcombe Castle 123, **125**
Letcombe Regis 123-4, **123**
Lewknor 162, **163**
Liddington 108, 110, **110**
Liddington Castle 108, **109**
litter 54, 57
long barrows
    see burial mounds
Long Distance Walkers'
    Association (LDWA)
    41, 43
luggage transfer 26

maintenance of path 63
mammals 67-9
Manger, The **116**, 116-17
Manton Estate/House 80, **81**
map key 199
map scales 95
maps 41-2
markets 23
    see also place name
Marlborough 73-7, **75**, **79**
Marlborough to Avebury
    walk 77, **78-9**, 80-1, **80-1**,
    82-3
medical insurance 25
Midland and South Western
    Junction Railway 106
minimum impact walking
    53-8

mobile phones 25, 41, 58
money 24-6, 41
Morris dancing 16, 119
motor vehicles on the
    Ridgeway 28
Moulsford Railway Bridge
    144, **145**
mountain-biking on the
    Ridgeway 28

national holidays 24
national nature reserves
    (NNRs) 61, 62
National Trails 7, 56, 61, 63
    certificates 199
    office 43
National Trust 24, 63
    properties 36, 85, 116
    shop, Avebury 86
Natural England 61-2
Natural History Museum at
    Tring 184-5, **187**
Neolithic structures
    burial mounds 91, 97, 98,
        122
    causewayed enclosures 98
    long barrows 115
    stone circles 80, 88-9, 91
North Stoke **146**, 146
North Wessex Downs
    AONB 61-2
Nuffield **155**, 157

Oaken Copse **153**, 155
Oakley Hill Nature Reserve
    63-4, 165, **167**
Ogbourne St George 105,
    105, 106
opening hours 24
outdoor safety 57, 58-60
Overton Hill 93, **93**, 98, **99**
Oxfordshire Way **159**

Pavis Wood **181**
Peddars Way 198
Pitstone 195
Pitstone Hill 192, **193**
post offices 24, 26, 33, 35
    see also place name
Princes Risborough 170-3,
    170, **171**
public holidays 24

public transport 21, 44-7,
    48-9, 50-1, 52, 53
    see also place name
pubs 20, 23, 24

racehorses 108
    see also horse gallops
rail services
    in Britain 45-6, **48-9**
    to Britain 44
rainfall 15
Ramblers 11, 41, 43
real ales 22
restaurants 23
    see also place name
Ridgeway Down **129**
Ridgeway Link Walk 37
Ridgeway Partnership 62-3
right to roam 58
rights of way 56-7
route finding 17, 106
Royal Society for the
    Protection of Birds
    (RSPB) 64
rucksacks 38

safety, outdoor 57, 58-60
Sanctuary, The **83**, 91, 92,
    93, **99**
sarsen stones 81, 90, 91, 115
Saunderton Lee **169**
Saunderton Tunnel 166, **169**
school holidays 24
Scutchcombe Knob **131**
seasons 14-16
Segsbury Camp 123, **125**
self-guided holidays 26-7
Seven Barrows burial
    mound 122
sheep fairs/markets 16, 132
Shirburn Hill **159**
shops 24, 33, 35, 53
    see also place name
side trips 36-7
signposts 17, 106
Silbury Hill **83**, 91, 92, **93**
Sites of Special Scientific
    Interest (SSSIs) 61, 62
Smeathe's Ridge **103**, 104
smoking 25
Snap 106, **107**, 108
South Stoke 144, **145**

Sparsholt 122
Sparsholt Firs **121**, 122
Special Areas of
    Conservation (SACs) 62
St Botolph's church,
    Swyncombe **156**, 158
St Mary the Virgin church,
    Wendover **178**, 181
Steps Hill **193**
stone circles **78**, 80, 88-9,
    89, 91
Stonehenge 88
Streatley 139-40, **139**
Streatley Warren **137**
Stukeley, William 88-9, 90
sunburn 60
Swan's Way 144, **145**
Swindon Stone 88, **89**
Swyncombe **156**, 158

taxis 46
    see also place name
telephones 25
    see also mobile phones
temperatures 15
Thames, River **139**, 143,
    145, **146**, **152**
toilets 54-5
    see also place name
torches 40
    emergency signal 58
tourist information 43
    see also place name
town facilities 33, 35
trail information 43
trail maintenance 63
trail maps 95-6
trains see rail services
travel insurance 25
trees 66-7
Tring 183, 184-6, **187**, 188
Tring Park 64, **182**, 183
Tull, Jethro 151-2
tumuli **93**, 97, **99**
two-day walks 37
Two Ridges Link walk 37

Uffington 7, 119, **119**, 120
Uffington Castle 116-17,
    116
Uffington White Horse 115,
    116, 116, 117, 118

village facilities 33, 35

Waden Hill **83**, 91, **93**
walkers' organisations 43
walking companies 26-7
walking seasons 14-15
walking times 95, 96
Wallingford 147-8, **149**,
   150-1
Wantage 126-9, **127**
water bottles/pouches 40
water, drinking 23, 58
water taps 23, 58, **104**, 106,
   113, **114**, **120**, 122, **154**,
   155, **155**, 157, **164**, 174,
   175
Watlington 160-1, **161**
Wayland's Smithy 91, **114**,
   115
waymark posts/waymarkers
   17, 106

waypoints 18, 200-2
weather forecasts 59
weekend walks 37
weights and measures 25
Wendover 176, 178-80, **178**,
   180
Wessex Ridgeway 77, **99**,
   198
Westbury White Horse 118
West Ilsley 131, **132**
West Ilsley Circular Route
   36
West Kennett **83**, 90, **93**
West Kennet Avenue **82**,
   90, **93**
West Kennet Long Barrow
   83, 91, **93**
West Overton 87, **93**
whistles 40
   emergency signal 58
White Horse Hill **116**, 118

White Horse Kite Flyers
   103-4
White Horse Trail **101**,
   102, 118
white horses 118
Whiteleaf Cross monument
   174, **175**
Whiteleaf Hill Nature
   Reserve 173-4, **175**
Wigginton 183, 184, **185**
wild camping 18, 55-6
wildlife 54
   see also flora and fauna
Wildlife Trusts 63-4
Windmill Hill 98
Withymend Nature Reserve
   145
Woodland Trust 64, 183
Woolstone 115-116

YHA hostels 18-19

TRAILBLAZER TITLE LIST

Adventure Cycle-Touring Handbook
Adventure Motorcycling Handbook
Australia by Rail
Cleveland Way (British Walking Guide)
Coast to Coast (British Walking Guide)
Cornwall Coast Path (British Walking Guide)
Cotswold Way (British Walking Guide)
The Cyclist's Anthology
Dales Way (British Walking Guide)
Dorset & Sth Devon Coast Path (British Walking Gde)
Exmoor & Nth Devon Coast Path (British Walking Gde)
Great Glen Way (British Walking Guide)
Hadrian's Wall Path (British Walking Guide)
Himalaya by Bike – a route and planning guide
Iceland Hiking – with Reykjavik City Guide
Inca Trail, Cusco & Machu Picchu
Japan by Rail
Kilimanjaro – the trekking guide (includes Mt Meru)
London Loop (British Walking Guide)
Madeira Walks – 37 selected day walks
Moroccan Atlas – The Trekking Guide
Morocco Overland (4x4/motorcycle/mountainbike)
Nepal Trekking & The Great Himalaya Trail
Norfolk Coast Path & Peddars Way (British Walking Gde)
North Downs Way (British Walking Guide)
Offa's Dyke Path (British Walking Guide)
Overlanders' Handbook – worldwide driving guide
Pembrokeshire Coast Path (British Walking Guide)
Pennine Way (British Walking Guide)
Peru's Cordilleras Blanca & Huayhuash – Hiking/Biking
Pilgrim Pathways: 1-2 day walks on Britain's sacred ways
The Railway Anthology
The Ridgeway (British Walking Guide)
Scottish Highlands – Hillwalking Guide
Siberian BAM Guide – rail, rivers & road
The Silk Roads – a route and planning guide
Sinai – the trekking guide
South Downs Way (British Walking Guide)
Thames Path (British Walking Guide)
Tour du Mont Blanc
Trans-Canada Rail Guide
Trans-Siberian Handbook
Trekking in the Everest Region
The Walker's Anthology
The Walker's Anthology – further tales
West Highland Way (British Walking Guide)

For more information about Trailblazer and our
expanding range of guides, for guidebook updates or
for credit card mail order sales visit our website:

www.trailblazer-guides.com

We've applied to destinations which are closer to home Trailblazer's proven formula for publishing definitive practical route guides for adventurous travellers. Britain's network of long-distance trails enables the walker to explore some of the finest landscapes in the country's best walking areas. These are guides that are user-friendly, practical, informative and environmentally sensitive.

● **Unique mapping features** In many walking guidebooks the reader has to read a route description then try to relate it to the map. Our guides are much easier to use because walking directions, tricky junctions, places to stay and eat, points of interest and walking times are all written onto the maps themselves in the places to which they apply. With their uncluttered clarity, these are not general-purpose maps but fully edited maps drawn by walkers for walkers.

'The same attention to detail that distinguishes its other guides has been brought to bear here'.
THE SUNDAY TIMES

● **Largest-scale walking maps** At a scale of just under 1:20,000 (8cm or 3¹/₈ inches to one mile) the maps in these guides are bigger than even the most detailed British walking maps currently available in the shops.

● **Not just a trail guide – includes where to stay, where to eat and public transport** Our guidebooks cover the complete walking experience, not just the route. Accommodation options for all budgets are provided (pubs, hotels, B&Bs, campsites, bunkhouses, hostels) as well as places to eat. Detailed public transport information for all access points to each trail means that there are itineraries for all walkers, for hiking the entire route as well as for day or weekend walks.

Cleveland Way *Henry Stedman*, 1st edn, ISBN 978-1-905864-91-1, 240pp, 98 maps

Coast to Coast *Henry Stedman*, 9th edn, ISBN 978-1-912716-11-1, 268pp, 109 maps

Cornwall Coast Path (SW Coast Path Pt 2) *Stedman & Newton*, 6th edn, ISBN 978-1-912716-05-0, 352pp, 142 maps

Cotswold Way *Tricia & Bob Hayne*, 4th edn, ISBN 978-1-912716-04-3, 204pp, 53 maps

Dales Way *Henry Stedman,* 1st edn, ISBN 978-1-905864-78-2, 192pp, 50 maps

Dorset & South Devon (SW Coast Path Pt 3) *Stedman & Newton*, 2nd edn, ISBN 978-1-905864-94-2, 340pp, 97 maps

Exmoor & North Devon (SW Coast Path Pt I) *Stedman & Newton*, 2nd edn, ISBN 978-1-905864-86-7, 224pp, 68 maps

Great Glen Way *Jim Manthorpe*, 2nd edn, ISBN 978-1-912716-10-4, 192pp, 50 maps

Hadrian's Wall Path *Henry Stedman*, 6th edn, ISBN 978-1-912716-12-8, 250pp, 60 maps

Norfolk Coast Path & Peddars Way *Alexander Stewart*, 1st edn, ISBN 978-1-905864-98-0, 224pp, 75 maps

North Downs Way *Henry Stedman*, 2nd edn, ISBN 978-1-905864-90-4, 240pp, 98 maps

Offa's Dyke Path *Keith Carter*, 5th edn, ISBN 978-1-912716-03-6, 268pp, 98 maps

Pembrokeshire Coast Path *Jim Manthorpe*, 6th edn, ISBN 978-1-912716-13-5, 236pp, 96 maps

Pennine Way *Stuart Greig*, 5th edn, ISBN 978-1-912716-02-9, 272pp, 138 maps

The Ridgeway *Nick Hill*, 5th edn, ISBN 978-1-912716-20-3, 208pp, 53 maps

South Downs Way *Jim Manthorpe*, 6th edn, ISBN 978-1-905864-93-5, 204pp, 60 maps

Thames Path *Joel Newton*, 2nd edn, ISBN 978-1-905864-97-3, 256pp, 99 maps

West Highland Way *Charlie Loram*, 7th edn, ISBN 978-1-912716-01-2, 218pp, 60 maps

'The Trailblazer series stands head, shoulders, waist and ankles above the rest. They are particularly strong on mapping ...'
THE SUNDAY TIMES

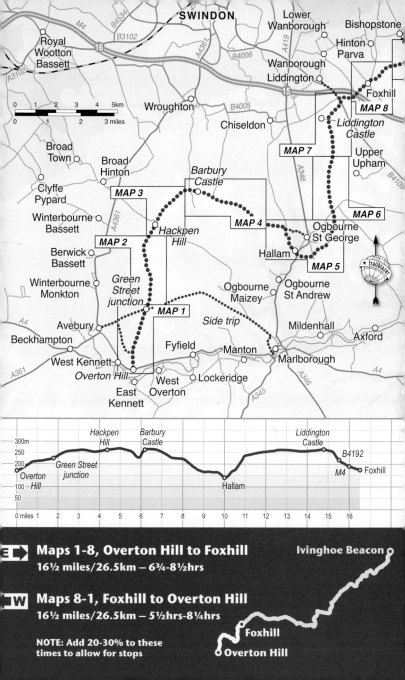

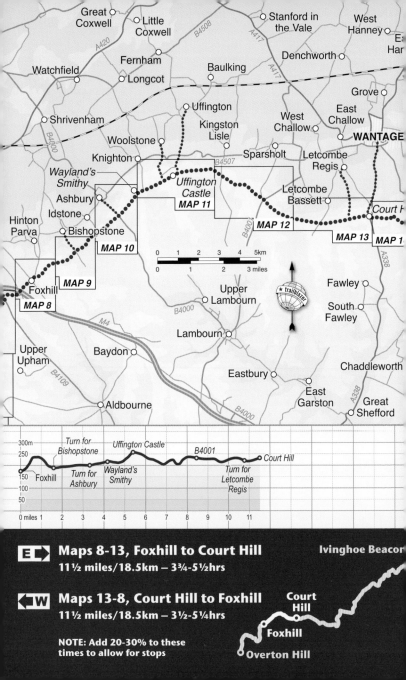

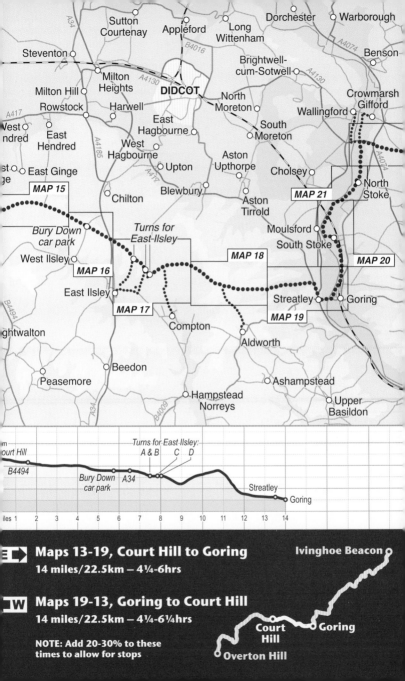

Maps 13-19, Court Hill to Goring
14 miles/22.5km – 4¼-6hrs

Maps 19-13, Goring to Court Hill
14 miles/22.5km – 4¼-6¼hrs

NOTE: Add 20-30% to these times to allow for stops

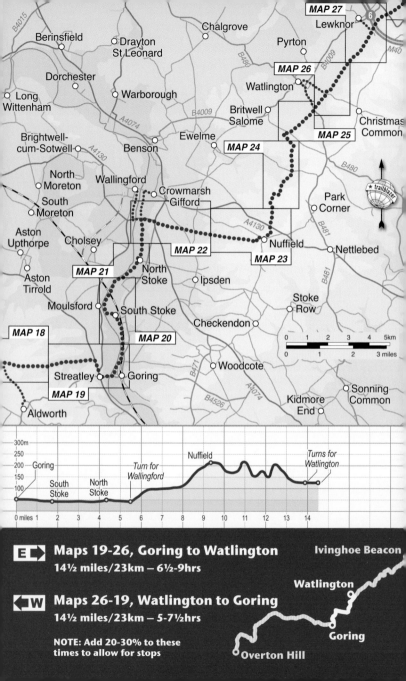

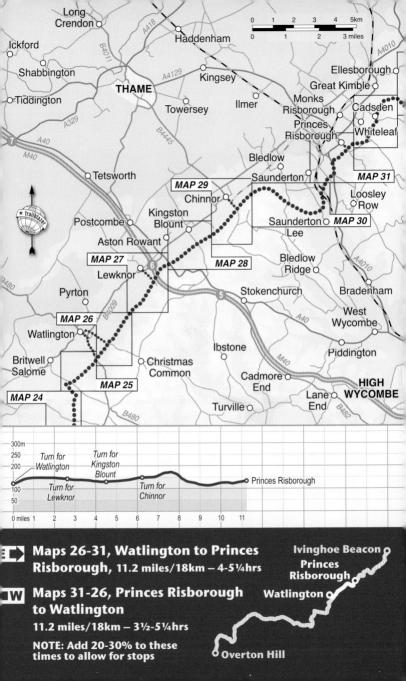

Long Crendon
Ickford
Shabbington
Tiddington
Haddenham
Kingsey
THAME
Towersey
Ilmer
Kingsey
Ellesborough
Great Kimble
Monks Risborough
Cadsden
Whiteleaf
Princes Risborough
Tetsworth
Bledlow
Saunderton
Postcombe
Chinnor
Kingston Blount
Aston Rowant
Lewknor
Pyrton
Watlington
Britwell Salome
Christmas Common
Ibstone
Stokenchurch
Saunderton Lee
Bledlow Ridge
Bradenham
West Wycombe
Piddington
Cadmore End
Lane End
HIGH WYCOMBE
Turville
Loosley Row

MAP 29
MAP 27
MAP 28
MAP 26
MAP 25
MAP 24
MAP 31
MAP 30

300m
250
200
150
100
50

Turn for Watlington
Turn for Lewknor
Turn for Kingston Blount
Turn for Chinnor
Princes Risborough

0 miles 1 2 3 4 5 6 7 8 9 10 11

0   1   2   3   4   5km
0   1   2   3 miles

➤ Maps 26-31, Watlington to Princes Risborough, 11.2 miles/18km – 4-5¼hrs

W Maps 31-26, Princes Risborough to Watlington
11.2 miles/18km – 3½-5¼hrs

NOTE: Add 20-30% to these times to allow for stops

Ivinghoe Beacon
Princes Risborough
Watlington
Overton Hill

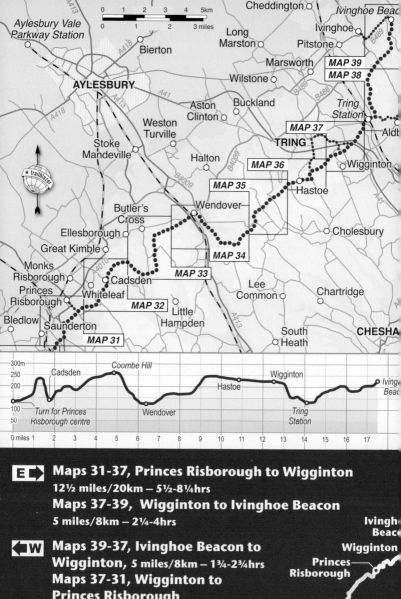

Maps 31-37, Princes Risborough to Wigginton
12½ miles/20km — 5½-8¼hrs
Maps 37-39, Wigginton to Ivinghoe Beacon
5 miles/8km — 2¼-4hrs

Maps 39-37, Ivinghoe Beacon to Wigginton, 5 miles/8km — 1¾-2¾hrs
Maps 37-31, Wigginton to Princes Risborough
12½ miles/20km — 5½-8¼hrs

NOTE: Add 20-30% to these times to allow for stops

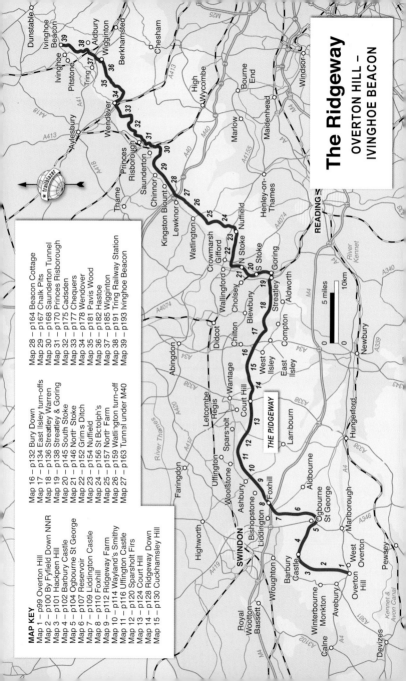

The Ridgeway
OVERTON HILL – IVINGHOE BEACON

MAP KEY

Map 1 – p99 Overton Hill
Map 2 – p100 By Fyfield Down NNR
Map 3 – p101 Hackpen Hill
Map 4 – p102 Barbury Castle
Map 5 – p104 Ogbourne St George
Map 6 – p107 Reservoir
Map 7 – p109 Liddington Castle
Map 8 – p110 Foxhill
Map 9 – p112 Ridgeway Farm
Map 10 – p114 Wayland's Smithy
Map 11 – p116 Uffington Castle
Map 12 – p120 Sparsholt Firs
Map 13 – p124 Court Hill
Map 14 – p128 Ridgeway Down
Map 15 – p130 Cuckhamsley Hill

Map 16 – p132 Bury Down
Map 17 – p134 East Isley turn-offs
Map 18 – p136 Streatley Warren
Map 19 – p138 Streatley & Goring
Map 20 – p145 South Stoke
Map 21 – p146 North Stoke
Map 22 – p152 Grim's Ditch
Map 23 – p154 Nuffield
Map 24 – p156 St Botolph's
Map 25 – p157 North Stoke
Map 26 – p159 Watlington turn-off
Map 27 – p163 Tunnel under M40
Map 28 – p164 Beacon Cottage
Map 29 – p167 Chalk Pits
Map 30 – p168 Saunderton Tunnel
Map 31 – p170 Princes Risborough
Map 32 – p175 Cadsden
Map 33 – p177 Chequers
Map 34 – p178 Wendover
Map 35 – p181 Pavis Wood
Map 36 – p182 Hastoe
Map 37 – p185 Wigginton
Map 38 – p191 Tring Railway Station
Map 39 – p193 Ivinghoe Beacon